The Lady and the President

THE LADY
and the
PRESIDENT

The Letters of
DOROTHEA DIX &
MILLARD FILLMORE

Charles M. Snyder

The University Press of Kentucky

ISBN: 978-0-8131-5474-9

Library of Congress Catalog Card Number: 75-3551

Copyright © 1975 by The University Press of Kentucky

A statewide cooperative scholarly publishing agency
serving Berea College, Centre College of Kentucky,
Eastern Kentucky University, Georgetown College,
Kentucky Historical Society, Kentucky State University,
Morehead State University, Murray State University,
Northern Kentucky State College, Transylvania University,
University of Kentucky, University of Louisville, and
Western Kentucky University.

Editorial and Sales Offices: Lexington, Kentucky 40506

To my wife,
MARY BURROWES SNYDER,
for whose aid and encouragement
I am ever grateful

Contents

Acknowledgments

For what must remain only a partial listing of persons and institutions contributing to this study I would like to go back a full century to single out Orsamus H. Marshall, an avid historian and collector of documents relating to Western New York. It was he who stimulated Fillmore's interest in the region's history and enlisted his aid in founding the Buffalo Historical Society. Marshall's son, Charles D., upon whom some of his father's enthusiasm for history rubbed off, preserved the Fillmore papers, and his administratrix, Hazel Koerner, presented Fillmore's Presidential papers to the Buffalo Historical Society. Worthy of mention too, is C. Sidney Shepard, who acquired the non-Presidential papers and stored them in his home until his death in 1934, and Grant Lindsley, a long-time employee of Shepard, who contributed his reminiscences of Shepard.

I would also single out Frank H. Severance for his painstaking collecting and editing of Fillmore papers, Francis Tiffany and Helen E. Marshall for their fine biographies of

[9]

Dorothea Dix, and Robert J. Rayback for his stimulating biography of Fillmore. I am indebted to Dr. James E. Perdue, President of the College of Arts and Science at Oswego, for the opportunity to collate and use the Fillmore papers and to the Research Foundation of the State University of New York for grants to assist me in tracking down Dix-Fillmore materials. I would also thank Miss Rosamond Lamb and the Harvard College Library for permission to reproduce Fillmore and Dix letters.

Helpful in uncovering more scattered Fillmore items were descendants of Calvin Fillmore; also, Fillmore Norfleet, a grandson of Charles Fillmore, the President's brother, and Mary H. McCann, a descendant of Glezen Fillmore, Millard's cousin. For details on Fillmore's youth in Cayuga County and East Aurora I am grateful to Robert J. Scarry and Amy A. Forden. I would also mention valued assistance given by Lester W. Smith and Arthur Detmers of the Buffalo and Erie County Historical Society, Professors Holman Hamilton and Albert D. Kirwan of the University of Kentucky, Robert E. Stephens of the Trenton State Hospital staff, and of the staffs of the Library of Congress, National Archives, the Smithsonian Institution, the New York Historical Society, the Massachusetts Historical Society and the Buffalo and Erie County Public Library.

Finally, I would like to acknowledge the continuing encouragement of my wife, Mary Burrowes Snyder, who has become as immersed in the lives and times of Dorothea Dix and Millard Fillmore as the author.

The Lady and the President

1
Beginnings

*A*merican women cast off from traditional moorings in the second quarter of the nineteenth century. With deliberation the ladies began to steer toward an uncertain future.

Propelling them was a tide of American achievement won by the labor and ingenuity of earlier generations on a virgin continent fabulously rich in natural resources. Material prosperity was liberating women from the heavier burdens of their mothers and grandmothers—but at the price of restricting their activities to the home. Here they were to practice the rites of fragile femininity and live in sublime accordance with the Victorian mystique.

American women, it came to be assumed, were created with mental powers peculiar to their sex. They were intuitive, not logical. They were unable to grasp higher mathematics, political theory, and philosophy. They were therefore unsuited for many positions. They were more spiritual and moral than men, and more delicate and modest. Women were ordained to

[13]

be helpers, teachers, and preservers, not competitors. Before these notions came into effect, Ruth Holmes Marshall, a young woman from Buffalo, New York, had emigrated as a bride to the frontier on horseback. She rode alone to the Illinois prairie and the upcountry of South Carolina. But in the age of Victoria her unmarried granddaughter, in her late twenties and the product of contemporary mores, had to be accompanied by relatives or friends whenever she traveled—and delivered carefully to the home of her host.

In this milieu few readers of the popular *Godey's Lady's Book and Magazine* found fault with its admonitions to avoid feminist groups and shun political issues. These only made sex conspicuous. Woman's sphere was not a public one, and there was nothing more unlovely than a female politician. Defects in the laws should be left to "our rulers and statesmen." [1]

The same publication advised women to join exclusively female social gatherings at which music, conversation, and kindred intellectual engagements were pursued. It told women to assist in the education of poor but talented youths. It told them, as mothers, to work in their homes for the cause of peace.

But there were misfits—young women, frequently daughters of professional families, who received at home liberal educations that went beyond the restrictive curricula of female schools. And there were unmarried women who rebelled against society's preconceived role for spinsters—a life of self-abnegation and sacrifice spent in ministering to others in the home and local community. Married and unmarried women chafed against the limited opportunities available to the professional woman. She might teach children, write for magazines that catered to conventional types, and occasionally find success as an "authoress" of novels. But prevailing assumptions of what was proper virtually eliminated all women from the business and civic worlds.

Dissidents drove an opening wedge into the system with the antislavery movement. Women's antislavery societies were not inconsistent with existing organizations for domestic and foreign missions. But when the South Carolina-born Grimke sisters obtained the platform of the predominantly male American Antislavery Society (the invitation had received the blessing of William Lloyd Garrison despite protests by some associates), a milestone was passed and a precedent broken. Women had addressed a mixed audience! When Angelina Grimke strayed from her text to advocate woman's rights, she was warned by the poet Whittier that her action was destructive to antislavery. Angelina retorted that women could do little against slavery while they were under the feet of men!

The temperance crusade was also a godsend to malcontents looking for a cause. They entered into it enthusiastically, and Susan Anthony and Frances Willard made their first platform appearances in its behalf.

Ultimately, in 1848, a handful of the female leaders of antislavery and temperance, headed by Elizabeth Cady Stanton and Lucretia Mott, assembled at Seneca Falls in western New York. There the ladies drafted a declaration of rights, paraphrasing the Declaration of Independence but amending it to read "that all Men *and Women* are created equal." Their declaration and resolutions were a call for a second American Revolution.

At mid-century the women's rights movement remained without an effectual national organization, and many of its goals would have to await the twentieth century. But it did not lack again for individual spokesmen and inspiration. Emma Willard in education, Elizabeth Blackwell in medicine, Clara

Barton in nursing, Harriet Beecher Stowe in literature, Margaret Fuller in philosophy, Amelia Bloomer in dress reform, and a tight phalanx of fellow workers were challenging Victorian concepts and providing guidelines for a new American woman.

One who challenged the concepts head-on was Dorothea Dix. As the advocate for improved care of the mentally deranged, Dorothea became a polished political strategist and an indefatigable tactician. She met on equal terms with top statesmen of her time, and she captured their support for her cause. To this slender woman from New England most of them also gave their respect. One of them, a President of the United States, gave special affection.

There is no record of the first meeting between Dorothea Dix and Millard Fillmore, but evidence of an early appointment and its approximate date is supplied by a letter written by a mutual friend and dated April 12, 1850. It introduces Miss Dix to Vice President Fillmore.[2]

Considering Dorothea's dislike for formal hearings and her preference for person-to-person relationships, they probably met in the Vice President's office, a high vaulted room a few yards from the entrance to the Senate chamber. The office, warmed and brightened by a classical marble fireplace, would soon become a robing room for the Supreme Court when the Senate moved into a new north wing. It was just a short walk down the poorly lighted corridors of the old Capitol from the Congressional Library, where Dorothea had improvised a headquarters to press for legislative action on a Federal land grant to provide hospitals for the indigent insane.

The fifty-year-old Vice President would have been hospitable and his manner impeccable. He was not unaware that women found him handsome. The heavy blond hair of his

youth had whitened prematurely, but his muscular frame remained athletic and his pinkish complexion radiated vitality.
At forty-eight Dorothea provided a physical contrast to the increasingly rotund Vice President. Tall and spare, she had dark
luxuriant hair that parted to frame an oval face and accentuate
large and beautiful blue eyes. Her plain dress, unadorned by
jewelry, suggested a natural dignity. Having demonstrated her
capability to direct statewide campaigns for the humane treatment of the insane, Dorothea would have shown the Vice
President a quiet confidence and dignity she had lacked as a
younger woman. Her innate shyness then would have pre-
cluded such an interview. Three months later, on July 9,
1850, Fillmore's importance in Dorothea's scheme of things
was enhanced unexpectedly when Zachary Taylor's death elevated him to the Presidency.

Between the two there appears to have been a special
meeting of minds and an immediate understanding of each
other's needs and aspirations. In this slender, almost frail, soft-
spoken woman Fillmore saw the personification of hope for
the most miserable of humankind. In the untried Chief Executive, facing a political crisis unprecedented in the nation's
history, Dorothea discerned a leader at once sensitive to sectional cleavages and committed to compromise and reconcili-
ation. Their early meetings laid foundations for a personal
friendship, a mutual trust, and, in time, a deep emotional involvement.

A relationship initiated in behalf of Dorothea's land grant
bill broadened to encompass the Washington scene, patronage, social reform, politics, and the sectional crisis. Both Fillmore and Dorothea seem to have assumed at the outset that
they spoke to each other in confidence, with only a few persons admitted on occasion to their privacy. The interview,
begun in the Vice Presidential office and later resumed in the

family quarters of the White House, soon incorporated the entire family. At times the relationship included Fillmore's wife,
Abigail, his son, Powers, twenty-two, and his daughter, Abby
(Mary Abigail), eighteen. Dorothea enjoyed the informality
of their home life and was a frequent caller. She preferred to
come and go as one of the family, and to avoid formal dinners
and receptions. She advised Abby on her reading and Abigail
on her health. She became a foil for Fillmore's humor and exchanged keepsakes with him.

When she left Washington to attend to the building of
asylums in the South, Dorothea sent to Fillmore detailed reports on political attitudes there. On one occasion, after she
forwarded laudatory newspaper editorials about his administration with additional praise of her own, Fillmore's next letter
joked about her flattery. But Dorothea did not see the humor.
She insisted that "high esteem" of his character and her
"friendly regard and esteem" were based solely on the President's "moral worth and strong mindedness." She spoke and
wrote, she said, only the "language of truth and soberness."
And while she did not consider a frequent exchange of letters
during her absence from Washington to be feasible, considering the claims on the time of both and the possibility that other
persons "in the strange world wherein we are dwellers" might
place a false interpretation on their friendship, Dorothea suggested that if Fillmore esteemed her, their correspondence
might continue indefinitely, "perhaps always." [3]

Abigail's death just after the termination of Fillmore's
term of office brought Dorothea closer to the stricken family,
and when Abby died unexpectedly a year later, she was momentarily distraught. She wrote to Fillmore: "I cannot be
silent. . . . I must mourn with you." [4] "My heart is aching
for you . . . [and] you have not at any time this week past
[been] out of my thoughts. . . . I sit here alone in my room

and think of you. . . . I am powerless to cheer your broken heart." [5]

If Fillmore's personal tragedies deepened their attachment, they also complicated their relationship. Dorothea, committed at least to one Victorian concept of what was proper, could not simply drop in to see a widower in Buffalo as she had visited a President in the White House. Whenever she made calls, she was attentive to conventions, and when their paths crossed in Europe in 1855 and 1856, she firmly reminded Fillmore that since he was no longer President *he* would be expected to call on her, not vice versa! [6]

Although the involvement between Fillmore and Dorothea was probably known to their closest associates, it has been long forgotten. Dorothea is not mentioned in the biographies of Fillmore. He is given few lines in hers. [7] The reason is apparent. The personal papers of Fillmore had been burned—or so it seemed—by a decision of his son, Powers, who provided for their destruction in his will. Historians had lamented this shortsightedness ever since Powers' death in 1889. But unobtrusively Charles D. Marshall, a Buffalo lawyer and one of the executors of Powers' will, moved the papers to his home a few blocks from the Fillmore mansion and stored them in his attic. There they remained until Marshall's death twenty years later.

C. Sidney Shepard, a cousin of Marshall who attended his funeral, purchased the papers in the attic, apparently without realizing that they contained Presidential manuscripts. Shepard had them boxed securely and expressed to his home in the quiet village of New Haven, New York. There under a stairway in the cool cellar of his sprawling house they lay for another sixty years, until their recent discovery. An examination in 1969 revealed that they exceeded ten thousand items and extended from Fillmore's youth to old age.

Equally surprising, Fillmore's letters to Dorothea became available simultaneously at Harvard University after they had lain in a private collection since Dorothea's death in 1887.

Thus overnight a correspondence of more than a hundred and fifty letters opens new perspectives upon two prominent, long-neglected Americans, with insights into their warm personal relations, their roles as national leaders, and the perilous times in which they lived.

2
Millard
Fillmore

EARLY YEARS

On July 9, 1850, President Zachary Taylor, the rugged hero of Buena Vista, died after an illness of five days. Physicians attributed his death to "cholera morbus" resulting from an overexposure to sunshine and an overindulgence in cold fruits and drinks. Unwisely, the President had participated too vigorously in prolonged ceremonies commemorating the nation's seventy-third anniversary. The festivities had taken place at the Washington Monument, then a stubby shaft just a few feet high. In accordance with the American system Taylor was replaced at once by Vice President Millard Fillmore.

In the early years of the republic the Vice Presidency had been filled by towering figures like John Adams and Thomas Jefferson. But the Twelfth Amendment, which separated the balloting for President and Vice President after the abortive coup of Aaron Burr and the Federalists to snatch the Presidency from Jefferson in 1800, had downgraded the Vice Presidency. In the ensuing half-century the office grew increasingly political in character.

Like most Vice Presidents after 1800 Fillmore would not have been considered for the top spot. He was hardly the equal of Webster as an orator, or of Clay or Calhoun as a congressional leader, or of Thurlow Weed or Van Buren as a machine politician. Yet his elevation to high station was not altogether accidental.

Unlike the apologetic Webster he was born in a primitive log cabin on January 7, 1800, on the frontier of central New York in the town of Summerville. His father, Nathaniel, and his mother, Phoebe Millerd Fillmore, natives of Vermont and Massachusetts respectively, had purchased a bounty lot there, sight unseen.

They soon lost the land due to a "bad title," a misfortune which Fillmore later termed a blessing. The lot was unproductive and isolated. They then leased a farm in Niles, a few miles away, on the west side of Skaneateles Lake, but this site also was sparsely settled, and opportunities for schooling were infrequent and of short duration.

From the age of ten young Millard could be spared only for brief periods from work on the farm. At fifteen he was apprenticed to a wool-carder and cloth-dresser at New Hope, a growing hamlet about a mile from his home. Here he worked from June to December, leaving the remaining months of the year for farm labor and schooling. He later recalled that while he attended the carding machines he placed a dictionary on a desk which he passed while feeding the machine and removing the rolls. ". . . In this way I could have a moment in which to look at a word and read its definition, and could then fix it in my memory." [1]

At eighteen during the off-season at the mill Fillmore taught a short winter term in a district school, an employment that probably tested his ability to handle the rod more than the alphabet. But it also taught him his academic inadequacies. He joined a tiny circulating library and the following winter earned the costs of a term in a short-lived academy by chopping wood for two days for each week spent in the classroom.

At the academy he met Abigail Powers, who like himself was a product of the New York frontier. Unlike him, however, she was spared the struggle against poverty and isolation. Though her father, a Baptist preacher, had died during her infancy, her mother, brothers, and sisters were able to provide her with a liberal education in their home in Kelloggsville, a short walk from New Hope. Abigail had opportunities to cultivate aesthetic tastes denied to most of her neighbors including a love of literature, music, and flowers. And if her personal charm and graceful movements drew Fillmore's initial attention, her intellectual interests and refinement revealed his inferiority and challenged him to better his situation.

Fillmore, nineteen, and Abigail, twenty-one, studied together and pooled their selections at the lending library. On days off, they strolled the narrow country lane connecting Kelloggsville with New Hope.

Their brief courtship was sidetracked when the Fillmore family moved to Montville, eight miles from Kelloggsville, and Abigail went to live with a brother at Lisle and teach in the village school. If the couple were lovers and had an understanding, it is obvious that they were willing to postpone the pleasure they found in each other until Fillmore had completed his apprenticeship and could afford housekeeping.

At Montville, however, Fillmore was offered a job as a law clerk by Judge Walter Wood, a local lawyer and landholder. The arrangements were made by his father, and Millard was unaware of them until his mother told him the good news at the dinner table. "The news was so sudden and unexpected that, in spite of myself, I burst out crying and had to leave the table, much mortified at my weakness." [2]

He purchased the unfulfilled apprenticeship and plunged into Blackstone. He remained in Montville when his parents and eight brothers and sisters moved again—this time to East Aurora, eighteen miles southeast of Buffalo.

The following Fourth of July the budding law clerk, now twenty-one, was drafted to deliver the oration in a grove adjacent to Mr. Wood's factory in Montville. As would be expected in any address to an audience sprinkled with veterans of the Revolution and their families who had suffered Tory and Indian depredations, his speech was a diatribe against British atrocities. But surprisingly, in the light of his later moderation, it was also a philippic against slavery.

A short time later Fillmore quarreled with Wood over his right to pick up fees by pettifogging before justices of the peace, and he terminated his employment.

"With four dollars in my pocket, I started [from Montville to East Aurora]," Fillmore recounted, "and arrived there the last of August or first of September, 1821; hoping like Micawber, that something would 'turn up.' " [3]

He taught school in the village for the winter and attended suits before justices of the peace on Saturdays. The next spring he taught at Buffalo until he entered the law office of Asa Rice and Joseph Clary as a clerk. Law clerking involved more than spending time in the office; he gathered information, served papers, and measured land. He purchased surveying instruments to facilitate the latter and to earn money on the side. Fillmore made rapid progress and, in little more than a year, was admitted to the practice of law. He was then twenty-three.

Evidence of the respect with which he was held by the Buffalo legal profession is suggested by his selection as the

Fourth of July orator in 1823, just a few months before he left the office of Rice and Clary. The honor came to him only at the last minute, when a more experienced speaker was unable to appear. Acknowledging the disappointment of the audience he apologized to the townspeople for his unpreparedness:

> He [Fillmore] is one who has always trod the humble walks of life, genius and learning have withheld their precious gems from his grasp . . . and his lips were never taught to lisp the sweet strains of eloquence to tickle and charm the ear, nor his limbs to form the graceful gestures to please the eye [and] nought but your united voices could have called upon him to this honorable station, and nought but a full faith in your charity and generosity could inspire him with confidence to attempt to address you on this important occasion.[4]

Considering the gaps in his education and the haste with which he produced his speech, it was a creditable performance. He recalled the causes of the Revoluton, outlined the functions of government, and demonstrated that the American system triumphantly fulfilled them. "What a happy constitution," he exulted. Adapting his remarks to his Buffalo listeners, he recalled the burning of the village during the War of 1812, and added the heroes of this conflict, Generals Scott and Brown, who had won engagements on the Niagara frontier, to their counterparts in the Revolution. He concluded with a call for peace and harmony and a reminder that the day they celebrated was not the birthday of a faction, but that of a nation.

Soon after the speech, Fillmore declined an invitation from Clary to accept a partnership with him, having decided to open an office in East Aurora. He explained later that he felt inadequate to compete with the more learned and experienced lawyers in Buffalo.

East Aurora, like hundreds of other villages in western New York, owed its existence to the combination of a fertile valley and a stream with sufficient power to operate a saw and turn a stone. It was surveyed a few years earlier by the Holland Land Company, and its first log house had now weathered nineteen winters. Since its erection gristmills and sawmills had been built on Cazenove Creek; also a small fulling mill and tannery. Near the center of a small quiet cluster of houses was a blacksmith shop, a framed school house, a Baptist church, a general store, and a tavern. The latter was operated by Fillmore's uncle, Calvin Fillmore. He had despaired of Cayuga's hard clay soil several years before his brother Nathaniel. Most residents were debtors of the land company, and ready cash was a scarce commodity.

But despite East Aurora's limitations, Fillmore's decision to open his office there may have been a wise one. He was the only lawyer in the community, and a variety of cases, most of them relating to land titles, mortgages, and debt collection, awaited him. He also handled cases for Clary and occasionally represented old neighbors in Cayuga, including Judge Wood. Apparently their differences had been forgotten. Fillmore became a pipeline to Albany when his Uncle Calvin was an assemblyman. He found little use for the surveyor's instruments he had acquired to supplement his income.

He was soon involved also in local politics, participated in local caucuses. He consulted with party leaders in Buffalo, and, of course, delivered the annual oration on Independence Day. It was a propitious time to go into politics. The abduction and disappearance of one William Morgan of Batavia in 1826, a crime linked in the popular mind to the Masonic Lodge as a means of averting Morgan's threat to publish the secrets of the Order, created a furor in western New York. Young men, ambitious to find a niche in politics, channeled the protest into a political party, Antimasonry. In a coalition with National Republicans it outstripped the Democratic party of Andrew Jackson.

Thurlow Weed, William H. Seward, and Francis Granger as well as Fillmore found Antimasonry a springboard to political leadership in New York. Sensing its potential among rural voters in Erie County Fillmore let it be known that he was available for the Assembly, and he led the local ticket to victory.

In setting out upon a political career not the least of Fillmore's assets was his appearance and manner. Just under six feet, he had a rugged physique spread over a broad and erect frame and the chest and shoulders of a woodsman—physical features common to several generations of Fillmores. Thick blond hair framed his broad and strikingly handsome face. His complexion was pinkish, his eyes blue and jovial. His voice was deep, masculine, and well modulated; his delivery, simple, direct, and unpretentious. He was not a showman on the platform and shunned the turgid figures of speech which were at that time so characteristic of orators. But his seeming sincerity, reasonableness, and confidence made up for his lack of eloquence. If not charismatic before an audience, he was magnetic on a reception line, at a cornerstone laying, or in the center of a circle of friends in a kitchen, drawing room, or caucus.

He was gracious and cordial, and had an infectious buoyancy. His clothing was not costly but it was sartorially correct, and his polished manner lent it an elegance. Women were flattered by his attentions.

With such physical attributes it is not surprising that political opportunity came his way early and that he attracted voters in an era when public opinion frowned upon a direct solicitation for support.

Fillmore's law office, a neat, one-story structure with a Greek entablature and two fluted Doric columns, was on Main Street. It became a gathering place in the evenings, where villagers talked politics and discussed the news. In hot weather they moved their chairs to the shallow portico, enduring the flies and dust in order to catch a cool breeze from Lake Erie. Fifty years later an old townsman recalled seeing Fillmore there, relaxing in an armchair, smoking his pipe, and exchanging anecdotes and gossip.[5]

Meanwhile, he was a frequent correspondent with book sellers in Albany, who supplied him, one by one, with the titles for his law library.

Three years after opening his practice and five years after leaving Cayuga County Fillmore returned to Abigail to ask her to marry him. It was probably his first visit since he had left Montville. In the absence of any evidence that he courted other young women in East Aurora, it would appear that he was simply waiting until he could fulfill a promise to her. There is no record that she had any other love interest.

His proposal was not the only surprise in store for her. Instead of the farm boy and apprentice of her youth she greeted a mature and immaculately dressed barrister (possibly jaded after a 150-mile stagecoach ride), clad in broadcloth with a tall hat and cane, probably a transformation beyond her fondest dreams.

Abigail accepted, but a sister, who was not at home to see the prospective groom, revealed her family's earlier reservations about the match in a confidential note:

I was as much surprised to hear of his visit as yourself. . . . Why did you not inform me more particularly how he appeared to you and whether you think him improved in etiquette, and how Mr. and Mrs. Powers [Abigail's brother and sister-in-law] was [sic] pleased with him, and what remarks they made of him.[6]

If Abigail was not a beautiful bride, she was nonetheless an attractive one. Tall, slender, and erect, she had an oval face and high forehead. Her nose was prominent and her mouth, straight and wide. Her luxuriant auburn-brown hair fell in curls, reaching her neck. Her large blue eyes were bright and expressive.

They were married quietly on February 5, 1826, in Moravia, at her brother's home and in the presence of her family. The Reverend Orasmus H. Smith, rector of the St. Matthew's (Episcopal) Church performed the ceremony. The couple departed immediately after the service for East Aurora.

For Abigail, settling in East Aurora was like turning back the clock twenty years to the frontier of her youth, but with the perspective of her generation, she anticipated improvements. They lived at first on the Fillmore farm, a quarter of a mile south of the village on the Olean road. With six children in the house, four of them in their teens, to do the chores, Abigail was freed to teach school. But within a year they were in their own small home, a few doors from Fillmore's office, and awaiting the arrival of a baby. Here, on April 25, 1828, Millard Powers Fillmore was born.

While few details of their East Aurora years remain, a poignant letter of Abigail's, written in snatches of time a few weeks after Fillmore's departure for Albany and during his first term in the Assembly, testifies to her devotion to him and indirectly to his affection for her:

January 16 [1830]
I have just received one of the most affectionate letters you have ever written. I was alone and gave vent to my feelings,

but I shed no tears of grief. . . . The perusal of your letter added new energies to my soul and tenderness (if possible) to my heart.

January 17

I am now alone and having laid our little son [aged nine months] on the bed to sleep, employ a few moments in writing, having again perused your *affectionate* favor, and to return thanks to kind Providence for so tender a friend. Though I regret the loss of your society more than I can express, I am far happier in having you at that distance with an assurance that you love me, than I should be in your society, doubting your affections. . . .

January 18, Sunday eve.
10 o'clock

. . . I have spent the day at home. Have felt more than usual lonely tho' not unhappy or discontented. Your society is all I have thought of. Have finished studying the maps of ancient geography. O, that you could have been here to have studied with me. . . .

January 19, 3 o'clock P.M.

Fearing I shall have no other opportunity tonight, will write one minute now; it is washing day. I have just got my work done and sit down, have been putting on the baby's red shoes, his others are worn out. I wish you were here to see him maneuvre. He laughs and stamps, and plays with his shoes. I wish you could read to me as you frequently have done after I sit down to sewing. . . . I am happy and proud in the thought that your heart is firm, and that no fascinating female can induce you to forget her whose whole heart is devoted . . . and who will continue to count the days until you are again restored to her arms. Good night my Millerd [sic]; a thousand blessings.[7]

In 1830 Fillmore reversed his decision to settle in East Aurora rather than Buffalo. Seven years after apologizing to a Buffalo audience for being inadequate, he was a highly successful lawyer, a member of the State Assembly, and, by general consensus, a man with a future. Joseph Clary's bid for his partnership was still open. Fillmore accepted it.

A few years later he established a partnership with Nathan K. Hall and Solomon G. Haven, whom he had guided into the profession as law clerks. The firm of Fillmore, Hall, and Haven was highly successful and soon had few peers in western New York.

By selecting Buffalo Fillmore was moving from an eddy to midstream. Rising from its ashes following the War of 1812 the thriving village was well on its way to become the metropolis of western New York. With a population of eight thousand, it was already the western terminus of the Erie Canal and principal port to the Michigan and Illinois frontiers. Without waiting for federal funds its citizens had erected a break wall to enclose a harbor at the mouth of Buffalo Creek and had constructed docks and warehouses to serve it. Upon the completion of the canal in 1825 it became the commercial heart of the village. The canal's junction with Lake Erie made Buffalo the jumping-off point for the West, and thousands of immigrants and millions of tons of goods were soon funneling through it. Speculators feverishly bought and sold waterfront property, and the community's first fortunes were garnered here. Alanson Palmer and Benjamin Rathbun became financial tycoons during these halcyon years, only to fall victims of overspeculation. But persons like Judge Samuel Wilkeson, Doctor John E. Marshall, and Ebenezer Walton built more solidly, and their families supplied Buffalo leadership for several generations.

A few blocks back from the harbor Joseph Ellicott's bold plans for a city were in evidence, although its population did not reach 18,000 until 1840. Broad Main Street was a hodge-podge of wooden structures, many unpainted, but farther up the street and on adjacent ones a few tall-columned houses and brick churches attested to its growing prosperity. Few scars from the War remained, but a note of incongruity was pro-vided by the Indians from the neighborhing reservations, who still walked the streets in blankets and moccasins.

The Fillmores purchased a house on Franklin Street, a block from the bustle of Main Street. The house was unpre-tentious but substantial for Buffalo in 1830; a rectangular frame structure with a doorway suggestive of the Federal mode in architecture. A neat white picket fence provided a modicum of privacy and served to keep neighborhood hogs and other untethered livestock out of the yard.

It remained their family home for twenty-eight years; here, two years after their arrival, the birth of Mary Abigail (Abby) completed the family circle. A sunny and responsive child, she shared her mother's interest in music, and became an accom-plished pianist and harpist. Abby had much of her father's vi-tality and self-possession, and a natural charm and dignity. A local newspaper reported, "though not beautiful she was so full of vivacity of intellect, of cordiality and of goodness, that it attracted more than any beauty." [8]

The Fillmores were soon at home in the social and civic life of Buffalo. During the winter months lake and canal shipping was suspended and the leading families enjoyed a long and spirited social season.

For eight months each year they attended to business, and then, as ice closed in on navigation, they gave over the four winter months to a gay social season. It had to be

provincial in scope but not in taste. "We were literally
ice-bound," explained a hostess, and "everybody stayed at
home, contributing to the general pleasure." [9]

With two small children, and with Millard in Albany and
later in Washington during sessions of the Assembly and
House of Representatives, the Fillmores' participation during
the early years was limited, but with the passage of time they
became an integral part of the circle. In contrast to the simple
village life they had known in Cayuga and East Aurora, "A
bright and undiscovered world [became] theirs. Formal dinners, chamber recitals, dances, visiting lectures, celebrities,
plays—all crowded their lives. The naive, impressionable
couple became enthusiastic devotees of this new world, and
throughout the rest of their lives they made its standards
and patterns their own." [10] If there was a difference in their
tastes, it was Abigail's preference for smaller and less formal
visitations with more intimate friends.

Fillmore's handsome appearance and gracious manners
made him a favorite with the ladies in Buffalo. The gallantry
with which he addressed Abigail and his polite attentions to
her were such as "a man usually bestows on a guest." On a
cold winter night after escorting her to the home of friends, he
quietly slipped away and returned to surprise her with the
flowers she had cut from her own conservatory, but had forgotten. "It was these small attentions, so natural to him, that gave
a distinct mark to the daily intercourse of their lives." [11] It was
proverbial in Buffalo that if women could vote Fillmore would
win any election.

Another tale reflects his chivalrous attitude toward women.
During the construction of the Suspension Bridge across the
gorge of the Niagara River an iron cradle was hung upon a
cable to negotiate the crossing. Fillmore, though a cautious

man, made the perilous passage, "simply because he could not
see a headstrong woman, till then a stranger, take that appalling journey alone." [12] The storyteller was not an eyewitness,
and the tale may be apocryphal.

The Fillmores joined the Unitarian Society in Buffalo. Its
trust in man was suited to the future President's optimistic
frame of mind, and its lack of creed, to his dislike for dogma
and ritual. He had never affiliated with a church previously
and was probably never baptized. Abigail, despite her identification with the Baptist church as a child, seems to have been
inactive as an adult. Their decision might be dismissed as
mere social climbing, had Fillmore not firmly believed in a
benevolent Providence. He had a Quaker's dislike for oaths,
believing they degraded religion. In the Assembly he once introduced a bill to eliminate test oaths from court proceedings
in New York and had defended it, despite opposition from
conservatives. But the legislature did not act on it.

In the Assembly and in Congress Fillmore was alert to
Buffalo's needs and gave especial attention to appropriations
for the canal and harbor. The response of the public could
only have been gratifying. Buffalo and Erie County voters
thrice elected him to the Assembly, and he was their four-time
choice for Congress. Only in his bid for the Presidency as a
Know-Nothing in 1856 would local voters reject him.

But his popularity at home and his sensitivity to the needs
of his constituents would not have carried him to the Vice
Presidency had he not been identified in New York with the
bill to abolish imprisonment for debt and in Washington with
the Tariff of 1842.

In 1831 citizens of New York who were unfortunate
enough to fall into debt might be committed to debtors' prison.
Even though creditors might be willing to withhold prosecution there was no state bankruptcy law to give the debtor a

new start. Fillmore decided to move into this controversial question, even though as an Antimason he belonged to a minority party, because he sensed there would be nonpartisan support for it. And by skillfully combining the abolishment of imprisonment for debt (popular among laborers) with a bankruptcy law (approved by businessmen) and an act making fraudulent bankruptcy a crime (a sop to creditors) he had a package which the Democratic majority in the legislature would accept. Its passage provided a model for similar action in other states.

Eleven years later in Congress as Chairman of the Ways and Means Committee he reported a protective tariff, a measure which manufacturers and laborers had sought ever since the Tariff of 1833 had provided for gradual reductions in duties over a period of ten years. The bill was adopted as the Tariff of 1842 and became almost the only victory which the Whigs salvaged from their glorious but short-lived "Tippecanoe and Tyler Too" triumph of 1840. Its subsequent repeal by the Polk Administration had served further to glamorize it among Whig stalwarts.

Fillmore's greatest handicap in his bid for the Vice Presidency was the less than enthusiastic support of Thurlow Weed, the "dictator" of the Whig party in New York. Weed's rise in the political hierarchy accompanied that of Fillmore, but he moved along a different path. Like Fillmore, he was a product of the New York frontier and a founder of the Antimasons. Unlike Fillmore, however, Weed preferred the game of politics to officeholding and made his mark as a party chieftain and publisher.

Shifting from Antimasonry as it lost its pristine momentum Weed helped to organize the Whig party. He moved from western New York to Albany, where he made the *Evening Journal* the leading Whig organ in the state.

He was impressed with the talent of William H. Seward and was instrumental in his election as Governor. In 1844 he groomed him for the Vice Presidential nomination. Meanwhile, Weed had also backed Fillmore when his constituency had been confined to the western counties, but once the latter's ambitions conflicted with Seward's, Fillmore was definitely Weed's second choice.

Fillmore believed that Weed supported him for Governor in 1844 in order to remove him from the race for Vice President and suspected that Weed anticipated, if he did not encourage, his defeat.

In 1847 Weed went along with Fillmore's nomination for Comptroller of New York and supported his election—his victory in the state's first popular election of a comptroller posing no threat to Seward's political future.

Fillmore's accession to the comptrollership marked a change in the home life of the family. Heretofore he had taken accommodations at roominghouses or hotels, leaving Abigail and the children at home. Salaries of public officials were low and the cost of maintaining the family in Albany or Washington would have been prohibitive. Now Abigail accompanied him to Albany in December of 1847 and set up light housekeeping while Powers, a recent graduate of Harvard College, entered upon the study of law. Abby enrolled at Mrs. Sedwick's School at Lenox, Massachusetts. Thus Fillmore and Abigail were in Albany during the portentous campaign of 1848.

The Whig Presidential nomination of 1848 was a cliffhanger involving the venerable Henry Clay, seeking a third nod from his party, and Generals Zachary Taylor and Winfield Scott. Northern delegates, disliking Clay's close ties with southern leaders, and discounting his prospects of success after two defeats, gravitated toward the uncommitted Taylor, currently a hero of the Mexican War. They finally obtained his nomination.

As in 1844 Fillmore and Seward were "favorite son" possibilities for Vice President, but Seward's ambitions were directed to the top spot. His only interest in the lesser post was to block Fillmore's nomination, lest it jeopardize his own future. Fillmore's ultimate choice has been attributed to luck and to his timely nomination and its clever justification by John A. Collier, an erratic anti-Weed delegate from the Southern Tier of New York. Both were certainly elements in his success, but his role in the Tariff of 1842 was well remembered, and he had been frequently mentioned among top Vice-Presidential candidates like Abbott Lawence, the cotton magnate from Massachusetts, and Thomas Ewing of Ohio.

During the jockeying for the nomination both Lawrence and Ewing were weakened by opposition within their own state delegations. At a critical moment Collier cleverly, but inaccurately, identified Fillmore as a Clay man and offered him to Taylor strategists as a means of propitiating the followers of the great Kentuckian. Fillmore proved acceptable to both Taylor and Clay partisans, and the impotent Weed could only withhold Seward's name from the balloting.

During the campaign that followed, Weed and Fillmore vied to be Taylor's spokesman in New York. At one critical moment just after the General, a political novice, had declared his willingness to accept a nomination from South Carolina Democrats (which he would combine with his nomination by the Whigs), a Whig mass meeting was called in Albany to reconsider their commitment. Both Weed and Fillmore worked frantically behind the scenes to shape the thrust of the decision, and at the last moment resolutions critical of Taylor were withdrawn. Later, each accused the other of preparing the hostile resolutions and each sought credit for sustaining him. Both Fillmore and Weed corresponded with Taylor in distant New Orleans, hoping to establish themselves as his lieutenant.

The campaign incorporated many of the features of the emotion-packed election of 1840. The Whigs avoided a platform to focus attention upon their hero, and Taylor marching groups and "Rough and Ready Songsters" were soon adding color and sound to the race. Meanwhile, the Democrats, with the controversial Mexican War to defend, were further handicapped by their nomination of Lewis Cass, a colorless elder statesman, and by the Free Soilers' nomination of former Democratic President Martin Van Buren.

The not unexpected result was a victory for the Taylor-Fillmore ticket over their divided opponents.

The campaign, of course, was a time of excitement for the Fillmores. Since a nominee did not campaign in his own behalf in this era, Fillmore stayed on the job as New York State Comptroller and used what, under other circumstances, would have been his leisure hours to attend his mounting political correspondence. And with the election won, he continued to perform the duties of his office, resigning just two weeks before his inaugural as Vice President.

He then proceeded to Washington to make himself available to the President-elect and, hopefully, to share in the distribution of the patronage. Abigail, meanwhile, returned to Buffalo without plans to attend the inaugural or take a residence in Washington. Abby accompanied her, expecting to obtain a position as a teacher.

In the ensuing contest with the Weed faction for the patronage Fillmore was no match for his better-organized and more resourceful rivals. Seward's election to the United States Senate in January enabled him to ingratiate himself with Taylor and his family, and in a few months he established himself as one of his closest advisers. Members of the incoming administration were soon bypassing Fillmore to consult with Seward and Weed.

Over the weekend preceding the inaugural on Monday, March 5, Washington came alive as thousands of visitors funneled into the District on railway cars, river craft, and horse-drawn vehicles to mingle with the forty thousand residents. By inaugural morning old-timers could not recall a similar push for the necessities as well as some of the frivolities of life. Early in the day a cacophony of bells, whistles, and drums, heard only quadrennially, demonstrated that it was that day of days. By midmorning the fashionably dressed vied with artisans and slaves for vantage points along Pennsylvania Avenue, while others threaded their way through puddles overflowing from late winter rains toward the Capitol steps for a closer view of Old Rough and Ready.

About eleven o'clock Fillmore set out from the Willard Hotel for the Capitol in an open barouche in company with the retiring Vice President, George M. Dallas. Many who witnessed their passage had difficulty distinguishing one from the other. Both were clothed in black broadcloth; both were broad-faced, clean shaven, and crowned with luxuriant white hair. But those on the front lines identified Fillmore's massive shoulders and the florid glow of his beaming face.

Arriving at the Capitol just before noon, Dallas escorted Fillmore to the Senate Chamber—it was the small semicircular room in the north wing of the old structure, for many years the chamber of the Supreme Court after the Senate occupied its present quarters in 1858.

The Chamber was already overflowing with legislators, glitteringly adorned members of the Diplomatic Corps, Supreme Court justices in traditional black robes, and crinoline-encased ladies. A few moments later Fillmore repeated the oath as it was delivered by Chief Justice Roger B. Taney. He then gave a short address in which he extolled self-government and the need for enlightened citizenship, but he was well aware that while his voice reached the back row of the gallery his audience was already focusing on the feature attraction to follow.

During these formalities in the Senate Chamber a second open carriage drawn by four matching gray horses drew President Polk and Taylor down Pennsylvania Avenue and up Capitol Hill. The carriage was preceded by twelve volunteer companies. Following were a bodyguard of one hundred horsemen and Rough and Ready marching clubs, with banners and music, from Georgetown, Alexandria, Baltimore, and Washington.

As Fillmore closed his remarks, the great door of the Senate opened, and Polk and Taylor marched down the aisle side by side. Pausing only long enough to line up the participants according to protocol, the assemblage moved out to the wooden platform on the Capitol's eastern portico, where Taylor took the oath of office and delivered his inaugural address. The venerable hero dedicated his administration to the welfare of the whole country and not to any particular section or interest, but he refrained from committing himself upon the great issues.

That evening Taylor and Fillmore drove through the quieted streets to look in upon three inaugural balls. They reached the third an hour before midnight at City Hall, where Taylor's appearance was the signal for a rendition of "Hail Columbia" by Gungl's famous band. The President and Vice President circulated among the diplomats, military officers, and politicians. They paid their respects to the bejeweled ladies, possibly reserving their warmest greetings for Taylor's attractive daughter, Betty Bliss, a three-month's bride who would soon replace her ailing mother as the President's official hostess. They greeted the glamorous Baroness Bodisco, the American wife of the Russian Minister, whose beauty and charm were the talk of Washington.

After dancing and dinner Taylor and Fillmore left the glittering spectacle at one o'clock. A scarcely noticed Congressman named Abraham Lincoln stayed on until four, and finally departed without his hat. An oversight in arrangements had caused it to be buried under tons of garments!

As Vice President, Fillmore presided over a Senate torn by sectional discord acerbated by the Mexican War. Grave issues had piled up on the congressional calendar which the outgoing Polk administration, though victorious on the battlefield, had been unable to resolve.

The California Territory, acquired from Mexico, changed overnight from a region of widely scattered ranches and missions to a gold rush. Seeking to stem the resulting chaos, residents petitioned for statehood. But Congress could not decide whether California should be free or slave. Territorial government was needed in the Utah and New Mexico territories, additional regions taken from Mexico. But again there was disagreement on the status of slavery. Texas had been annexed as a state, but the settlement of its debt and western border begged a solution. The Underground Railroad was carrying increasing numbers of slaves to freedom in Canada and proving the inadequacy of the half-century-old fugitive slave law. The South demanded its revision and enforcement. Free Soilers and Abolitionists countered with a campaign to prohibit slave trading in the District of Columbia, a practice they branded as a national disgrace.

Amidst threats of disunion and personal vendettas, Fillmore maintained an outward calm, which undoubtedly helped to blunt animosity. During one heated Senate debate in mid-

April the diminutive Senator Henry S. Foote of Mississippi drew a five-chambered pistol from his pocket and aimed it at the unarmed but aggressive Senator Thomas Hart Benton of Missouri, who had advanced menacingly toward him. During the resulting confusion Fillmore pounded his gavel and called for the sergeant-at-arms, but he was ignored. Fortunately, Foote was disarmed, and after the new Vice President made repeated calls upon the senators and the gallery for order, business was resumed.

Realizing that as presiding officer he lacked authority to discipline the members should the need arise, Fillmore addressed the Senate to explain the problem and to underline the need for definite procedures. The senators listened with respect and had his remarks entered into the Journal, but they took no other action.

Fillmore astutely avoided any personal commitment throughout the protracted debates on problems. But he confided to President Taylor that if he were forced to break a tie on Clay's compromise bill, which sought a solution to sectionalism by combining the major issues into a single "omnibus bill," he would support it, including concessions to the South. In taking such action he would repudiate Taylor, who had accepted Seward's advice to insist upon free soil (the Wilmot Proviso) in the territories obtained from Mexico, and let the chips fall where they might. Commenting upon Taylor's position, one authority recently noted that he had led the country to the brink of disaster, and had he lived out his term, the nation might have been torn by disunion and civil war a decade before Lincoln's election.[13]

As it turned out Fillmore was spared this decision as Vice President. Instead the agonizing crisis was dumped into his lap by his unexpected elevation to the Presidency.

Taylor's health had not been robust since his inaugural,

but his condition was at no time considered alarming. One Thursday, July 4, 1850, he attended festivities at the Washington Monument, and, according to varying reports, cooled himself with "cucumbers, cherries and cabbage," or "bread and milk and cherries," or possibly "copius draughts of iced milk and water." The milk and cherries version is best remembered.[14]

The following day he was sick with "cholera morbus," and three days later his condition was grave. Fillmore was called from his chair in the Senate on Monday morning and conveyed to the Executive Mansion where he joined members of the Cabinet in a vigil outside the President's bedroom. The old General lingered through that day and the next, but died late Wednesday night.

A short time later Fillmore received the Cabinet's formal notification of Taylor's death at his lodging in the Willard Hotel. After acknowledging it, he closed the door to spend a sleepless night pondering his next steps, and reviewing in those hours "his own opinions and life." He could think of no definite solution to the nation's ills, but he resolved "to look upon this whole country, from the farthest coast of Maine to the utmost limit of Texas, as but one country." [15]

At noon the next day, at a joint meeting of both Houses and in the presence of the Cabinet, Fillmore repeated the Presidential oath of office. Hours later the members of the Cabinet resigned—it was a poorly-kept secret that the majority were closer to Weed and Seward than to Fillmore. Fillmore faced the impasse alone. No President had previously undertaken the responsibilities of the office at such a perilous moment.

Perplexed, and obviously fumbling to find his way through the shoals of sectionalism, he steered toward nationalism and compromise. Evidence may be found in his choice of advisers.

Without exception he named moderates including the incomparable Daniel Webster as Secretary of State. Webster's recent Seventh of March oration in the Senate—familiar to generations of Americans—had been a reprimand to sectionalists and a defense of the Union. Thomas Corwin of Ohio in the Treasury, John J. Crittenden of Kentucky in the Justice, and William A. Graham of North Carolina in the Navy department were seasoned and moderate Whigs. The same could be said of Charles M. Conrad of Louisiana, Fillmore's Secretary of War, and Alexander H. H. Stuart of Virginia, his Secretary of the Interior. If the personnel appeared to favor the South, it was because several of Fillmore's original choices declined appointment.

His selection of N. K. Hall, his former law partner, as Postmaster General, reflected his mortification over the patronage under Taylor and an unwillingness to entrust it to anyone but a long-time associate. Hall had served in Congress, but was scarcely known beyond western New York. His appointment raised eyebrows in Buffalo and drew the fire of the Weed-Seward faction of the party.

Turning to the stalled compromise Fillmore indicated to congressional leaders that he would sign the bill as drafted or accept its contents as separate bills if this approach should be more feasible. The latter approach was attempted and the log jam was at last broken. Congress approved the bills one by one, and dispatched them to the waiting Executive. On September 9 he signed the bill giving California statehood under a constitution denying slavery. On the same day he added his signature, first, to the Texas and New Mexico Act, defining the western boundary of Texas and compensating her for land combined with New Mexico, and creating the New Mexico Territory, leaving the legality of slavery to the inhabitants, and second, to the Utah Territory Act, with the same stipulation regarding slavery as that contained in the New Mexico Act. On September 18 he signed the Fugitive Slave Act, the most controversial of the five measures. Two days later he accepted the bill prohibiting the slave trade (but leaving slavery untouched) in the District of Columbia.

That evening Union members of the House of Representatives serenaded Fillmore and Webster, the latter for his Seventh of March speech in defense of the compromise. The President bowed his acknowledgment from a window of the White House, and Webster came to his doorstep in a dressing gown. "Now is the winter of our discontent made glorious summer," he responded, "by this son of York." [16]

During these tense and significant weeks in the national capital Abigail Fillmore closed their home in Buffalo and made preparations to join her husband. Abby, in turn, discontinued her teaching, and Powers interrupted his law studies to accept an appointment as his father's private secretary.

During these weeks also Fillmore received communications from Dorothea Dix, and her first call at his Executive Office—incidents that would open another meaningful chapter in his life.

But Fillmore, to be sure, was not permitted to relax and enjoy a calm after the storm. Abolitionists repudiated the Fugitive Slave Act and made Fillmore the target of their wrath. Charles Sumner, the Abolitionist politician, seeking Webster's vacated seat in the Senate, declared that the act ranked with the tyranny of Appius Claudius, Louis XIV, Charles I, and George III and, in signing it, Fillmore had sunk to the "depths of infamy." "Better for him had he never been born; better for his memory and the good name of his children, had he never been President." But after his election to the Senate Sumner accepted Fillmore's invitation to dinner and found him willing to consider his appeal to pardon two "slave stealers," who were serving sentences in the District of Columbia prison.[17]

In New York the Weed-controlled State Whig Convention at Syracuse refused to endorse the compromise and Fillmore's hand in obtaining it. Fillmore's adherents directly confronted the Weed-Seward faction on the compromise and lost. Instead of accepting defeat with as little mortification as possible, they bolted the convention, and, as the Silver Greys, organized independently. The move virtually closed the door to any Fillmore-Weed rapprochement.

Shortly thereafter Pennsylvania Abolitionists rescued a fugitive slave at Christiana, and steeled by this success, Abolitionists in Syracuse and Boston staged similar rescues. Fillmore answered with a proclamation justifying the use of the armed forces to enforce the law, but his action only inflamed northern opinion. The unpopularity of the Fugitive Slave Act probably cost him a nomination for the Presidency in 1852 and possibly an election in his own right.

Yet, despite these setbacks, most Americans accepted the compromise, and Fillmore's tenure remained relatively harmonious and prosperous. His foreign policy was vigorous, but not jingoistic. He rebuked filibusterers seeking to plant the American flag in Cuba and Nicaragua, where southern expansionists hoped to acquire slave territory now that it had no place to spread within the national domain. But such men as the indomitable William Walker would not be dissuaded. One expedition to Cuba, headed by Narciso Lopez, ended in his death, and fifty of his followers were killed by a firing squad—some of them sons of the planter aristocracy. Fillmore resisted pressures to retaliate against Spain.

In the Hulsemann letter (drafted by Webster) Fillmore expressed the nation's displeasure with Austria's suppression of a Hungarian uprising led by Lajos Kossuth, "the Noble

Magyar." The United States, he insisted, sympathized with struggles for popular constitutions and national independence, and the people were willing to take their chances "and abide their destiny."

During the ensuing excitement, Congress voted funds to rescue Kossuth from a prison in Turkey, and the American Minister at Constantinople provided transportation for him to New York aboard the battleship *Mississippi*.

Fillmore also dispatched Commodore Matthew Perry on his epochal naval and diplomatic expedition to Japan, where a combination of tact and force and the awesome sight of seven smoke-belching warships led the Shogun to open ports of the Celestial Empire to the United States and subsequently to the Western world. The mission was not completed during Fillmore's tenure of office, but it remained one of his most cherished achievements.

On the domestic front Congress was disposed to enhance the beauty of the long-neglected capital of the nation. The splendor of the city at the close of the nineteenth century could scarcely have been imagined at this time. Some of the "magnificent distances" of Jefferson's tenure were now partially filled, but a decade later Henry Adams noted: "As in 1800 and 1850, so in 1860, the same rude colony was camped in the same forest, with the same unfinished Greek temples for workshops, and sloughs for roads."

The Capitol, though inadequate, was imposing, as was the Executive Mansion on Pennsylvania Avenue. The same might have been said of the classically designed marble palace which housed the Treasury Department. But the State, Army, and Navy departments warranted only plain brick structures. On the undeveloped Mall the newly erected Smithsonian Institution with its incongruous medieval towers offered a contrast to the neoclassical mode elsewhere.

Congress now made appropriations to enlarge the Capitol substantially by the construction of two massive wings, one to house the Senate, the other, the House, and to raise a new and massive dome. It turned over many of the details to the Chief Executive. On July 4, 1851, Fillmore laid the cornerstone and Webster delivered the principal oration.

Funds were also voted to landscape and beautify the Capitol grounds and to establish a library in the White House, a project which Abigail had pressed upon her husband. Like President Kennedy, Fillmore selected the books carefully, after consulting with Edward Everett and other scholars, and Abigail housed them in three- and five-tiered mahogany cases around the walls of the Oval Room on the second floor. She furnished the room tastefully with Victorian appointments, including couches and chairs. She also moved her piano and harp there, and it became the family's favorite living room. (Many years later Fillmore was credited with installing the first bathtub in the White House, but it turned out to be a joke traced to the satiric pen of H. L. Mencken.[18])

Details for the landscaping in the District were turned over to Andrew Jackson Downing, the Superintendent of Public Grounds, but Fillmore kept his hand in it. One improvement, which was directly related to the recent prohibition against the slave trade in Washington, was the razing of two slave pens which had stood across the street from the Smithsonian building. Fillmore also helped to supervise the planning and construction of the United States Asylum for Soldiers and Sailors.

Meanwhile, he attended to the duties of his office with equanimity. He was cordial to callers, plain spoken, yet seldom lacking in dignity. He was attentive to office seekers, but avoided commitments until he had taken time for reflection. He used the patronage to reward his supporters and dismissed the more partisan Weed men, particularly in New York. In Buffalo, for example, the collector of the port was an outstanding critic of Fillmore, whom Taylor had refused to remove. Now the axe fell. But Weed had most of the experienced men in his corner, and personal loyalty to Fillmore often proved a poor substitute for experience. To counteract the enormous influence of the *Evening Journal* Fillmore helped to found the Albany *Register,* but again he found no one who could match the resourceful Weed as an editor and editorialist.

Fillmore established guidelines for his department heads, leaving sufficient latitude for them to operate effectively. And none, including the prestigious and formidable Webster, forgot that they were members of a single administration and responsible to the Chief. He did not mistake the trees for the forest.

Fillmore opened the Executive Mansion to the public with a cordiality unexcelled by his predecessors. He began slowly, however. The death of Taylor dampened the capital's social life temporarily; furthermore, Abigail and his son and daughter had not been in Washington at the time of his accession, and it was not until October that they were settled in the White House. Also, Fillmore's heavy schedule accompanying the formulation of the compromise had been a deterrent.

But by the spring of 1851 Fillmore and Abigail were receiving Thursday mornings from ten to twelve. Levees were scheduled for Friday evenings from eight to ten. These receptions featured band music, but there was no dancing. Sarah Polk, the vivacious, but fundamentalist, wife of President James K. Polk, had ruled in 1845 that card playing and dancing were out of place in the White House, and the Fillmores did not reverse her decision. Alcoholic beverages were also exceptional, especially at larger and more formal receptions. At dinner Abigail's wine list was ample, but Fillmore seldom tilted his glass. He needed no artificial stimulant to spur his conviviality.

Thursday evenings were reserved for larger dinner parties, and occasionally Saturday evenings as well. A typical dinner, beginning with soup and fish, and offering the guest a choice of nine entrées, including "larded sweet-breads with mushrooms," and as many as four desserts, concluded with fruits, coffee, and liqueurs. It was served by six waiters, whose costumes included white gloves.[19]

Not regularly scheduled were smaller dinners in the family dining room. On one such occasion Webster and Corwin, Mr. and Mrs. A. H. H. Stuart, Mr. and Mrs. N. K. Hall, Congressman and Mrs. James Brooks and their daughter, and several others joined the Fillmores. Miss Brooks sang with accompaniment by her mother on the harp, and Webster displayed his talent as a conversationalist.

A highlight of one of the morning receptions in the winter of 1851–1852 was the presence of Fillmore's aging father. The papers announcing his arrival noted that it was the first time a President had entertained his father in the White House, and Washington's officialdom and citizenry turned out in unexpected numbers. They were received by father and son, and the family resemblance was unmistakable. Tall, straight, and rawboned, the stereotype of a frontiersman despite his eighty years, the elder Fillmore was at once the focus of attention. One guest paused to inquire how he might raise his son to be President. "Cradle him in a sap trough," was the prompt reply. Like his son, the grizzled veteran of two frontiers was ever ready with an answer.[20]

Thirty-one years before and from a distance of 150 miles he had advised Millard, then an apprentice of Judge Wood, that it was impossible for parents not to feel anxious for their absent children, "well knowing from experience how this world is beset with snares, temptations and dangers, and considering how apt youth are to be led astray by the allurements of pleasure and find themselves ruined before they discover the tempting bait, I was much rejoiced at reading how well you was [sic] provided with the means of paying for your board. I hope the kindness of your benefactor will not be met with ingratitude, but pursue your studies and become renowned for wisdom and virtue." [21]

The old man enjoyed the attention, and after the last guest had passed by he confided to a friend that he would not have marked out a pathway to the Presidency for his son, "But I cannot help feeling proud of it now that he is here." [22]

Edward Everett, who succeeded Webster in the State Department after the latter's death, shared an impression of a Presidential dinner with his wife. Upon his arrival he was asked to draw a number to determine his escort. He found Mary Abigail's name on his card—she was acting as hostess for her mother, who had absented herself out of respect for a sister who had recently died. "I had the honor to take in Miss Fillmore," he reported, "a pretty, modest, unaffected girl of about twenty, as much at ease at the head of the Presidential table as if she had been born a princess." The President, he added, "is just fifty years old, a very handsome man, and wholly unaffected with the cares and labors of his office." [23]

As Fillmore's term reached a close visitors frequently filled the saloons and halls to overflowing. The friendly Washington *Intelligencer* referred to a reception as "one of the largest and brilliant ever known here . . . [testifying] with distinctness the unfeigned respect and regard entertained by the people of our city, residents and strangers, for the excellent Chief Magistrate, whose term of office, equally advantageous to his country and honorable to himself, is so near its close." [24]

Few Presidents have received more plaudits from a grate-

ful citizenry. In his thirty months in the White House Millard
Fillmore was praised by the people of the nation as much as by
his friends in New York State or Buffalo.

Not the least of his admirers was Miss Dorothea Dix.

3

Dorothea Dix

EARLY YEARS

$\mathcal{S}$ even weeks after Millard Fillmore's elevation to the Presidency he received a four-page communication with the enigmatic signature, "Y'r. Known Correspondent." [1] Whether the correspondent was known to him at the time of its receipt remains undetermined, though the chirography, with its high, speedily shaped, and often inscrutable characters, would soon become familiar to him.

If the signature suggested modesty, the contents contradicted it. The letter was a call for an independent administration, free from the domination of Henry Clay or other politicians of the Whig hierarchy.

A second missive a day later under the same pseudonym contained a brief apology for seeming to impugn his ability to handle the duties of his office—and another admonition to be a "noble, truthful, self-relying, independent leader and ruler of our government." [2] A third communication a week later requesting an interview bore the signature "D. L. Dix." [3]

If Fillmore was puzzled over the identity of "Y'r. Known

[53]

Correspondent," he scarcely needed an introduction to Dorothea Dix. Her humanitarian crusade had carried her name
across the nation, and her annual quest for a federal land grant
for the indigent insane had made her a familiar figure in the
national capital.

Though "Y'r. Known Correspondent" made no reference
to herself, Fillmore might have gained insights into her personality by reading between the lines: a professed reluctance
to interject herself into his affairs; but, having done so, to
come directly to the point, submitting facts as she saw them,
standing upon principle, and revealing an obvious impatience
for those who accepted less in the name of expediency. There
was a sense of mission, and an assumption that God was looking over her shoulder.

Yet, there was also much that he could not have discerned.
Beneath the professional façade was a lonely spirit seeking in
her work the satisfactions which had eluded her in her personal life. Those who penetrated the public image found a
woman, warm, responsive, and loyal.

The forces that guided this forty-eight-year-old spinster
into such an unlikely career went back to her childhood. Dorothea Lynde Dix was born on April 4, 1802, at Hampden, a
cluster of crude slab and log cabins on the Maine frontier. She
was the daughter of an erratic Methodist evangelist and pam-
phleteer, and a possibly mentally retarded mother. The Reverend Joseph Dix was not a typical frontiersman, having grown
up in Worcester, Massachusetts, and attended Harvard College. But his collegiate life was cut short by his marriage, a
breach of conduct that resulted in his expulsion by the Harvard overseers.

Little is known about his bride, Mary Bigelow, who may

have been some eighteen years his senior. According to the Dix tradition she was poor, ignorant, and uncouth, possibly illiterate, and certainly unwanted by Joseph's parents. But she seems to have offered the security which thus far had eluded their son.

Joseph's marriage forced him to find an occupation. And having nothing better, he agreed to manage a land tract on the Penobscot River, which his father, Doctor Elijah Dix, had acquired for speculation. But Joseph soon tired of it and turned to preaching. A poor and uncertain provider, his home was a stopping place between his junkets along the backwoods. For his wife and daughter, it was little more than a workshop where they folded and hand-stitched hundreds of religious tracts.

Life for Dorothea was a constant struggle. Added to the pamphlets were the multitudinous chores incidental to the frontier and the burden of caring for two younger brothers— cooking and cleaning, carrying wood and water, feeding, clothing, and comforting—responsibilities that her hapless mother was unable to handle. Consequently Dorothea matured early, and developed a mental toughness she retained through adulthood. But physically she was frail and hollow chested, and susceptible to an inflammation of the throat and lungs which worsened with overwork and fatigue.

Almost nothing is known of her education, but her natural interest in reading overcame the disadvantage of irregular school attendance. Her father's theological works, the tracts that she handled, helped to fill the void. She made occasional trips to Boston to visit her grandparents at their fine brick home in Orange Court, where her imagination was stimulated by the costly furnishings, the glass in the windows, the lawn, garden, and stables. She also saw the sights of Boston beyond

its premises from the seat of her grandfather's wagon and listened to his travelogue of the city and his reminiscences of
Revolutionary War times. She was a precocious child.

Dorothea seems to have imbibed religion from her father,
but there is no evidence that she was receptive to free-will
Methodism. Her God was the stern Deity of Calvin. An association with liberals in her young adulthood broadened her
concepts, but her basic beliefs remained unshaken. She was a
steward of God, and his purpose and direction were omnipres-
ent in her personality.

Details of her adolescence are also meager. She refused to
speak of them, avoiding the subject on one occasion with a
cryptic, "I never knew childhood." Her family moved several
times and settled for a time in Worcester, where she had
greater opportunities for companionship and education. But at
twelve she was in Boston with her widowed grandmother,
Dorothy Lynde Dix, after possibly running away from home.

There is a tradition that Dorothea taught elementary
school at Worcester when she was fourteen and that several
years later she fell in love with her cousin there. But only her
residence with her grandmother can be stated as fact.

Grandmother Dix, or Madam Dix, as she was usually designated, took her responsibilities seriously, and inculcated
such Puritan virtues as work, discipline, responsibility, and
service in her impressionable granddaughter. But she denied
Dorothea the tenderness, warmth, and affection she craved.
Whatever the grandmother's shortcomings, however, she provided her granddaughter with a well-managed home and a
routine in which neatness, order, and punctuality were viewed
as virtues. Meals were served on time, and there was a schedule for household duties, instruction, religion, and recreation.
She also encouraged her to renew her studies. Dorothea was

an eager student and a voracious reader, but reading was seldom a mere pastime; it had to have a purpose.

Dorothea looked back on her school days in Boston at this time as the happiest of her life. She formed an abiding friendship there with Ann Heath of Brookline. To Ann she was "Thea," and with her she found a companionship she had never known with a sister or a mother. When they were not together they poured out their innermost thoughts, their joys and sorrows, their satisfactions and frustrations, in hastily written notes. Dorothea was usually the petitioner and confessor, Ann the adviser and consoler.

Dorothea's affection extended to the entire Heath family, and she seemed to find relief from loneliness by identifying herself with their vicissitudes. The correspondence continued for more than fifty years, and it offers the most revealing record of Dorothea's adolescence and young womanhood that has survived.

Her residence in Boston, the "Athens of America," afforded intellectual stimulation unmatched anywhere in America. By 1820 the bustling commercial center of forty thousand was at the threshold of a ferment in literature, theology, philosophy, and social reform which would make it the center of the Flowering of New England. Dorothea found the sermons of William Ellery Channing, with their forecast of broader horizons for man, to be thrilling intellectual confrontations. She was flattered to accept his invitation to teach a class of children in the Sunday school of Federal Street Church.

Her letters to Ann Heath are sprinkled with observations upon Channing and his conservative critics, and the controversies attending his speaking and writing. The two young women also found Channing's young and handsome assistant at Federal Street Church, Ezra Stiles Gannett, an inviting subject. They followed the rumors of his romantic attachments and speculated upon his marriage. "I heard not long since that this season had proved fatal to Bachelors," Dorothea playfully advised Ann, "and that the few survivors were making hasty preparations for changing their *singleness* of heart, lest they should be pointed out as *solitary* monuments, and be looked upon with no complacent regard by the candidates of the other sex." [4] Dorothea met Gannett at Ann's home. He was cordial, but not romantically inclined.

Dorothea took advantage of her residence in Boston to attend sermons and lectures by local and visiting intellectuals, but her shyness deterred her from active association with them, even after she had won recognition as an author and teacher. In a letter to Ann she noted that in church she had seen Elizabeth Peabody, Doctor Channing's young amanuensis who was already acclaimed as an exceptional teacher and conversationalist. Dorothea had *"more* than *half* a mind to speak to her *after service,"* but "Was restrained by the consideration of the *time* and *place,* also by a doubt how I might be received." [5]

On the occasion of General Lafayette's first visit to Boston on his triumphal tour of America in 1824–1825, Dorothea was invited to a reception in his honor at the home of Doctor H. S. Hayward, whose daughters had been her close friends since school days. She related her mixed emotions to Ann:

> This evening I am to be presented to the Marquis; dare not think what I may appear like but fear, very like a simpleton. I half dread going, but I may never again enjoy the opportunity, so shall summon all my courage and confidence to meet the emergency in the case.

She was favorably impressed with the aging hero and also with his son, but after the honored guests had departed, one of her friends asked her why she had looked so sober all evening and inquired whether she had not found the General handsome. "I did not criticize his features, I was thinking of his deeds," was her poor repartee.[6]

Her sense of inadequacy led her to avoid purely social gatherings. "I have little taste for fashionable dissipations, cards, and dancing"; she confided to Ann, "the theatre and tea parties are my aversion and I look with little envy on those who find their enjoyment in such transitory delights, if delights they may be called." [7] Unwittingly, in rejecting such social activities Dorothea was cutting herself off from other young people and jeopardizing her chances for marriage.

This personal insecurity continued through her life. She repeatedly declined invitations to formal affairs, including those in the White House when she was in Washington.

By contrast, she came to relish more informal associations, many of them with the socially and intellectually elite: Doctor Channing, the Rathbone family in England, Francis and Matilda Lieber, Julia Ward Howe and her husband, Samuel Gridley Howe, Secretary of the Navy and Mrs. James C. Dobbin, Senator and Mrs. John Bell of Tennessee, President and Mrs. James K. Polk, President and Mrs. Millard Fillmore, and others. And at times she looked upon the masses with a patronizing attitude. While she deplored the misery of the Irish, whom she saw at firsthand on a tour of the Emerald Isle in 1854, she considered their emigration to the United States "the curse of a vicious population sent over to people our now fast corrupted and over-burthened country." [8] This is not to say that Dorothea was a nativist. In the election of 1856 she regretted Fillmore's acceptance of the chauvinist American

(Know-Nothing) nomination for the Presidency, and only her personal attachment to him resolved her misgivings. She was critical of the thousands of poor in Scotland and England for contributing their pennies, and of Harriet Beecher Stowe for accepting them by the thousands, for her condemnation of slavery in *Uncle Tom's Cabin*.[9] In fact, slavery itself drew no anathema from the great humanitarian.

But her repugnance for "purposeless" socializing did not deter her from "purposeful" church-related activities. She participated actively in an Orphan Sewing Society and extended her involvement to visitations of the "abodes of want and disease." She wrote to Ann of one home:

> Oh, how much misery is sheltered in this place. I have never before got so much excited, so completely overcome. I am today ashamed of myself, but I cannot bear such scenes; if I can by any means render myself useful, I do and will; but my mind, meanwhile, is ill at ease. . . . I am to go again this afternoon to see what more can be done for two poor suffering females.[10]

But her primary concern at this time was not social reform per se but her own immediate career. At nineteen she decided to open an elementary school in her grandmother's house, and she threw herself into the work with the intensity and abandonment that would be her trademark.

Her obligation was to prepare the children for grammar school at eight, and the curriculum included the rudiments of reading, writing, and arithmetic, training in manners, and the memorization of selected verses and a broad familiarity with the precepts of the Scriptures.

At the outset Dorothea found the teaching elevating. She declared that she loved to watch the progress of a young being

and found satisfaction in her humble efforts to advance the
feeble on their paths of toil. It was like sowing seed on good
ground:

> What greater bliss than to look back on days spent in use-
> fulness, in doing good to those around us. The duties of a
> teacher are neither few nor small but they elevate the
> mind and give energy to the character.[11]

But her physical strength was unequal to her strenuous
activity. On New Year's Day of 1822 she pondered upon her
work and health. She was suffering from a hard cough, and
she speculated upon the possibility that she would not live to
see another spring:

> Today I am almost sick; the pain in my side and chest
> is almost constant; but I am going to nurse myself very
> carefully and dare say I shall be relieved soon. If I could
> speak in school without feeling a constant desire to cough,
> I should suffer much less; but you know there can be little
> silence on my part, surrounded as I am with those who are
> putting "perpetual questions." [12]

Her poor health sometimes forced her to absent herself
from school and to remain in her room. But the change
afforded her little relaxation. She advised Ann,

> I am so much accustomed to a methodical appropria-
> tion of my time that now [that] I am compelled to relin-
> quish the ordinary duties of the day I feel restless and anx-
> ious. I do not like vacations out of season, but I must per-
> force submit to this present necessity, and bear the cross as
> I ought, with submission. . . . And I try to think every-

thing is ordered for the best. It must be so, for none but the Atheist would dare another belief.[13]

Her continued ill health finally induced Dorothea to close her school and devote her time to study and writing. She particularly enjoyed composing hymns and devotional stanzas. Her keen memory gave her an instant recall of numerous passages in the Scriptures and religious commentaries, and versifying became a form of recreation. She scattered bits of poetry through her letters and occasionally rose from bed to jot down a fleeting thought.

She had also undertaken a child's book of knowledge, and she now took time to complete it. *Conversations on Common Things*, published in 1825, was a compendium of about three hundred short subjects ranging from history to science. Her purpose, she noted in the preface, was to stimulate young minds to seek useful information through life and "fit them to lay up treasures which would not like riches of this world take to themselves wings nor yet by moth or rust be corrupted." The book filled a void in children's literature and was at once a best seller. In fifty years it went through sixty editions!

She also edited a book of *Hymns for Children*, many of which seem to have been her own productions, two volumes of devotional passages and poems, titled *Evening Hours* and *Meditations for Private Hours*. She authored *Moral Tales*, short stories about children in which the principal characters personified virtues or faults: the punctual boy; the girl who forgot her manners and whispered in church; and the "dainty boy," who cut up three times as much as he ate. She edited *The Pearl or Affection's Gift: A Christmas and New Year's Present* and *Garland of Flora*, booklets filled with sentimental poems, ancient and modern.

Dorothea's output was an impressive, if not a notable accomplishment, and she had done it in less than five years. The royalties were lucrative and, combined with her grandmother's estate, provided her with an independent income.

When she was not writing she was engaged in ambitious reading programs. During a few weeks' visit with a Miss Gourgas in Weston, Vermont, in January of 1826 she divided her time between reading, needlework, walking, and riding, when the weather permitted. "Cowper, Montgomery, Wordsworth and Percival daily contribute to our social intercourse," she noted. They had completed Swinburne's and Hasselquist's travels and Cooper's *Pilot* (which she considered a waste of time), and were currently engaged in Robertson's *Scotland*.[14]

But after a few years a career of writing and reading lost its appeal. It lacked the activity she needed and did not seem to be the proper fulfillment of her duty to God and man:

> We are not sent into this world mainly to enjoy the loveliness therein; nor to sit us down in passive ease; no, we were sent here for action; the soul that seeks to do the will of God with a pure heart fervently, does not yield to the lethargy of ease.[15]

Dorothea's dislike of ease was not unlike that expounded years later by a dynamic Theodore Roosevelt in a famous speech in Chicago.[16] Thus she reopened the school in her home, and for good measure undertook a charity school in the loft of her grandmother's barn in the afternoons. "Why not, when it can be done without exposure or expense," she observed to her grandmother, "let *me* rescue some of America's miserable children from vice and guilt?" [17]

Dorothea continued both schools for several years, but her ceaseless pace inevitably took its toll. She was compelled repeatedly to take vacations "out of season."

Aware of the disparity between her concept of service and her frail physique, Doctor Channing advised her to adjust her plans of usefulness to the will of God. "We make *these* the occasion of self-will, vanity, and pride as much as anything else. May not one of your chief dangers lie there?" [18] To help her unwind he engaged her to tutor his children during several summers at Oakmont, near Narragansett Bay, and a winter on St. Croix. She found her association with the Channings enjoyable and relaxing, and she basked for a time in the Caribbean sunshine. But she could not resist the temptation to use the opportunity to study the natural history of the island and to convert the tropical paradise into a workshop. She returned with collections of exotic plants, shells, and rocks—and with notebooks filled with excerpts from religious works of ancient and modern periods.

She became one of Channing's enthusiastic disciples, and her months of close association provided opportunities to converse with him upon theology, transcendentalism, and social reform, but she was a better listener than conversationalist and did not respond to him with the spontaneity of Elizabeth Peabody. For the latter, Channing's approval became an entrée to the select circle of Boston intellectuals including Margaret Fuller, Bronson Alcott, Emerson, Theodore Parker, Orestes Brownson, and Channing. But Dorothea remained outside.

Back in Boston Dorothea was drawn into the movement to provide secondary education for girls. Several public and private schools had been founded, and a high school for young women was being tried experimentally. She decided to conduct a school in her grandmother's spacious home and to convert the second floor into a dormitory for boarding students. As might have been expected she placed emphasis upon character building, religion, and morals, and also stressed natural history and French.

Evidence of Dorothea's awareness of new trends and her interest in science is suggested by the incorporation of astronomy and mineralogy into the curriculum. And when she could not find room for the former in the regular schedule, she reserved several evenings a week, and offered it then to the upper classes. "I had some hesitation as to the expedience of undertaking it," she explained. "It will require much time and you will know that even now I have little unoccupied . . . [but] I think I shall make the attempt. There are hours when I feel equal to almost every undertaking and again times are singularly changed, and I find every energy enfeebled." [19] The school was an immediate success.

Many years later, after she had gained renown as a reformer, several of her students were asked about their old school days and their recollections of Miss Dix. They remembered her high standards and strict discipline, her emphasis upon moral training, the habit of introspection to identify and cleanse imperfections, weekly reports of these self-examinations, and solemn and probing personal interviews on Saturday evening. The whole suggested a monastic austerity, lightened somewhat by her personal attention to their welfare.

They also remembered Dorothea's tall, slender, and slightly stooped figure, her large and expressive eyes animating a pleasant, but rather plain face; her delicacy and femininity which belied her almost indefatigable energy.

One student, who entered the school at sixteen, declared that Miss Dix had fascinated her from the outset. "Next to my mother, I thought her the most beautiful woman I had ever seen. She was in the prime of her years [thirty], tall and of dignified carriage, head finely shaped and set, with an abundance of soft, wavy brown hair." [20]

Dorothea conducted her school for girls for five years, but was then compelled to close it because of a recurrence of poor health. To the burden of teaching and administration, she had added the care of her grandmother, now past ninety. It was more than her frail physique could bear, and by the spring of 1836 she was beaten. She was confined to her room in a state of exhaustion; and worse, she was hemorrhaging from the lungs.

Fearful that she would refuse to take the rest required for recovery, her friends interceded to urge her to go to Europe to convalesce. She was reluctant. The crossing was boisterous in the spring; at best it would require several uncomfortable weeks. She had planned no European itinerary. But she eventually was persuaded and sailed on April 22 in the company of several friends.

After a fatiguing crossing she arrived in England completely prostrated. She might have expired on the Liverpool docks had not a letter of introduction from Doctor Channing enabled her to reach the family of William Rathbone at Greenbank, several miles from the city. Subjected to frequent hemorrhaging and a piercing pain in her side, she spent several months in bed, and remained a semi-invalid for many weeks thereafter. Surprisingly, she relaxed and accepted the tender ministrations of her attentive hosts.

Almost by chance Dorothea's misfortune had dropped her into a nerve center of England's cataclysmic transition from a rural to an urban society. The vast Dingle slum had mushroomed adjacent to Liverpool's great docks, and William Rathbone, as a Liverpool merchant and Member of Parliament, was engaged in a variety of philanthropic projects designed to aid the downtrodden. As her condition improved Dorothea was drawn into the discussions of the family and the many visitors who stopped there, and her awareness of suffering in both England and America was sharpened.

"Hearts met hearts, minds joined with minds," she noted,

"and what were the secondary trials of pain to the enfeebled, suffering body when daily was administered the soul's medicine and food." [21]

Eighteen months after her surprising arrival at Greenbank she prepared to turn homeward; her European tour had scarcely taken her beyond the sound of the rushing tides which swept past the Liverpool harbor.

Dorothea's return to Boston in the fall of 1837 was joyous. Her health was improved and she had only the fondest memories of her lengthy visit with the Rathbones. But it required only a few months of relative inactivity to rekindle her old restiveness. She was reluctant to return to teaching, and at thirty-five, with little in her past to suggest it, saw no likelihood of marriage. Grandmother Dix had died while Dorothea was in Europe and her two brothers were now self-supporting. To avoid the rigors of a New England winter she went to Alexandria, Virginia, and Washington for a few months. She frequented the Congressional Library and visited historic sites, but found tourism unrewarding.

No day or hour, she gloomily reminded Ann Heath, should lack a useful purpose. There were sufferers to comfort, the wandering to lead home, and the sinner to reclaim. "Oh, how can any fold the hands to rest and say to the spirit, 'take thine ease for all is well'!" [22] She groped for a mission to make her life meaningful and satisfying.

Her answer came on March 28, 1841, in the guise of an invitation from a friend to teach a Sunday school lesson to about twenty women in the East Cambridge House of Correction. No record remains of her text or her reception by the prisoners. But among the pathetic little group she observed that several women were obviously insane. She also found their room unheated, poorly ventilated, and stinking. When she approached the jailer he replied that a fire was not needed and would be unsafe. Outraged, she took the matter to court, and obtained a promise that the rooms would be warmed.

The incident might have ended here if she could have forgotten the misery of the insane, and if she had not had an uneasy suspicion that other houses of correction in Massachusetts were equally offensive and degrading. Thoroughly aroused, she decided to find out, and with notebook in hand she inspected almshouses and jails from the Berkshires to the Cape. A fragment from her copious notes reads:

> Leicester Alms House, June 15, 1842
>> Town farm: House not neat; greatly wanting repairs.
>> Inmates: 7, five over 60 years; no insane; no idiots; religious service about once a year, pastoral visits very rare; few books.
>> Aged woman—son seized her property. taken to poor house at E. Bradford; chained to block. Has, since I visited the poor house, died.[23]

Eighteen months later, with her evidence assembled and tabulated, she drafted a petition to the state legislature:

> . . . I come as the advocate of the helpless, forgotten, insane, and idiotic, men and women; of beings sunk to a condition from which the most unconcerned would start with real horror; of beings wretched in prisons, and more wretched in our almshouses. . . . If my pictures are displeasing, coarse and severe, my subjects, it must be recollected, offer no tranquil, refined, or composing features. . . .
>
> I proceed, gentlemen, briefly to call your attention to the *present* state of insane persons confined within this

Commonwealth, in *cages, closets, cellars,* and *pens, chained naked, beaten with rods* and *lashed* into obedience. . . .

Groton: . . . There is no window, save an opening half the size of the sash, and closed by a board shutter; in one corner is some brickwork surrounding an iron stove, which in cold weather serves for warming the room. The occupant of this dreary abode is a young man, who has been declared incurably insane. He can move a measured distance in his prison; that is, so far as a strong, heavy chain depending from an iron collar which invests his neck permits.

Shurburne: . . . The person who conducted me tried with a stick, to rouse the inmate; I entreated her to desist; the twilight of the place making it difficult to discern anything within the cage; there at last I saw a human being, partially extended, cast upon his back amidst a mass of filth, the sole furnishing, whether for comfort or necessity which the place afforded.

The indictment concluded with a stirring call for action:

Men of Massachusetts, I beg, I implore, I demand pity and protection for these of my suffering, outraged sex. . . . Gentlemen, I commit to you this sacred cause. Your action upon this subject will affect the present and future conditions of hundreds and thousands. In this legislation, as in all things, you may exercise that wisdom which is the breath of the power of God." [24]

The petition became a storm of controversy, and Dorothea was berated and defended in dozens of presses. Despite her attempt to make the contest one of issues rather than personalities, local officials felt pilloried and termed the memorial a pack of lies.

In the face of the determined and sometimes frenzied opposition, her petition might have been defeated or at least postponed had she not previously enlisted the assistance of an able corps of supporters. Doctor Samuel Gridley Howe, a Boston philanthropist, who had offered his services to the Greeks in their struggle for independence and pioneered in the education of the blind, corroborated her evaluation of the Cambridge jail, and led the drive for passage in the legislature. Horace Mann, who had introduced bills to provide more enlightened care for the insane in the legislature thirteen years earlier, came to her aid, as did Doctor Channing during his last illness and the young and brilliant Charles Sumner.

Behind the scenes Dorothea counseled the legislators, demonstrating a quiet confidence and persuasiveness which she had not revealed earlier.

The result was a decisive victory, and an appropriation to enlarge the already existing mental hospital at Worcester. It became the first monument to her crusade.

It has not been ascertained whether Dorothea's special concern for the plight of the insane predated her inspection of the East Cambridge House of Correction or if she was aware of newer therapies. It can be assumed, however, that she was conversant with the work of Doctor Philippe Pinel in Paris and William Tuke at York. She may have met the latter's son Richard during her visit at the Rathbones. Pinel's publication of a treatise on mental disease in 1791 marked the beginning of a rational and scientific approach to the treatment of the insane. He advocated a humane system, the removal of restraints from the victims, and occupational therapy. His treatise became a guidebook for reformers in Europe and America.

Shortly after the publication of this book, William Tuke established the York Retreat, applying the principles of Pinel to provide better care for fellow Friends who were mentally sick. It became a model for other institutions and a laboratory where students might observe the new therapy in operation.

Whatever her deficiencies may have been at the outset, Dorothea became an advocate of Pinel and Tuke and was soon in contact with American leaders. But the immediate need was the creation of hospitals or lunatic asylums, as they were called at this time, where humane methods could be introduced. She made it her first order of business, and she did not deviate from it for many years.

With an initial success in Massachusetts assured, she was eager to repeat the formula elsewhere. Her response to a call from Rhode Island was a letter to the Providence *Journal* titled: "Astonishing Tenacity of Life," a shocking account of the maltreatment of Abram Simmons in a dungeon in Little Compton:

> "He's here" [said the attendant], unlocking the strong, solid iron door. . . . An iron frame interlaced with rope was the sole furniture. The place was filthy, damp and noisome; and the inmate, the crazy man . . . there he stood, near the door motionless and silent, his tangled hair fell about his shoulders; his bare feet pressed the filthy wet floor; he was emaciated to a shadow. . . . In moving a little forward I struck against something which returned a sharp metalic sound, it was a length of ox-chain connected to an iron ring which encircled a leg of the insane man.[25]

Finding several wealthy donors, Dorothea was saved a statewide campaign to provide a building program, and Butler Hospital at Providence became her second monument. A year

later New Jersey succumbed to her pressure, and the State
Lunatic Asylum at Trenton was a reality. It was her first
wholly new state hospital, and she proudly referred to it as her
"first-born child."

Meanwhile, she had initiated action in Pennsylvania,
New York, Maryland, Ohio, Kentucky, and Tennessee. By
1845 she could report to the Rathbones that she had covered
ten thousand miles in three years, and had visited eighteen
state penitentiaries, three hundred county jails and houses of
correction, over five hundred almshouses, and had assisted in
establishing six hospitals for the insane.

Traveling by stagecoach, steamboat, canal packet, and railroad when available, often at great inconvenience, stopping at
homes of friends or at boardinghouses and hotels, Dorothea
continued her circuits North and West with occasional side
trips to the Canadian provinces in summer and the South and
Southwest in winter, despite its demands upon her precarious
health. Her procedure followed what became a familiar pat-
tern: investigation; publicity; legislative action, with her ever
ready counsel from a convenient location at the capital. Yet she
remained flexible, revising her plans, itineraries, and time-
tables to fit local situations. She traveled alone and handled
her own correspondence.

In the process Dorothea learned a good deal about politics
and politicians, accepting the latter as necessary, but scarcely
respectable instruments in her mission. She also attracted a
corps of enthusiastic supporters, who opened their doors to
her, looked after local arrangements, and worked with her as
she needed them. The experience broadened her perspective,
teaching her to live with defeat—albeit reluctantly—and sustaining her through a second and third campaign to gain an
objective.

Though she had changed little physically during her forties

—her tall spare figure, the characteristic parting of her hair yet untouched by gray, and the grace of her movements would not have suggested the passage of a decade—a closer scrutiny would have revealed a self-confidence that had been lacking earlier. Her repeated successes, the demand for her services, the deference with which people approached her, and an increasing dependence upon her decisions seemed to add to her stature. She spoke and wrote with greater assurance, and her manner sometimes became authoritarian. When displeased she could be abrupt and even petulant.

Her developing "professional" image, however, did not appear to affect her less formal and more personal relations with old friends. On her travels, and for brief periods between them, Dorothea made their homes her own, often on short notice. Families like the Robert Hares of Philadelphia cherished her association, and were ever ready to receive her. Her friendship often extended to the children, and she corresponded with both Mrs. Hare and her daughters. She also took a deep interest in Doctor Robert Hare's career as a chemist and essayist. She introduced his works to President Fillmore and sponsored their friendship.

Yet, if sojourning with friends was a solace from the strain of her strenuous rounds, and much to be preferred to rooming-houses and hotels for the amenities of life, it did not provide a home and family. In her letters to Ann Heath she sometimes alluded to this void—a void she had felt from childhood.

In 1848 Dorothea deviated from her routine to stake out a claim for a federal land grant to the states for the care of the indigent insane. Congress was voting extensive tracts from the huge public domain for railroads and facing pressures from lobbyists for grants for other purposes including pensions and homesteads. And Congressman Justin Morrill would soon petition Congress for land grants for the so-called land-grant colleges to support agricultural and mechanical arts. Why not use it, she argued, to ameliorate the lot of the indigent insane? On June 23 she petitioned Congress for a grant of five million acres.

Her strategy in Washington was consistent with her practices in the states. She established a headquarters and remained as long as her presence was required, sometimes a few months, sometimes an entire session of the Congress. One of her letters in 1849 affords a view of her operations and her appraisal of the forces at work to float or scuttle her bill:

> Specially and prominently, at this particular time, I am watching and guarding the 5,000,000 bill. Through the courtesy of my friends in the Senate and House, a special committee room is assigned to my use in the Capitol. I am neither sanguine nor discouraged. I think the bill may be deferred till next session. A new difficulty is to be combated, the President [Polk] having declared to his Cabinet that he will *veto* all and every land bill which does not make a provisional payment to the general government. I suppose this will be gotten over by a small premium upon every acre sold. I, fortunately, am on good terms with Mrs. Polk and the President, knowing well all their family friends in Tennessee and North Carolina. The Vice President, Mr. Dallas, the intimate associate of many of my Philadelphia friends, is warmly in favor of the bill. I have decidedly declined the interposition of the State Legislatures, preferring to rely on the "uninstructed" deliberations and acts of the two branches of Congress. The public interest is involved for *all* the states, and those who will vote negatively do so on constitutional grounds, imaginarily involving the federal integrity.[26]

Failing passage, Dorothea left Washington to resume her work in the states: Louisiana, Mississippi, and Alabama receiving her attention in the fall of 1849. The burning of the Alabama state capitol at Montgomery turned a likely victory into defeat. The building had been occupied for only a few months when, in the midst of a heated debate over apportionment, burning embers began to drop from the ceiling. A hasty exit saved the more than one hundred members from the holocaust.

The fledgling state felt the pinch, and a call for retrenchment became irresistible. "I think, after this year," Dorothea complained, "I shall certainly not suffer myself to engage in any legislative affairs for a year. I can conceive the state of mind which this induces to be like nothing save the influences of the gambling table, on such unlooked for, and often trivial, balances do the issues depend." [27]

But her depression was only temporary. Days later she was in Washington to do battle for the land-grant bill.

In response to a repeated request from an old friend for more information about her activities, Dorothea outlined a typical day at work, and, for good measure, added a few details about her weekends and social affairs. Few of her letters are as self-revealing: the efficiency with which she organized a seventeen-and-one-half-hour day, and the restrictions which she placed upon her social life, and the begrudging, and almost apologetic, acceptance of it:

In the morning till lately I have risen at 4¼. After the duties of the first hour, I write till 8½ when I breakfast— with my knitting in my hand at intervals—and hear the morning paper read by the Professor [Johnson]. At 10 I go to my place in the Congress Library at the Capitol, and remain there 5 hours or more till 3 P.M. or past, when I return to 12th Street. Read letters or papers till 4½ when we dine. I sit with the family till six o'clock; go to my room and write till 8, when I return to the parlor, take tea and remain with book or basket till 10, at which hour I retire to my room for the night, sometimes employed till an hour or two later, but not often.

On Sundays at 8 A.M. I go to the penitentiary and either remain till 1 P.M. or come into the city in time for morning service. I do not go to church either afternoons or evenings. Saturdays I frequently go to Baltimore to the prisons and hospitals returning at 8 P.M. My correspondence with attending business consumes most of my day.

Now for the dissipations, the fashionable life, you think I lead. *One* day from 12 till 4 since I have been in Washington dating from December 6th I have appropriated to returning calls—and left about 50 cards; except them I am still in arrears. Three visits only I have paid, *viz*: dined at the President's; was one of three hundred friends at the Mansion of the Secretary of the Navy; one of two hundred at a very select party given by the Hon'ble J[ohn] A[lsop] King to the Heads of the Departments, leading officers and families of the Army and Navy and the Foreign Ministers. So you see I am not greatly dazzled by the attractions of gay life in Washington, and probably if I remain here I shall not find myself consenting to be again in public. . . .

I board at Professor Johnson's, 12th Street near E. The family consists of the head thereof above named, Mrs. Johnson, her sister, Miss Donaldson, and a young nephew and niece, adopted children.

Thus I am quiet and follow my pursuits without interruption. My friends, the Henry's, are at lodgings in the same neighborhood.[28]

In the fall of 1849, dissatisfied with the limitations of the five-million-acre bill of the previous session, Dorothea now doubled the acreage and asked for an additional two and one-half million acres for the blind, deaf, and dumb. She was hopeful that the Whig administration of General Taylor would prove more amenable than its Democratic predecessor. But the time proved inauspicious. Congress was absorbed in Clay's Omnibus Bill, designed to settle the momentous and divisive issues stemming from the Mexican War. Lesser matters languished in committee.

On July 10, 1850, however, Dorothea faced a nearly unknown quantity. President Taylor was dead, and the almost obscure Millard Fillmore occupied the Executive Mansion.

Did the change of leadership portend success or failure for her bill? She prepared to make Fillmore's acquaintance more closely.

4

Getting
Together

1850–1853

*C*orrespondence in the nineteenth century was almost
as indispensable to friendship as to politics or social
reform. At a time when travel was limited by the pace of a
horse and curtailed by the discomforts and costs of the road,
letters substituted for verbal conversation.

Beyond their utility as purveyors of news and gossip, letters were at once an outlet from routine and a means of sharing thoughts with relatives and friends. Such outlets were
rare in the workaday world of the mid-1800s. Letters were also
highly valued as records. Frequently they were folded carefully for filing and sometimes even cataloged by recipients.

Victorian letters were also badges of respectability, testi-
monials to the American success story. By 1850, thousands of
Americans who had started life in humble circumstances had
achieved material prosperity. But their grip on the social lad-
der was slippery. Aware that they were judged by social usages
—and especially by their speech and writing—these persons
struggled for self-improvement. They purchased pocket dic-

tionaries and handbooks on letter-writing containing models suited to almost any situation, occurrence, or relationship.* They joined reading circles, and supported lyceums and other popular lecture series. In most American communities competence in letter-writing was important enough to warrant instruction of children in epistolary mechanics and in the obligation of maintaining punctual correspondence.

An inspection of prevailing mid-century conventions in American letter-writing reveals that salutations were formal and the use of given names exceptional. "His Excellency" was appropriate for a President, "The Honorable" for a legislator, and "Esquire" for a lawyer or highly successful businessman or landholder. A niece or nephew might write "Dear Uncle," but never append his given name, though use of a surname would be appropriate. The signature, whether that of a man or woman, was ordinarily the initials of the sender.

Dorothea Dix and Millard Fillmore, like their contemporaries, devoted part of almost every day to correspondence. If letter-writing could not be fitted into daylight hours, it was completed by candlelight. Such fidelity had the built-in satisfaction of generating a heavy volume of incoming mail.

Victorian mores spilled over into their letters. Formalities were scrupulously observed. In her letters to him, Dorothea addressed Fillmore at first as "His Excellency, The President." She later settled on "My Dear Sir and Friend." Her closings were apt to be less formal ("Stedfastly yours," was her favorite) but she consistently signed her name "D. L. Dix," never "Dorothea."

---

* One such handbook is exhaustively titled *American Fashionable Letter Writer, Original and Selected, Containing a Variety of Letters on Business, Love, Courtship, Marriage, Relationship, Friendship, etc. with Forms of Complimentary Cards, To the Whole Are Prefixed Directions for Letter Writing, and Rules for Composition*. It was published by W. & H. Merriam, Troy, New York, in 1845.

Fillmore's salutation was almost always a formal "My Dear Miss Dix." His style, direct and unpretentious, was similar to his manner of speech. However, in expressing what was undoubtedly his sincere admiration for Dorothea's ministrations to the insane, Fillmore was sometimes effusive and hackneyed —traits suggestive of his gallantry toward females. His characteristic closing was a simple "Your friend, Millard Fillmore."

At the outset Dorothea's letters were usually brief. There simply was no need to write long letters. Fillmore was abreast of affairs in Washington and her reserve would not permit her to dwell on personal matters. Since the President was available to callers, she preferred to take important matters to him at his office.

But there were exceptions: the rumor of an unwise (in her judgment) appointment might elicit Dorothea's passionate appeal for reconsideration. In these situations she dashed off her thoughts with such abandonment that her writing became well-nigh indecipherable—abbreviations and scant punctuation complicated a timesaving scrawl she termed hieroglyphics. For additional emphasis she sometimes capitalized and underlined important items. There were many letters to write, and Dorothea seldom had time to be philosophic or reflective.

However, when Congress adjourned and she took to the road to attend missions throughout the States, Dorothea felt a personal need to inform Fillmore of her work. She wrote to him of her successes and failures, and the dispositions of mind she encountered in her travels. And since her itinerary had no rigid schedule, she did not ask that he answer her letters. The satisfaction of finding an occasional response waiting at her address in Trenton, New Jersey, or of having one forwarded, was a sufficient reward.

Fillmore's rejoinders were sometimes short—invitations to his office or his home in the White House. When Dorothea was out of Washington he sometimes delayed an answer until he had received several missives, attributing his tardiness to the pressures of office. When he did respond, Fillmore's concern was for her crusade and welfare. His pleasure in conversing with her, and his high spirits emerge from the pages.

After leaving the Presidency Fillmore was a more punctual correspondent, but he sometimes found that retirement provided few topics of interest, particularly when he was addressing a woman who scoffed at suggestion of a vacation or a slower pace.

But Dorothea's satisfaction came from his personal interest and his reassurance of personal well-being. She never found Fillmore's letters commonplace.

During Fillmore's term in the White House the Fillmore-Dix correspondence contained fifty letters, twenty-four by Dorothea and twenty-six by Fillmore. There are references to possibly twelve additional letters which are missing. The initial letter by Dorothea is dated August 30, 1850; the last, a missive from Fillmore, is dated February 23, 1853, nine days before the termination of his Presidency.

The correspondence, which was initiated by Dorothea in behalf of her land-grant bill for asylums for the indigent insane, indicates Fillmore's support of this legislation and of Dorothea's broader crusade for humane care of the insane. It also reveals Dorothea's enthusiastic approval of Fillmore's leadership and an almost immediate friendship based on mutual respect and the enjoyment each found in the other's company.

Two lengthy letters from Dorothea provide a striking eye-witness account of the secession crisis in South Carolina in 1850. Others document the vicissitudes of her land-grant bill, her personal identification with Fillmore's Presidency, her affection for the Fillmore family, and her numerous calls at the White House. Fillmore's letters, though more matter of fact, indicate both a dedication to duty and an ability to find relaxation from the cares of office. They also reflect the pleasure he found in his associations with Dorothea, whether they were her more formal appearances in his Executive office or her less formal visitations.*

ৰ§ 1. To MILLARD FILLMORE

Dorothea was alarmed that Fillmore's inexperience might tempt him to turn over Executive power to Henry Clay or other leaders. She was particularly disturbed by a rumor that he would name Richard H. Bayard of Philadelphia as Secretary of the Interior. She regarded Bayard as a mere henchman of Clay. Preferring not to use her own name, she signed the letter "Y'r. Known Correspondent."

Fillmore subsequently appointed Bayard as chargé d'affaires at Brussels, Belgium.

August 30th [1850]

It is not Sir without great hesitation that I obtrude opinions on your notice, and only urgent motives would move me

* The letters are reproduced here as the correspondents wrote them except for minor changes in punctuation.

To separate Fillmore's identification notes at the bottom of Dorothea's letters from the text, they have been enclosed in brackets. Brackets have also been used to indicate insertions made by the editor for clarity or identification. Gaps in the text caused by mutilation of the manuscript are indicated by brackets, and a question mark has been inserted within brackets when the reading is doubtful.

The Dorothea L. Dix and Millard Fillmore letters published in this volume are in the following depositories: *Letters by Dorothea L. Dix:* Numbers 1 to 3 and 6 through 24, Buffalo and Erie Co. Historical Society. Numbers 4 and 5 and 25 through 105, State University of New York, Oswego. *Letters by Millard Fillmore:* Numbers 1 through 8 and 10 through 69, Harvard College Library. Number 9, Massachusetts Historical Society.

to express views which may seem to your mind uncalled for. I have now but very few moments at command, and must proceed rather bluntly to my subject.

I learn with no less surprise than mortification that Mr. [Richard H.] Bayard of Philadelphia is pressed upon your notice as a suitable person for filling the vacant secretary-ship [Department of Interior], and I know of but one individual of note who could possibly press such a nomination. It has been said indeed, both in Maryland and in Pennsylvania, that Mr. Clay was likely to rule our new President as he most disastrously swayed the Cabinet during Ex-President Tyler's Administration. As I have some singular facts which would throw light on this subject if opportunity should ever offer, I shall take the [liberty of] communicating them.

Mr. Bayard has a very *mediocre* reputation; is by many called a good sort of man. That he is certainly singularly forbearing and amiable in some domestic relations, and in admitting the intimate friendship of his patron [Clay] is too well known to need comment, and too special and unwelcome a topic to be more explicitly dwelt upon.

Your popularity Sir, I need not announce as a fact of which you can be ignorant, is rising—and that steadily. All my private correspondence proves this. But allow me to say it would have a singular check were you to bring Mr. Bayard into your councils. There are many who esteem you; there are many who will love and honour you, but it must be as a noble, truthful, self-relying, independent leader and ruler of our government, not as the (pardon my speaking so very plainly) not as the tail of one whose long public career has often been advanced and distinguished by great acts and great efforts, but of late years who has shown how entirely all could be merged that is wise and honourable, in a petty not a great *ambition*.

I feel how abruptly I write. I see how partial you may declare my judgment, but I speak, I do assure you Sir, with a true regard to your interests and those of our country, and from *certain* knowledge of many facts you cannot know.

Please destroy all my letters. I need not add my name, for I am no insidious anonymous correspondent.

If you are embarrassed in choice of a good and business man for the vacancy referred to, who is likely to be more faithful to you or more able, and bringing with him more virtuous and honourable relations of a domestic character than J[ames] G[ore] King of New Jersey? But there are others beside who would stand fast, and are more able than *"the nominated."* ["Y'r. Known Correspondent," Wash'n., Sept. 3, 1850. Against Appointment of Mr. Bayard of Penn'a. to office of Sec'y. of the Interior.]

❧ 2. To MILLARD FILLMORE

Dorothea was apprehensive about appearing overzealous in her letter of August 30. She hastily drafted a second missive. Though more temperate, she again warned Fillmore against the influence of Clay. She also cautioned him about Senator Robert A. Tombs of Georgia, one of the most powerful of the southern Whigs.

Dorothea's quotation from the "wise historian of kings" appears to have been taken from Shakespeare's Coriolanus, *Act 1, 6th scene, line 51: "Know you on which side they have placed their men of trust."*

As before, she signed her letter "Y'r. Known Correspondent."

Washington, D.C.
August [31], 1850

To His Excellency,

The President,

I feel Sir, that an apology is absolutely due to you for the exceedingly informal, not to say illegible, communication which I forwarded yesterday; and which I do very much fear implied or seemed to imply, a doubt of your ability to conduct your own and the nation's affairs. I cannot forget the grave and touching remark which fell from your lips with your accession to the Presidency, "Henceforth I suppose I must expect to hear but little truth." And certainly much that might assist the soundest and least fallible judgment will hardly reach you.

But Sir, I have not the extravagant self-conceit of supposing my suggestions in general, likely to be of importance. And this unaffected conviction has deterred me from writing for no inconsiderable time; and what I have penned has been inevitably so broken and imperfectly defined as to be entitled to but slight consideration I fear.

Perhaps you will smile at my declaration that I am extremely sensitive to your success and your reputation. I certainly do wish that your administration may be distinguished for a strait-forward [sic], *honest* policy, rather than be remembered as a brilliant but unsound period. It is said, probably not altogether without reason, that business is sadly in arrears in the Departments, and there are not wanting persons who clamour for "redress of grievances." These intimations, like most loud sounding complaints, I do not doubt are exaggerated, but also they do not float on empty air, but have support on a tangible basis.

"Know," says a wise writer, the historian of kings, *"Know the men that are to be trusted"*; but how is this to be? The possession of *knowledge* involves both time and opportunities. Neither of these are "handservants at command." And you Sir are compelled to receive the opinions of others and to act thereon.

I wish in all my heart you had at your right hand [Gustavus A.?] Henry of Tennessee, a really upright and conscientious able man, or some other sound heart and mind whom I might name. Providence *defend* us from the Georgian candidate [Senator Robert A. Tombs], as from the Clay's man of Pennsylvania. In one case *the Tombs* will hold fast his prey; in the other he will be plastic friable *Clay* indeed!

It seems to me that the holiest service true-hearted friends can do you, is to *pray* for you, for in these Godless days, one seems floating on a shoreless ocean.

We know that the honest exercise of private judgment, faithfully gone about, does by no means end in loss to the governing party, and the governed are apt to know a free and independent course.

I conclude sir, with expressing for you an interest sincere and respectful, and a mind honouring your distinguished station.

Very respectfully,
Y'R. "KNOWN CORRESPONDENT"
["Y'r Known Correspondent," Washn, D.C. August–Rec'd. Sept. 1/50]

◄§ 1. To DOROTHEA DIX

In his initial response to Dorothea's letters (her pseudonym could not have been effectual), Fillmore indicated that he had called on her at her roominghouse while he was on an evening stroll. He had not found her at home.

September 6 [1850]

The President acknowledges with pleasure Miss Dix's note and the accompanying papers, the marked passages of which he has perused with pleasure, and herewith returns the same.

Miss Dix can not regret more than he does the misfortune of not seeing her the other evening. It is seldom he makes a call, but as he regards her as the guardian angel of his administration, he intends still to have the pleasure of seeing her, and will be happy therefore in some of his evening walks to make her a call.

Friday
Sept. 6.

3. To Millard Fillmore

Dorothea had failed to keep an interview, and now requested another.

[September 8, 1850]

To the President,

I hardly know how to express my keen regret at failing to see you Sir, yesterday P.M. A commission from the excellent Professor [Joseph Henry, Director of The Smithsonian Institution] engaged me, and various reasons impressed me that I might have the honour of seeing you for conversation on some important subjects perhaps today. I am not insensible to what or how much I ask in respectfully requesting that if consistent with your onerous obligations you will grant half an hour to your correspondent; and if convenient name the time when I may hope to see you.

I am quite sure of entire disengagedness today from claims either at home or from abroad.

Respectfully,
D. L. Dix

Mrs. Kennedy is proving the renovating influences of the mountain air, and Mr. Kennedy [Joseph C. G., Superintendent of the Census in 1850] set off this morning to join her and attend her return in October.

H Street, 8th September.

[Miss D. L. Dix, Sept. 8, 1850, requesting an interview]

4. To MILLARD FILLMORE

With obvious pride, Dorothea presented a lithographic drawing of a new hospital for the insane in Tennessee, The Central Hospital for the Insane at Nashville. It was opened in 1852.

September 14, 1850

To

His Excellency,
  Millard Fillmore
  President of the United States
Miss Dix respectfully asks permission to offer to
  The President
a copy of a Lithographic Drawing of one of
the Thirteen Hospitals for the relief of the insane
which she has had the happiness to assist in causing
to be established in the United States and in the
British Provinces in America.

H. St. Sept. 14th. 1850

[Miss Dix. Sept. 13. Rec'd. 14, 1850; answered Sept. 15.]

᪷§ 2. To DOROTHEA DIX

*Fillmore sent an immediate note of thanks for the litho-
graph, and added a short, but lavish, tribute to Dorothea's
services for the insane.*

Washington, Sept. 15, 1850

My Dear Miss Dix,

Accept my sincere thanks for your kind note, accompanied
by a Lithographic print of the Hospital for the Insane in Tennessee. The building presents a beautiful appearance, and
when I looked upon its turrets and recollected that this was
the 13th monument which you had caused to be erected of
your philanthropy and disinterested devotion to the cause of
the unfortunate, I could not help thinking that wealth and
power never reared such monuments to selfish pride, as you
had reared to the love of mankind. For these kind offices to
suffering humanity and helpless misery, your name will endure when these assylums [*sic*] shall have crumbled to the
dust, and the Pyramids themselves shall be scattered to the
winds. Heaven grant that your noble example may, in some
future age, inspire some other gentle sister to devote herself, as
you have done, to the relief of the wretched and destitute.
May Heaven reward you for your disinterested devotion.

With the highest regard and most sincere respect,

I remain

Your friend

MILLARD FILLMORE

᪷§ 3. To DOROTHEA DIX

*Fillmore was not at home for a call from Dorothea. He
acknowledged her letter, noted her anxiety over her land-grant
bill, and indicated his support of it.*

*He also extended his thanks for a bouquet she had sent or
delivered to the White House.*

Dorothea's note of September 21 has not been located.

Washington, Sept. 22, 1850
9 P.M.

My Dear Miss Dix,

I have this moment received and perused your note of last
evening, and regret now more than ever that I missed you. I
perceive that you feel anxious and sad. I can not wonder at it!
I wonder your patience has held out so long; and that you can
speak with so much equanimity of the provoking and vexa-
tious "delays" in Congress. But yours is a goodness that never
tires—a benevolence that never wearies—a confident hope
that seems never to desert you. None but the most disinterested and self-sacrificing can have such faith, or display such
all-conquering perseverance. May Heaven at last crown your
noble efforts with success.

Accept my thanks for your kind remembrance in those
beautiful flowers. They lie upon the table before me, beautiful
and lovely as blushing innocence, and fragrant as the works of
disinterested love for suffering humanity.

This will be to me a busy week. But possibly in some of
my evening prominades [sic] I may see you a moment. Certain
I am that the portolas of this mysterious mansion would open
at your magic touch or "Sesame" at any moment.

If I can do any thing to aid you in your work of mercy,
command me and I am at your service. But do not despair. It is
always darkest just before day, and your fondest hopes may yet
be realized.

I am, with the deepest
Sympathy in your anxiety.
Sincerely yours
MILLARD FILLMORE

❧ 4. To Dorothea Dix

Fillmore expressed his regret over the loss of the land-grant bill, but anticipated its ultimate success. The bill had been approved in the House of Representatives, but was rejected by the Senate.

Seeking to comfort Dorothea, he facetiously speculated upon the possibility that she might concentrate as much attention upon a man as she devoted to the "suffering world."

Though Fillmore had occupied the White House a few days after President Taylor's demise, he was still awaiting the arrival of his family from Buffalo.

Dorothea's note of September 27 is missing.

Presidential Mansion
Sept. 27, 1850

My Dear Miss Dix,

I have really been too busy to read the papers, and therefore was not aware that you had had the misfortune to lose your bill for the relief of the Insane, till I received your note this evening. I sympathise with you most deeply at this calamity. Your noble and disinterested exertions deserved a better fate. But do not despair. Hope on—Hope ever! Your quiet but well directed efforts will, eventually, I doubt not, be crowned with success. My philosophy is, that all things are for the best. In our short sighted views we are often inclined to think otherwise. But rest assured, that where we have done our duty, God will eventually bless our work.

I suppose you are soon to leave the city, and I fear I may not have the pleasure of meeting you again, unless you and professor Henry will do me the honour to call and take tea with me on Sunday evening at 6. —Do come and see how a bachelor lives and it may induce you hereafter to take pity on

some lonely gentleman and concentrate that affectionate tenderness upon one object that now circles in its embrace a
suffering world.

But excuse this badinage and believe me when I say, that I
shall expect you and you must not disappoint me. I regret to
say that there is more truth than poetry in my bachelor like
condition, for I can not hope to see Mrs. F. here for 3 weeks
yet to come. When less occupied this will seem a long and
lonesome time.

I am truly and sincerely your friend

MILLARD FILLMORE

ᥱᥤ 5. To Dorothea Dix

*Upon the defeat of her land-grant bill Dorothea left Wash-
ington to attend to business in Philadelphia, Harrisburg, and
Trenton. Presumably she had written to Fillmore relative to
her plans before her departure.*

*The following fragment seems part of Fillmore's response
to her.*

[Oct. 3–6, 1850 ?]

. . . Still I hope to see you on your return. Do call with or
without the professor as may be most convenient or agreeable.
I am very lonesome and can not expect my family for a week
to come, and possibly more; but when they come they will be
happy to see you.

I am as ever

Truly your friend,

MILLARD FILLMORE

6. To Dorothea Dix

Several of Dorothea's letters during September and October are missing, but Fillmore reviews her projected itinerary. His increasing fondness for her is evident in the exchange of keepsakes, his assumption that she considered his letters confidential, and the relaxation he enjoyed in her presence.

Oct. 7, 1850

Well Miss Dix,

I am a poor correspondent. I read your letters with great interest but have no time to answer.

I wrote you two or three days since and before I sent off my message received yours from Trenton, and addressed you there. Now I have just received your flattering letter from Philadelphia, and today you are in Harrisburg, and day after tomorrow will be again at Trenton, where I trust you will receive the little package I sent.

I am now writing at 10 o'clock in that snug little office, which you fancied so much, and where you furtively obtained that little token of remembrance to which you so kindly and playfully allude. I really wish you had taken something of more value and more deserving so kind a remembrance. Possibly the little token which I sent at Trenton may occasionally beguile a weary and lonely hour in your round of perpetual mercy. It was not what I desired but the only thing I could find worthy of your acceptance.

I can not but be amused at your observations upon politicians. You consider them as a race, ambitious and selfish. I am sorry to admit the truth of this charge. I am satisfied that no man can long exercise the appointing power without becoming utterly disgusted with his species. The *courtier* of a monarchy is the *demagogue* in a republic. They fawn on power whether in the Prince or the people. And it appears to me that the desire for office is increasing. They rush from the remotest corners of the republic to the Capitol like famished wolves. The contest is truly ferocious and disgusting.

But pardon me, I am disclosing *"state secrets."* But I trust all is safe. I have never doubted that a woman could keep a secret, and hence the freedom with which I write to you.

I wish indeed that you were here this evening for an hour's conversation. It appears to me that it would be a delightful relaxation—a kind of intellectual treat. But I am chained to the car of state and you are pursuing your noble work of charity. God Bless you. Good night.

M[ILLARD] F[ILLMORE]

◆§ 7. To DOROTHEA DIX

Fillmore again alluded to their exchange of keepsakes and acknowledged the receipt of a letter and pamphlets from Dorothea. He then commented upon the problem of the criminal insane and the numbers and distribution of the insane by states as recorded in the recent census.

Jenny Lind, the "Swedish Nightingale," was one of Phineas T. Barnum's "discoveries." Under his astute management her tour of the United States was a box-office triumph.

Neither Dorothea's letter of October 12 nor the Lunatic's poetry to Jenny Lind has been found.

Washington, Oct. 20, 1850

My Dear Miss Dix,

Yours of the 12th came duly to hand, and today I received your note, enclosing the Lunatic's poetry to Jenny Lind,

which is a very creditable production. I am not certain but the
partition which separates madness from genius is much thin-
ner than most of us suspect.

How I regret that I disappointed your anticipation of the
bouquet. I thought of it at the table, and intended to send a
servant up with it immediately, but our rambles over the
house and your interesting conversation so engrossed my mind
that I forgot it.

But I am gratified to perceive that you cherish so highly
the little paper folder. It being so mere a trifle I flatter myself
you would not value it so highly, were it not for the association, either personal or local. And that reminds me that here I
am alone in the same little office which you admired so much.

I see you are busy in your good work. May Heaven reward
you!

In looking over the pamphlets which you sent me I was
struck with the large number of Insane in some of our penitentiaries, and horrified at some statements that they were insane when convicted and sent to prison.

I was also surprised to see how much larger the number of
insane was at the North than at the South.

If I recollect right the percentage was as 2 to 1 in some
cases and South Carolina had a less number of Lunatics in
proportion to her population than any other state in the
Union. But I confess I have little faith in the statistics collected in our decenial census. Your information may be from a
more reliable source. But if not I must think there is some
mistake.

I perceive the plan of the assylum [sic] at Trenton differs
much from that in Tennessee. But I should think the forms
more light and airy. It must be a source of unallayed felicity to
sit as you now do and see the misery you have averted, and

contemplate the happiness which you have produced. That you may long enjoy it is the prayer of your friend

MILLARD FILLMORE

✑§ 8. To DOROTHEA DIX

By mid-December Dorothea was again in Washington to renew her struggle for the land grant. She stopped at the White House to see the Fillmores and forwarded reading matter to President Fillmore.

Washington, Dec. 29 [18]50

My Dear Miss Dix,

This is the first leisure moment I have found to answer your kind note of the 24th inst. and to return my sincere thanks for the books which accompanied it. But do tell us to what denomination the *Prayer Book* belongs. I perceive it differs somewhat from that generally used by the Episcopalians, and yet the ritual appears to approach nearer to theirs than to any other with which I am acquainted. The truth is I am quite ignorant on those matters, having no taste for *sects* and *forms* in matters of religion.

I regret that you did not spend the evening with us when you called the other day; but we are generally disengaged except on Thursday and Friday evenings and we shall always be happy to see you at your convenience.

I am truly and sincerely your friend
MILLARD FILLMORE

✑§ 9. To DOROTHEA DIX

On the last day of the year Fillmore wished Dorothea a "happy new year," and enclosed a Bible as a gift.

My Dear Miss Dix,

I beg you to accept the accompanying Bible as a slight testimony of my esteem for your active benevolence in the cause
of suffering humanity. That you may enjoy many returns of a
"happy new year" is the sincere prayer of your friend

MILLARD FILLMORE

Dec. 31, 1850

✿§ 5. To MILLARD FILLMORE

*For the first time Dorothea interjected politics into her
correspondence in a request that Fillmore confer with Senator
James A. Pearce of Maryland to facilitate her land-grant bill
in the Senate.*

*Dorothea's request that her solicitation of his aid remain
confidential seems to have stemmed from her understanding
of the legislative process rather than her modesty.*

[January, 1851]

Miss Dix respects, and asks to renew her request of the
President that he will merely urge on Mr. Pearce the desir-
ableness of carrying through *the Land Bill* for the relief of the
Insane, the *present session.*

It is a matter of exceeding importance; and it is believed
that delays now, will ruin the measure.

Miss Dix respectfully prefers another request: That none
of her written communications may be seen by other eyes than
his to whom they are directly addressed, always excepting
Mrs. Fillmore from exclusion.

The chirography has been recognized upon the table; only
by a friend it is true.

⇜§ 6. To Millard Fillmore

Dorothea forwards to Fillmore a favorable, but unidentified, notice in the press.

Congress Library
Feb'y. 24th, 1851

To His Excellency,
The President,
Dear Sir,

I have the pleasure in sending to you a paper in which you and your deeds are so pleasantly and favorably noticed and discussed that I desired to have you see the two articles in which your name is honored. You do not need to receive their expressions of good will, but still they are not likely to be indifferently regarded.

Respectfully and cordially,
Your friend,
D. L. Dix

[D. L. Dix, Wash., 24 Feb. /51, sending newspaper]

⇜§ 7. To Millard Fillmore

Dorothea seeks Fillmore's assistance to obtain a copy of Henry R. Schoolcraft's History of the Indian Tribes of the United States.

Congress Library
Feb'y. 27th, 1851

To the President
Dear Sir,

I much desire to possess a copy of Schoolcraft's History of the North American Indians; and which has lately been published by authority of Congress. I am told that by application to you I can be furnished with this work through your order—a request to the officer of the Department in which the books are deposited to be distributed as directed. If it is proper that this request should be complied with, I shall hold myself much obliged to yourself for the kindness of a favorable consideration of my wishes, and much gratified at receiving the work through your intervention and authority.

Respectfully and cordially your friend,

D. L. DIX

[Miss Dix, Wash., Feb. 27/51 asking for copy Schoolcraft's History of Indian Tribes.]

◄§ 8. To MILLARD FILLMORE

Dorothea acknowledged her receipt of Schoolcraft's work on the Indians and asked Fillmore to convey her thanks to Senator Pearce for his assistance in winning Senate approval for her land-grant bill. It had passed in the Senate by a vote of 36 to 16.

Congress Library
March 3d, 1851

To His Excellency, Millard Fillmore
My dear Sir,

I have received and beg to acknowledge with expressions of grateful obligations, the valuable work of which you have made me the possessor, accompanied with such friendly expressions, as greatly enhance the value of the gift.

Permit me to subscribe myself sincerely and respectfully

Your friend,

D. L. DIX

If opportunity shall offer will you Sir, please to say to Mr. Pearce of Maryland that I have expressed to you a high sense

of obligation for his able conduct of *the Land Bill* in the Senate.
[D. L. Dix, Mar. 3, 1851, acknowledging receipt of book.]

❧ 9. To MILLARD FILLMORE

*Dorothea recommends Titian Peale for a position in the
Patent Office. He was a son of Charles Wilson Peale, the
noted portrait painter.*

*Alexander D. Bache was Superintendent of the United
States Coast Survey.*

                                    12th Street, Thursday Mg.
                                                  [March 6]
To His Excellency, The President
Dear Sir,

I do not like to presume in offering suggestions on any
subjects, but I think you will allow me to speak in favor (not
from motives of good-will or friendly considerations so much
as from a conviction of *ability* and *worth*) of Mr. Titian Peale
as a person who might be *relied* on for the faithful discharge of
duty, to fill the *office* of *Examiner* in the Patent Office, two of
which are, it is understood, to be appointed at this time. Mr.
Peale can present credentials of far greater weight from Mr.
Bache and Professor Henry than any I can give, but he has I
may say a character and reputation which is the best support
in asking a position involving important responsibilities and in
posing very grave obligations.

I need say no more to enlist your favorable consideration in
regard to Mr. Peale, and am with sentiments of sincere respect

                                               Your friend,
                                               D. L. DIX

[Miss D. L. Dix, Wash. Rec'd. March 6/51. Recom'd. Mr. Peale for Examiner in Patent Office. Answered 7.]

✎§ 10. To MILLARD FILLMORE

The House failed to approve the Senate's land-grant bill and upon the adjournment of Congress on March 4, the disappointed Dorothea prepared to leave Washington for South Carolina and Georgia, where state action for hospitals was pending. But she had no intention to accept defeat.

She bid the Fillmores a friendly farewell.

[Between March 7 and 9, 1851]

Miss Dix' friendly and respectful regards to
The President,

In reply Sir, to your inquiry if I desire the letter in behalf of Mr. Peale to be communicated to the Secretary of the Interior, I would submit the subject and decision to your judgment. I should hesitate in doing so myself, having a very slight acquaintance only with Mr. Stewart [Alexander H. H. Stuart], and not considering it quite well to suggest appointments to those who hold officially the right of their distribution. I indeed, have a clear conviction of Mr. Peale's ability as declared by many competent judges.

I would inquire if you have received from four to six packages within six weeks enclosing newspapers and two short notes. The papers contained articles from leading journals, South and West, commenting on your character and administration in such terms as it seemed to me were as just as they were discriminating; and I thought the perusal of the marked passages would be alike gratifying to yourself and family.

I do not attach great importance to this questioning which has arisen from your failing to receive the note of acknowledgement forwarded the morning after receiving the valuable work of which you were so obliging as to make me the possessor. The envelope also contained a note to Mrs. Fillmore, which I regret chiefly that to omit writing was not considerate on my part, to say the least.

I beg to present to Mrs. and to Miss Fillmore my parting compliments and friendly regards. I am about proceeding to South Carolina (that state where the Bishops forbid prayers for the President!) and to Georgia to renew efforts in behalf of the neglected insane: the more needed, that an inconsiderable *minority* had power over a large majority to defeat the measure.

I have had so much at heart. Defeated not conquered; disappointed not discouraged. I have but to be more energetic and more faithful in the difficult and painful vocation to which my life is devoted.

I beg Sir, to offer to you sincerest wishes for your health, happiness and public success, and am with respect and friendly regards,

> Yours,
> Sir very sincerely,
> D. L. Dix

[Miss D. L. Dix, Ans'd. Mar. 9.]

❧ 10. To Dorothea Dix

Fillmore again offers his sympathy to Dorothea upon the loss of her land grant and wishes her God speed on her journey.

Washington,
March 9, 1851

The President acknowledges with pleasure the receipt of
Miss Dix's note of today; but did not receive the note to which
she alludes in reference to the History of the Indians, and he
received only one paper, but that contained a very flattering
article for which he is most obliged. Mrs. F. desires him to say
that she owes Miss Dix many thanks for her kind note naming
a dress maker.

The President sympathises most deeply and sincerely with
Miss Dix in the loss of her bill in Congress, but is gratified to
perceive that her faith is unshaken, her hope yet strong, and
that she is to go forth on her mission of mercy to the afflicted
with the same courage as though all had been prosperous. May
God speed her going and protect her from all harm.

[Millard] Fillmore

11. To Millard Fillmore

*Writing from Charleston, Dorothea offered her impres-
sions of the public mind in the South. She found Virginians
and the Whig press there favorable to Fillmore and compromise. But in South Carolina, she reported that the delusion of
the populace entitled them to be classified with the insane.
Dorothea's strong sense of nationalism is evident in her scorn
and anger over the agitation of the secessionists.*

*The proclamation to which she refers was Fillmore's threat
to use troops to enforce the Fugitive Slave Act. It followed the
rescue of Frederick "Shadrack" Williams from a federal marshal in Boston.*

*Her memory was faulty when she referred to articles by
Mary Lowell Putnam in the* North American Review. *The*

article was in the Christian Examiner, *XLVIII (May 1850),
444–448. Francis Bowen's article was in the* North American
Review, *LXX (January 1850). Both were reviewing a book
by A. de Gerando,* De L'Esprit Public en Hungrie depuis la
Revolution Francaise. *Interest in Hungary at this time was
aroused by an abortive revolution against Austria.*

*Doctor Lieber, an 1848 exile from Germany, was a warm
supporter of Dorothea's crusade. He was a member of the
faculty of South Carolina College in Columbia.*

Charleston, S. C.
March 23d, [1851]

Dear Sir,

Though I cannot suppose that my letters will prove any
high value written in great haste at brief periods of compara-
tive leisure, as I pass from one part of the country to another, I
yet persuade myself that they will not be wholly deficient in
interest as they will chiefly relate to popular subjects of discussion, and may some times touch on points of such moment as
to engage your notice.

The proceedings of the legislature at Richmond, together
with deliberations of the State Convention, formed the sole
topics of conversation in private circles when I was there last
week. No confidence was expressed in the results which might
follow these public movements. The general opinion was that
incompetent men had been chosen to perform very responsible
works, and as for reforming the laws it was not supposed that
those who are undertaking to mend what Jefferson, Madison
and other distinguished statesmen had done with deliberation,
and many would say with wisdom, would accomplish for the
State any benefit whatever.

Your measures were often adverted to in terms of just appreciation and approval, and often in quarters where it would

not have been surprising to have heard contrary sentiments.
The editors of Whig papers sustain your course with spirit
and decision in the Middle States; our New Englanders are
just now somewhat angry upon the subject of the Proclamation, but not the thinking and reliable portions of the population I should judge.

Here in South Carolina the delusion of the citizens seems
fairly to entitle them to be classed with the insane. In their
estimation South Carolina is the universe: They have not the
slightest perception of their inability to hold out against the
Federal Government, nor the nations of the World if need be.
But in fact they evidently rely on England for aid during the
coming year, as if England having already sacrificed so much
on her own part was likely to take part with this feeble state
against the 30 Sisters! I have maintained that all the bombast,
declamation and legislation touching secession was just the
passing ebullition of passionate politicians and excitable men
who had really no great influence; and as an argument in support of my view I remark, that the public credit does not
waver, states do not fall, merchants transact business on the
accustomed basis, etc. Now it is manifest that the first overt
act would depress stocks to twenty or twenty-five percent.
Some sapient member of the House last winter offered a resolution, directing inquiry how many *millions* the banks could
furnish when called on for loans to support *the war!*—not considering that the banks were a "mighty" feeble reliance in such
extremity.

The Governor Whitemarsh B. Seabrook, when the measure for calling a convention was passed, ordered a "feu de joie"
of 100 guns in front of the Capitol. He is a young man in
more than one sense; yet impetuous, inexperienced, a disun-
ionist and an agitator as he is, the fortunes of the citizens seem
to rest with him. He can at any hour summon the Convention,

and proceed to announce secession and its consequent decrees.

It is said by the few who do reason dispassionately on these questions that within six months the great declaration will be made; that *then,* Virginia and Pennsylvania are prepared to interpose mediation, to act as arbitrators, to soften the *keen sense* of "injury through oppressive aggressions,"(!) which stimulate these southrons to seize the sword and brandish the spear!

It is singular how inconsistent men and rulers are! A few years since, Mr. Samuel Hoar, a reputable citizen of Massachusetts, was sent to Charleston to exercise his profession peacefully in the courts of the state in behalf of free Negroes arriving in the capacity of stewards or sailors on northern and other vessels. Nothing was said or done by Mr. Hoar on his arrival which could offend or injure the good people here; yet he was compelled by them to leave the city forthwith, and to forego all of the rights of an American citizen. Last winter the *British* Consul proceeded to Columbia, bearded the sovereign authority in its stronghold, the Capital *demanded* what one of our own citizens quietly pleaded for; *insisted* on the passage of a protective law, and returned in triumph, not one of these "chivalrous persons," perceiving that a foreigner had ruled them in the most highhanded manner, while they shortly before refused to listen to a mild argument in a court of justice from one of their own countrymen!

I found Judge [Andrew P.] Butler [United States Senator] here on arriving, and learnt that he had this week been present at a political meeting and social celebration, where he had *seemed* to propound sincerely the most ultra opinions. I say *seemed,* for I really suppose that now as on a former occasion, the wolf's coat was worn in order to secure by an adroit movement, by and by, some saving influence. The toast given by the Senator reads thus: "The measures of a tyrannical majority;" in the language of the eloquent Burke, "They are dragon's teeth, and will spring up armed men." And by another, "The Governor of South Carolina—he has the head, the heart, and the hand suited to the times." Drank with three times three, and immense applause!

On the whole, from all I see and hear, it is certain that a crisis is anticipated. These people are possessed with the most ultra and heathenish notions of *honour,* and will plunge into the gulf when they only look to stand on the pinnacle of Fame, and exhibit their worth to an admiring world!

I will not ask to hear from you Sir, in reply to my letters— they require no special answer—and I am moving from place to place with little delay at any point. I shall be at Columbia at the end of next week.

By this time I trust you are in possession of my missing note of acknowledgment for your obliging and kind gift of Schoolcraft's valuable book. I am rather exact in all business matters, as in those which embrace attention to the courtesies of life, and regret that I should have seemed to you so negligent of your kind consideration of my gratification.

My health is not so good as when I left Washington, but I still indulge the hope that I shall not find it absolutely necessary to suspend my journies [sic] of humane obligation.

Permit me to offer, through you, friendly regards to Mrs. Fillmore and to your daughter. I command to her notice, if she has not already seen them, two very able articles on Hungary, by Mrs. Mary Lowell Putnam in late numbers of the *North American Review,* and which place [Francis] Bowen [editor of the *North American Review*] in a not very distinguished position as a *correct* historian.

If I did not feel it was transcending my duty, and passing upon forbidden ground, I should urge you to send Dr. Francis Lieber abroad, to some European nation as chargé d'affaires or some such station, that while he was a credit to his country on this side of the Atlantic, for honesty and good sense, he might also have leisure to write an historical work and access to documents necessary thereto, which would be valuable to his own times and be authority for succeeding historians. I have thought there might be a mission created to Switzerland; but over that I am not well informed in these matters.

Respectfully and sincerely your friend,

D. L. Dix

[Miss D. L. Dix, Charleston, S. C., March 23/28/51.]

❧ 12. To Millard Fillmore

From Columbia, the very heart of the secessionist movement, Dorothea described the agitation in one of her most incisive letters. She refuted the claims of the radicals that they could create an independent nation and belittled the current efforts of South Carolinians to free themselves from economic dependence upon northern manufactures and credit.

She also offered some interesting observations upon the backward state of transportation in the interior of the state. Dorothea misquotes the London Spectator, *possibly because she was writing from memory. However, she did not alter the purport of the article, which reads: "His tolerance of slavery is fitted to conciliate the good-will of the Southern States; his Protectionist leanings, to render him a favorite in New England. But the unlucky Fugitive Slave Law has involved him in an angry dispute with the men of Massachusetts; and the knotty question of State rights threatens to set him at loggerheads with the North Carolinians" (March 15, 1851, No. 1185, p. 241).*

Two favorite southern spas, Sulphur Springs and Warm

Springs, were in Buncombe County in western North Carolina.

Dr. Lieber's "Laura" was a study of Laura Bridgeman, a blind, deaf mute who had been taught by Samuel Gridley Howe.

Columbia, S. C.
April 8th, 1851

To the President,

Dear Sir:

Though I cannot delude myself with the idea that my letters are especially interesting, I hope on the contrary that they may sometimes occupy a portion of your time not fatiguingly. Detained in Charleston by illness, a threatened attack on the lungs, and from which I have not yet recovered, I make but slow advances in the work which I have assigned for myself this year. I am preparing to explore the surrounding districts, and notwithstanding I am "from the North" it is my good fortune to be cordially and kindly received.

The Carolina Senator Butler who so correctly designated you as our "mild and just President," has been very active in his own district; but while he *seems* to share the hot-headed spirit of hot-headed politicians here, who shout secession at the corners of the streets, it is whispered that more sensible plans are framed, and that wiser opinions are covertly urged in private circles. I confess, I like better the noble, manly spirit which prompts to speak the whole truth, dispassionately and clearly at all times, and to set forth correct principles of action, especially when the unreflecting are in haste to rush headlong into a ruinous contest.

It is curious to see how little the journals of the day reflect the true state of affairs, and equally curious to notice how

completely ignorant of their own internal weakness and fee-
bleness of resources are most of the people here. Rarely leaving the state, they are not able to compare the prosperity of
this with other states of the Union. Lately some enterprising
citizen established a shoe manufactory in Charleston; and
some equally enterprising planter sowed his fields with *broom-
corn*, and the cry is raised through out the country that South
Carolina with her *newly developed* elements of prosperity is
rapidly rising above dependence upon the *North*. They will
wear shoes of their own making; they will sweep their floors
with "native brooms"!

A tannery is now contemplated! But the great triumph is
the grand scheme of ruining northern manufacturers. They
shall have no cotton from their plantations, *nay more;* no rice
from their swamps!

The latest example of maritime prosperity seems to have
crowned the whole ideal, "Glory Monument." "In eight
months *three* vessels have been built by several of our capital-
ists (!) of 340 tons burthen, and are now nearly rigged and
ready for service. We thus see that South Carolina can build
her own ships and compete with other states on the waters."

I suppose that these mighty merchantmen are part of that
future fleet which Prentice [George Dennison Prentice, editor of the *Louisville Journal*] wittily says will refuse to direct
their course at sea by the North Star!

I was amused looking over this week the *London Spectator*
to see some odd comments on "Trials of President Fillmore
. . . who though rather in favor with New Englanders on
account of *Protectionism,* had created the most furious opposition to his administration by his violent, *passionate* Fugitive
Slave Proclamation, and that he was in equal difficulty with
North Carolina for his implied aggressions on state Rights.

What will be the result?" inquires the *intelligent* editor! The
English in *general* know about as much of American History
and Geography as they do of affairs in Central Asia or Africa.

In Charleston I saw but few except Unionists; here nearly
every person I have met is really or ostensibly a secessionist,
and both parties speak with the greatest contempt of the measures of their opposites. The Anarchists are making Capsicum
[peppery] speeches; projecting vast projects, and quoting the
Iliad; the Unionists write letters, converse in parlors, or discuss
affairs at the corners of the streets, and pray God to give common sense or restore understanding to the opposite party.
"Barnwell Rhett [fiery secessionist and successor to John C.
Calhoun in the Senate]" said a high spirited woman in
Charleston to me, "Barnwell Rhett is a mean base hypocrite, a
man false to every principle and sentiment of honor. He has
created a whirlwind, and is frightened at his own necromancy.
But he is weak as a puny infant to disturb the Union; the
Union is safe. *He* may *seem* to shake it, or fancy that he does.
But as a feeble arm can disturb the steadiness of the Druid
Stone, he rocks it in vain; even the stalwart arm of a giant
Washington cannot cast it from its base; the Union cannot be
destroyed!" If there are South Carolina women to speak out
boldly in such ringing tones, and that amongst the highest
circles of their proudest aristocracy, we may not doubt that the
wordy boasted chivalry will be silenced.

General Hamilton's [former Governor James Hamilton]
letter, this week published, is producing a marked effect; for
though he is not esteemed in private circles, nor popular
amongst the people at large, he has dared to utter unwelcome
truths so fairly and fearlessly, that others rally and come into
his support, who have from motives of *expediency* been heretofore passive. If Hamilton should now be honest, pay his

debts, and retrieve his reputation, he might rise to an enviable distinction.

But I must conclude this letter. I forget that you may not wish to read a volume.

I shall proceed to Milledgeville, I hope the first part of May. But I do not speak very confidently of my plans, for my yielding health compels me to modified exertion. Should you have the curiosity to glance at the map of South Carolina, you will see just west from Columbia 105 miles the town of Marion, to reach which it is necessary to proceed to Charleston, embark on a freight *flatboat* steamer, drawing two and a half feet water, put to sea (in fine weather), run for the mouth of the Pedee river and ascend till Marion is reached, for *positively, except* on *foot,* there is no other way of reaching that part of the state. There is not a carriage road at all! And a member of the legislature declares it cannot be reached on horseback. So to accomplish 105 miles, I have to go 510 at the least; and this is no quick time, avoiding the night air on the river as a pestilence. After April, it is declared to be certain death to be exposed to it. The planters forsake their estates throughout the rice country, that is, those in the maritime districts, and go to Charleston or hasten to Buncombe or to the Northern States; that is, heretofore they have chiefly resorted to the North, but now I suppose they will compromise their offended feelings, and forgetting the want of sympathy shown by the honest Rip Van Winklers [poor whites], will prefer to breathe the air of *their* mountains and eat *their* bread, to indulging the Yankees by patronizing the fish and fogs of Newport!

With respectful and friendly regards to Mrs. Fillmore, I am yours Sir, with sentiments of sincere esteem and friendship.

D. L. DIX

Dr. Lieber requests permission to offer through me most respectful regards. His "Laura" paper has been attacked here by some wise and learned theologians for inculcating *un-biblical* doctrines; not supporting the Mosaic account of the origin of language! In other words, Dr. Lieber is attacked and maligned for not teaching as they say, that language was *perfect* and *complete* from the *beginning;* that with the creation of man, also was made the whole *grammar* and *vocabulary* of language! Of all fanaticism, the fanaticism of ignorance is the most hopeless.

[Miss D. L. Dix, Columbia, S. C., April 8/15/51.]

✥ 13. To Millard Fillmore

There appears to have been an eight-month interruption in the correspondence between April and December.

Dorothea had escaped the dread pestilence and exposure to "night air" in low lands of South Carolina, but she returned to the North in a state of exhaustion, suffering a racking cough and an inflamed throat. She was immobilized and her activity limited to an occasional letter. Her convalescence lingered into the autumn. In December she was unable to take her accustomed place in Washington.

Meanwhile, with the Compromise of 1850 behind him and Congress adjourned, Fillmore was freed from the heavy pressures of his first nine months in office. In May, with other notables, including Daniel Webster, he attended the grand opening of the Erie Railroad from Cornwall on the Hudson River to Dunkirk on Lake Erie. He participated in local celebrations at dozens of stations along the route. In June he sailed down the Chesapeake Bay to Fortress Monroe, and then to Richmond, returning by way of Fredericksburg. In August he visited White Sulphur Springs in western Virginia with stops at Harpers Ferry and Winchester in the Shenandoah Valley. A month later he was in Boston to take part in the festivities marking the completion of a rail connection with Canada, a tour which encompassed points from Portland, Maine, to Newport, Rhode Island.

During August and September Abigail and Abby escaped the oppressive heat of Washington to join Fillmore at Newport and bask in the ocean breezes there.

Meanwhile, Fillmore appeared to be unaware of Dorothea's poor health.

In December, hopeful of returning soon to Washington, Dorothea addressed Fillmore to seek his advice on the handling of the land-grant bill in Congress prior to her arrival.

Trenton, New Jersey
Dec'r. 11th, 1851

To His Excellency, Millard Fillmore
My dear Sir:

Certainly in connection with your name, the old adage loses its force, "out of sight, out of mind"; if my own sincere and respectful regard did not hold you fresh in my memory, I am sure that frequent reference to "the President" would prevent forgetfulness and avert indifference.

When your political opponents give the distinguishing pronomen of "The good and just" it would be strange if those whose opinions harmonize with those you hold, and whose opportunities of a near personal acquaintance increase and make durable their esteem, should not have you "often in remembrance." I do not feel at liberty to occupy your time, and engage your thoughts on myself alone, nor my interests, and have forborne to address letters merely social and friendly when the frequent impulse has prompted epistolary communication. I cannot say how long this regard for your more weighty and authorized engagements *might* have prevailed over my inclinations if I did not now wish to avail myself of your correct judgment and experience on a question which is in my estimation of very great importance.

It is not therefore that I consult you as President of the United States, but as an individual whose knowledge and good sense may dispel my uncertainties. When you have leisure will you suggest to me what you deem the best modes of taking up and conducting the "Ten Million Land Bill." This embraces interests too important to be abandoned; and in their importance to admit any but most careful measures following mature deliberations.

To whom, when, and how then shall this grave trust be confided? I have not supposed that anything would be gained to the cause by proposing it earlier than February; am I correct in this view? Now I cannot come to Washington to give personal care and influence to the measure. The severe, protracted and dangerous illness to which I was subject during the whole summer has left me as yet with but little reliable strength, and though I have been able to employ my pen much, all special fatigue and exposure by journies [sic] are positively forbidden by my medical advisers, who assure me that by present care I may soon be fully reestablished.

I arrived here from New York a few days since, going first to Philadelphia; and am under positive treatment for cough and inflamation of the throat. My friends and physicians have indeed wished to exile me from labor and care to the Antilles; but those Hesperides, "the blessed Isles," I have resolutely turned from; and as a sort of compromise, have consented to adopt a sort of Catholic penance by coming into "Retreat." And add to this a modified Quaker rule of "sitting *silent*" for several weeks. Every evil has its good, and every ill an antidote. If I may not move abroad, I shall have the more leisure for devising plans for future usefulness. And, if I cannot speak, I can meditate and write, and occasionally take up the neglected arts of needlework.

But all these personal details are not of moment to claim your thought. And I hasten to conclude this letter with the sincere expressions of my respectful regards and friendship, with which I am cordially yours,

D. L. DIX

[D. L. Dix, Dec. 11. Rec'd 13, Ans'd. Dec. 13th.]

≈§ 11. To DOROTHEA DIX

Prior to Dorothea's letter of December 11, Fillmore may not have known that she was in Trenton. He immediately replied, expressing his concern for her health.

He offered only general suggestions regarding procedures she might follow in pushing her land-grant bill.

Washington, Dec. 13, 1851

My dear Miss Dix,

I have your kind note of the 11th inst. and I am exceedingly pained to hear of your illness; but hope soon to hear that you are again restored to health.

I can not however help admiring your philosophy, or rather Christian resignation, under your affliction.

I have been wondering every day since the session commenced, what had become of that *"Angel of Mercy"* to the poor afflicted insane, and was constantly hoping that I should soon see your cheerful face.

I hardly know what answer to give to your question. I think however that it would be well to have the petition at once presented and referred, so as to obtain as early a report as possible. But I can give no advice as to the proper persons to

take charge of it, further than this; as both Houses are democratic, it seems to me a member of that party, all other things
being equal, would be likely to exert the most influence, where
it will probably be most wanted.

With my sincere prayers for your speedy restoration of
health, and for your success in your humane mission, I am
truly and Sincerely your friend

MILLARD FILLMORE

·◆§ 14. To ABIGAIL FILLMORE

*Still confined in Trenton, Dorothea wrote to Abigail Fill-
more to recommend a specialist in New York who might pre-
scribe a treatment for her impaired vision. She enclosed it in
a letter to Fillmore in which she offered her analysis of the
Kossuth "mania."*

Trenton, N.J., Dec. 23 [1851]

To Mrs. Fillmore,

My dear Madam, I received lately from New York two
pamphlets which were sent me by a friend who was at the
time under treatment of Dr. Turnbull for impaired vision; and
who expressed the hope of being permanently benefitted
through his skill. Another whose hearing has gradually declined, promises to give me the result of her experience after a
fair trial of the disability to cure the trouble under which she
suffers much inconvenience. Dr. T. is not considered a Char-
latan in his practice in New York, where he has been I understand but a short time, but I am always slow to give confidence
to those who propose so much; it is not just to say that there is
apparent reason for accepting the opinion that Dr. Turnbull
can benefit, if he cannot perfectly cure many of his patients.

Allow me to offer my respectful and friendly salutations
with others who join to express the good wishes appropriate to

the approaching annual festivals, and in wishing you a "cheerful Christmas" and "Happy New Year."

I wish you through your whole life peace and prosperity.

Yours cordially and sincerely,

D. L. Dix

[Miss D. L. Dix, Dec. 23'd, 1852 (1851).]

◄§ 15. To MILLARD FILLMORE

Lajos Kossuth, the Hungarian revolutionary, arrived in New York early in December aboard the United States warship Mississippi. *He had been freed from a prison in Turkey by the intervention of the British and American governments. The identification of the abortive Hungarian revolt with freedom, and Secretary Webster's approval of popular constitutions and national self-determination in the Hulsemann Letter, combined to prepare a hero's welcome for Kossuth as he disembarked. The clamorous scene was reminiscent of Lafayette's arrival in 1824. His reception in Washington was also a personal triumph, but Fillmore, forewarned by Dorothea, carefully avoided a commitment to restore him to power. The White House dinner party in Kossuth's honor, which seated thirty, was dwarfed by Seward's gala banquet which had a guest list of three hundred.*

Trenton, N. Jersey
Dec'b. 24th [1851]

My dear Sir,

I enclose for Mrs. Fillmore two pamphlet notices of Dr. Turnbull's method of treating cases of visual and auricular defect. If you judge proper, you will please give them to Mrs. Fillmore, who may think proper to consult Dr. Turnbull on some convenient opportunity.

The *Kossuth Mania* still rages "in these parts." It has seemed to show evidence of being a self-curing disease, and the only really serious cause of anxiety it creates is the fact it chiefly aids more fully to develope [*sic*] that Americans are not one of the most, but *the* most, excitable people inhabiting this mundane sphere. I do not think we so much have occasion to blame Kossuth as an agitator and disorganizer, as to rebuke those who with such ready facility are disorganized. Kossuth was brought to our shores by an act of Congress: he may well say that *he was no party* to our negotiations with the Turks; and if we rescued him from the autocrat and the tyrant in removing him beyond the machinations of Russia and of Austria, we pledged our faith to the Ottoman Porte who held the Hungarian in ward, to give him an Asylum on our shores. It is not proposed, I imagine, to get up a new Crusade, and to assist in spreading war with all its sanguinary horrors over the European Continent. And this point it seems to me he should be made to apprehend distinctly if not before he reaches Washington, at least when he shall have come within direct communication with our government. I confess I was *glad* to read the courteous, but very timely remarks of Judge [John] Duer at the dinner given to Kossuth by the New York Bar. He should understand that his doctrines are a little too free when *he* charges the American people in the matter of their duties as citizens.

I have without intending it filled my paper, and briefly as comprehensively add *my thanks and good wishes and thoughts.*

I hope to be in Washington by the middle of January.

Respectfully your friend,

D. L. Dix

[Miss Dix, Dec. 24/51.]

⟡ 16. To MILLARD FILLMORE

Dorothea had arrived in Washington by January 22, 1852.
A few days later she drafted a note to Fillmore introducing
two of her friends. Ballard may have been Joseph Ballard, a
Boston merchant, who was interested in philanthropies.

Miss Dix' respects to President, and asks permission to introduce Mr. William Henry Churchman, of the Institution
for the Blind, Indianapolis, Indiana, who is desirous of paying
his respects to our honored Chief Magistrate. Mr. Churchman's singularly successful labors in conducting the Education
of the Blind is his title to kind and respectful consideration
from all who esteem and appreciate a good life devoted to useful ends.

Mr. Ballard attends Mr. Churchman, and shares his natural earnest wish to be honored by an introduction, to the President, while both are slow to encroach on his occupied time and
engagements.

G Street, three doors from 15th Street North
January 28th, 1851 [1852]
[Miss Dix, Wash., Jan. 28/52, Mr. Churchman.]

⟡ 17. To MILLARD FILLMORE

Dorothea seemed to feel the need to advise the Fillmores
in a rather formal letter that she was in Washington before
she resumed the informal relationships of the previous year.
Possibly she had been disappointed at not receiving a word of
welcome from them during the previous week.

Washington, D.C.
January 31st, 1852

To the President,
  Dear Sir,
  I cannot believe that were I a Staunch Catholic I should have any chance of canonization on the ground of patience under some annoyances and privations; for example, I have borne with no real equanimity, which indeed has not been outwardly spoken or manifested, the circumstance of having been nine days in Washington without having seen you for any conversation at all.

  Part of this time I have not been well enough to be abroad, but chiefly I have been deterred from seeking to see you by not knowing when I had any chance of finding you disengaged from either the cares of business or other society. I am a little exclusive in my tastes and habits, and do not court what is indiscriminate and general. In association with those I esteem, I seek mental intercourse and expression without the presence of numbers, or the restraints of mere ceremony.

  You as well as Mrs. Fillmore have heretofore indulged my choice of seeing you when your Mansion has not been open to the public, and if I may ask a similar indulgence again, and can know when my visits will not fall at unseasonable times I shall be gratified to resume a personal acquaintance which is as agreeable as I hope the sentiments of friendly regard conducting to it may be lasting.

                    Your friend respectfully and cordially,
                                                  D. L. DIX

Honorable Millard Fillmore
Executive Mansion
[Miss Dix, Wash., Jan. 31/52, Interview]

ᴥ§ 12. To Dorothea Dix

Fillmore reassures Dorothea that she has an open invitation to the White House and urges her to come without ceremony. He also reveals that Abigail is in New York consulting the eye specialist Dorothea had recommended.

March 9, 1852

My Dear Miss Dix,

I received your two kind notes, read and returned the paper about Kossuth, and intended to write you. But really I have scarcely a moment which I can call my own.

Mrs. Fillmore as you have probably heard is in New York. She has gone to test the skill of Dr. Turnbull; but my daughter is here and we shall both be most happy to see you whenever and as often as it may suit your convenience. Do come without ceremony.

I forgot to mention when I wrote you before, that the Documents which you desired from the Indian office I requested the Commissioner to send. Have they been received?

Hoping to see you soon I remain

Your friend

Millard Fillmore

ᴥ§ 18. To Millard Fillmore

Obviously pleased at the warmth of Fillmore's invitation Dorothea plans to join Abby and Fillmore for dinner.

Annapolis, March 11th, 1852

My dear friend,

I received your note just as I was departing for this City, having arrived from New Jersey and Pennsylvania by the Express Train the preceding evening. I had not a moment for seeing friends, nor for writing during this flight into and from Washington. I propose returning on Friday evening, and will dine with you on Saturday, or take tea and spend the hours with yourself and Miss Fillmore on Sunday evening (not as a visitor), but quietly as a family friend. I have but time to wish you ten thousand blessings—of mind, and outward good without stint or measure. I wish you may have for friends (but where they shall be sought and found), men honest and right-minded as yourself; —and sincere as yourself.

Respectfully,
D. L. Dix

19. To Mary Abigail Fillmore

Enclosed with Dorothea's note of March 11 to Fillmore was one to Abby asking her to drive Dorothea from her lodging house on G Street to the White House.

Annapolis
March 11,1852

My dear Miss Fillmore,

I have something worth showing you. If you have *no engagement,* I accept your and the President's invitation "at any time," making the special time Saturday at dinner. Should you be driving abroad, will you take me up, *en passant,* also, the *heavy tomes* which I hold "in trust" for your amusement and that of your friends.

In haste, cordially
your friend,
D. L. Dix

[Miss Dix, Annapolis,
Mch. 11, 52.]

⋙ 13. To DOROTHEA DIX

Fillmore writes to confirm Dorothea's acceptance of an invitation to dinner.

Washington, March 12th, 1852

My Dear Miss Dix,

Your two kind notes from Annapolis were received this morning, and I can assure you it will give myself and my daughter great pleasure to have your company at dinner tomorrow at ½ past four. I shall expect you without fail, and I must reserve the rest that I would say until that time.

I am truly
Your friend
MILLARD FILLMORE

⋙ 14. To DOROTHEA DIX

Fillmore writes an informal and friendly tribute to Dorothea in recognition of her support and advice. Her letter regarding the Maryland judgeship is missing.

Abigail had returned from New York, and the family was expecting Dorothea to join them in a family dinner.

Washington City
March 24, 1852
Wednesday morning

My Dear Miss Dix,

It is strange to me how you find time to accomplish every thing and especially every thing good. But so it is. You are my mentor; my good genius; not any evil genius like that which haunted the footsteps of the noble Brutus, but my friendly, charitable, confiding guide like the Mentor of Ulysses which followed and directed him through all the tangled mazes of an

eventful war and more eventful journey to his quiet and retired home, and the undying affection of his constant and Devoted Penelope.

But I took up my pen merely to thank you for your kind
note of yesterday; and for the information which it contained
on the subject of the vacant Judgeship in Maryland. It was
however too late to affect my decision, but it was a source of
real pleasure to know my own judgment confirmed by so disinterested and competent a judge as yourself.

I will not suspect you of flattery because you disclaim it,
but I fear that you sometimes view my acts with too partial an
eye to be just. But instead of regarding this as flattery I am
disposed to look upon it as an evidence of friendship, and I can
assure you that it is fully reciprocated on my part.

Mrs. Fillmore joins me in the request that you will favor
us with your company at a private family dinner on Saturday
at 4½ P.M. I expect no one else.

I am truly
Your friend
MILLARD FILLMORE

✑ 20. To MILLARD FILLMORE

*Dorothea insisted that her admiration for Fillmore was
genuine and her praise was not flattery. "I see and feel and
know this." Her "life-objects," she added, were too absolute
for her to correspond frequently; furthermore, a frequent exchange of letters might be misunderstood by others.*

Monday Ev'g.

My dear Sir, and most excellent friend,

I have not as yet referred to the contents of your note on
Friday Evening as I arrived from Baltimore, save to the con-

cluding passage which *bade* me to the Executive Mansion.
One expression allow me to say I cannot pass without review. *I*
at least am neither "a too partial friend," nor blind interpreter
of character. *I know* that you are a good and upright man, and
a sound statesman. I have both pride and pleasure, as an
American, in noting your course. I study the history of your
administration with gratitude and thanksgiving, that "amidst
the scores unfaithful found, one mind shows sound and true."

With a clear and careful aim you have directed our National affairs safely and prosperously; navigating the ship of
our destiny past shoals and sunken rocks, and maintaining her
onward course in deep secure waters. Your career manifesting
in its progress no mean or vain ambition, has conquered faithlessness and envy, and jealousy and pride, and vain glory.
Thousands are added to your list of friends; the bad alone, if
any, are enemies.

Now if I *see* and *feel* and *know* this, I do not consider it
flattery to tell you these results. I honour and respect you far
too sincerely to *offend* your, or my own, mind by fulsome
praise and vain words.

I shall not always reiterate the truths at which I have
glanced, but if you esteem my friendship of any worth, if you
attach any value to the brief, but to me, pleasant interchange
of our thoughts and opinions, our written communications will
continue and perhaps always; more or less interrupted indeed,
but not wholly broken off. How can I write then to you, or
speak when I am your fireside guest, without allowing occasional expression of the *right* sentiments I entertain toward
you, and the *high* estimate I have of your character. I assure
you that you have no other hold on my friendly regard and
esteem than that which is based on the precept I have of your
moral worth, and clear strong mindedness; and could I sup-

pose you really deficient in the first and wanting in the last, the fabric my friendship has built for its serious affection would very quickly crumble to dust. After this you must know that I write and speak the language of truth and soberness.

In regard to a frequent correspondence, I have the idea that the many claims more urgent than those of friendship hold on your time must limit the use of your pen, and my life-objects are too absolute for me to be a valuable correspondent or very frequent one. Beside it is by no means certain in this strange world wherein we are dwellers that other persons would place the right construction on a frequent exchange of letters, and it is a very good rule to concede in such a case somewhat to the faults and follies of society, happy that the tribute paid into that mixed treasury is only the surrender of a portion of innocent letter-writing.

I must take leave lest your patience shall not be in measure with my pages, and praying that the blessing of the Father rest always on your life and its duties, I repeat that I am as sincerely as respectfully and affectionately your friend,

D. L. Dix

[Miss D. L. Dix, Wash.,
March 26 (29?) 52.]

◄§ 15. To Dorothea Dix

Fillmore again is apprehensive regarding Dorothea's health.

April 1, [1852]

My Dear Miss Dix,

I have but a moment to express my regret at hearing of your illness. I sincerely hope you may be better by Saturday so as to give us the pleasure of your company at dinner, which will be at 3½ instead of 4½ as heretofore.

The morning is bright, beautiful and *inviting*, but I am a prisoner of state and can not enjoy it.

Truly your friend,
MILLARD FILLMORE

◄§ 21. To MILLARD FILLMORE

Dorothea drew upon her background in natural history to satirize the ambitious but, in her judgment, ill-advised plans of distinguished horticulturist and Superintendent of Public Grounds Andrew J. Downing. He wanted to provide the public grounds next to the Executive Mansion with a pond fed by the foul water of the canal. In one of her most expressive letters she flays the proposal and reveals her tastes in architecture and decoration.

The canal ran along the southern margin of the White House grounds and had been built to connect the Potomac River with the Eastern Branch (Anacostia). It carried more sewage than vessels.

The Washington Monument languished for a lack of contributions, and remained a stump rather than a majestic spire.

The fears of Dorothea and Professor Henry were not realized. Downing died in a steamboat accident in July of 1852 leaving only a few loops of trees and shrubs on the Smithsonian grounds completed. Subsequently the purer water from the Potomac River at Great Falls was carried by an aqueduct to Georgetown to provide Washington with ornamental fountains and pools. But it was not until Buchanan's Presidency that Washingtonians beheld this sight.

April 5th, [1852]

Dear Sir,

Please be prepared for a *movement of the waters.* "Ah yes, but what does the President think," is now the inquiry. I have somewhat to tell you concerning that *beautiful* sheet of water which is to adorn "the grounds" and afford at one and the same time, variety to the landscape, a capacious receptacle for certain organisms which do much multiply in stagnant waters, and are alembic for generating those miasmatic airs which act as subtle poisons on the brain, and too often of a sudden insidiously extinguish the clear light flame of the lamp of life. That same "Lake," "Pond," "Hole," as it is indifferently designated, and "the waste" of which is supplied by a *ditch* transmitting the foul waters of the adjacent canal (into which flows all the city drainage), is subject of critical remark and conversation, it seems, in various quarters by certain persons who *do* presume to question the correctness of Mr. Downing's taste, and the soundness of his judgment.

Professor Henry and others calling to see me, the former suddenly inquired if I had examined Mr. Downing's plans for embellishing the Public Grounds, especially those connected with the Executive Mansion. I replied that with but little leisure, I had but slightly observed any of the public *improvements,* but that to the extent of notice given, I could not fail to remark the failure of "the Landscape Manufacturer," in taking advantage of the Natural beauties at his disposal, and his preference for what was artificial, and of questionable value; especially, a casual observer would discover his ambition to emulate the Ancients by restoring what was obsolete and long ago condemned in ornamented and ornamental grounds, I observed that the city of Washington seemed peculiarly under that curse to which Mr. Jefferson pointedly referred as being inflicted upon the *whole* country. There, for example, was the

Washington Monument, not yet raised to one-fifth its proposed elevation, but already furrowed by the ravages of decay;
and destined, it would seem, to be not a Monument to the
venerated memory of the Country's honoured Father, but a
type of the defective judgment of *well-meaning* persons, but
not very discriminating.

And then in near proximity stands the Smithsonian edifice
(or mass of deficient edifices), a monstrous pile of misshapen
towers, arches, columns, etc., a reproduction of the defects of
by-gone semi-barbarous periods, a strange blot on the brow of
advancing science and a strange commentary on the *aims of*
those who were rather boastful in their announcement of the
high purpose of "cultivating the arts" and diffusing "useful
knowledge."

And now we see advancing upon the Public Grounds, a
party (pick, spade and barrow in hand), for what, to dig and
delve? to *execute* a hole; to fill this "Kentucky Bear Wallow"
as it might fitly be called, with not Heaven's pure element, the
crystal waters, but, as toiling on, "while still the wonder
grows," the amazed spectator sees these labours day by day
proclaim a new success and revel in beauties yet concealed by
the veil of futurity.

Yet is the result not all obscure: this noble toil, this high
endeavour, it has produced "a Frog Pond," and "a Molehill
Mount!" For my part, since I am consulted, I heartily recommend that with least possible delay all varieties of the Order
Batrachia, Genus *Rana,* found by the *"Exploring* Expedition,"
should forthwith be collected *there,* for the study of the curious Herpetologist, while their varied and mellifluous notes
should charm the senses and beguile the cares of the Chief
Magistrate of the United States.

"But what does the President think of the Pond," resumed
Professor H[enry] "for I have some hand in this?"

Good Sir, may your shadow never be less, but the President, the President, I replied illatively [?], I am not the exponent of the President's views, only this I know, he is reported a man of sound sense, and a gentleman of taste. Granting these propositions, he is bound to condemn the whole of this vicious artificial production. Take timely warning of a friend, "If our good President does not veto this proceeding, look for no distant action on the part of the *Board of Health*. All experience shows the certain mischief resulting from such festering pools of rank foul waters![")] The Professor could bear no more, but declares that "Downing's Death Hole" shall be speedily brought under consideration at the President's!

If you have no time to read such paper messengers, do not think I shall complain at omissions.

Respectfully and Sincerely your friend,

D. L. DIX

[D. L. Dix, April 5/52, In regard to water pond below Presit's House.]

ᴥ§ 22. To MILLARD FILLMORE

There was urgency in Dorothea's request for an immediate conversation with Fillmore. She did not explain it.

Monday Mg.

April 26th [1852]

To the President

My dear Sir,

Urged by very strong motives of a private nature (relating to individuals), of public and political (relating to State affairs), and of personal (relating to yourself as Guardian and just Executor of a most difficult Wardship), I wish *half an hour's* conversation with you today, or this evening.

I think you know me well enough to be *sure* I should not
make this request except urged by *positive* notices both of obligation and judgment. I will not say that feeling has not a
share in this, but I think that a keen sense of justice prevails
over feeling.

I do not know that any remedy can be had for a serious
evil, but I at least, in a great wrong perpetrated by a responsible individual high in office, shall have the satisfaction of
your opinion, whether under *all* the circumstances you can or
can not interpose. I have serious doubts, but am clear in the
duty of seeing you.

I must leave town early tomorrow. I have much to occupy
today. Be so kind as to name the time, if any, that you can see
me *this day* from 8 A.M. to 9 P.M. *as will least* interfere with
your engagements, only saying that from 12 M. to 3 P.M. mine
are presumptory and not transferable.

With sincere respect and friendship,

D. L. Dix

[Miss Dix. Ap'l. 26/52, Interview. Ans. 26.]

◄§ 16. To DOROTHEA DIX

*Fillmore, obviously, gave top priority to Dorothea's request
for an interview.*

Washington City,
April 26th, 1852

My Dear Miss Dix

I have your note of this morning requesting an interview
on a matter of public business, which it will give me great
pleasure to grant, and I only regret, that I had not received it
in time to have invited you to come and breakfast with us. But

as it is, I will see you either at three o'clock, or will be happy to have you come and dine with us at half past four, as may best suit your convenience. I write in great haste, but am truly yours

MILLARD FILLMORE

꿎 23. TO MILLARD FILLMORE

Again, Dorothea's business would not wait. She would see Fillmore immediately after his breakfast.

The President
  in *desmains proper,*
  Has the President ten minutes to spare after Breakfast. If this is *quite convenient,* Miss Dix will await his leisure in the red parlour, or where he shall direct.
  To Mr. Fillmore more sunny congratulations on the *advent of May* than the sky exhibits.

D. L. DIX

[Miss Dix, May 1/52. Interview.]

꿎 17. TO DOROTHEA DIX

Fillmore has a bouquet delivered to Dorothea.

Saturday Evening
May 15, 1852

My Dear Miss Dix,
  Please to accept the accompanying *bouquet* as a slight testimony of the respect and esteem, with which your disinter-

ested devotion to the cause of suffering humanity, has inspired
your

Sincere friend,
MILLARD FILLMORE

[Miss D. L. Dix at Mr. Peale's, G. Street.]

~§ 24. TO MILLARD FILLMORE

Dorothea introduces a Mr. Avery.

To His Excellency
   Millard Fillmore,
   Miss Dix' respects and asks permission to introduce to the
President, Mr. Avery of Massachusetts, a gentleman whose
respect for the Chief Magistrate of the Republic inspires the
wish to be indulged with a personal interview.
Baltimore, June 2d, 1852.

[Miss Dix, June 2/52. Mr. Avery.]

~§ 18. TO DOROTHEA DIX

*Fillmore pardons two "slave stealers" who were languish-
ing in a Washington jail despite the probability of unpopularity and sectional overtones.*
   *On Saturday, April 15, 1848, Daniel Drayton, with funds
supplied by Abolitionists, engaged Edward Sayres, Captain of
the schooner* Pearle *(out of Philadelphia), to transport seventy-
seven slaves from the District of Columbia to Frenchtown,
New Jersey. The fugitives were loaded into the hold and the
ship embarked on schedule. But at the entrance of the Chesa-*

peake Bay an adverse wind induced Sayres to drop anchor. Meanwhile, on Sunday morning some of the owners of the missing slaves, including Dolly Madison, reported their losses, and an informer revealed their flight aboard the Pearle.

An armed posse hurriedly set out in pursuit on the steamship Salem, reached the Pearle early the next morning, and boarded it before Sayres could get underway. They brought Drayton and Sayres and the fugitives back to Washington and confined them in the District jail. Amidst rumors of mob violence against Drayton and Sayres Abolitionists and the more vocal defenders of slavery argued the matter in Congress.

Drayton and Sayres were subsequently fined and imprisoned for "'transporting" slaves from the District. After four years, petitions for their release were signed by more than one-half of the slaveholders in Washington, and Senator Sumner interceded with President Fillmore to obtain pardons. The latter complied on August 11.

Sumner sent a carriage to the jail for their deliverance beyond the District, lest disapproving residents should be tempted to intervene.

Fillmore makes no mention of his disappointment at not receiving the nomination of his party for a full term. He had just lost the nomination to General Winfield Scott after a convention stalemate that required fifty-three ballots to resolve. A handful of Webster supporters from New England had held the balance of power. Scott's support came from the Free Soil faction of the party, and his victory was facilitated by the Weed-Seward control over the New York delegation.

Fillmore gave no outward sign that he sought the nomination; once it was lost, he accepted defeat with his accustomed resignation.

Washington, Augt. 13, 1852
Friday 7 A.M.

My Dear Miss Dix,

Drayton and Sayers [Sayres] are out; and doubtless I shall be abused and misrepresented for pardoning them. I perceive that a false telegraphic report came back from Baltimore last night by the evening papers, stating that they were sentenced to 50 years imprisonment and had been confined only two. But I have a conscientious conviction that I have done my duty, and am therefore quite indifferent to these assaults, but some of my friends are much alarmed. I should despise myself, if I feared to do right because of popular prejudice or clamor.

I return the interesting letters which you sent, and am in *great haste.*

Truly yours,
MILLARD FILLMORE

✒§ 19. To DOROTHEA DIX

Dorothea's land-grant bill was approved in the House of Representatives by a vote of 98 to 54, and Fillmore immediately drafted a congratulatory note to her. However, the bill was subsequently sidetracked in the Senate, when opponents offered a series of amendments which would have added millions of acres for their own special interests.

It was a bitter blow to Dorothea's hopes.

Washington, Augt. 17, 1852

My Dr. Miss Dix,

I have your note and congratulate you and the country on the passage of your bill through the House by so large a majority. "Patience has done her perfect work," and you have triumphed.

Truly your friend,
MILLARD FILLMORE

◄§ 20. To DOROTHEA DIX

Fillmore agreed to take another look with Dorothea at the prospectus for the Government Hospital for the Insane. Designed as an asylum for the personnel of the armed forces, it was authorized by Congress on October 13, 1852, and opened in January of 1855. It was situated on high ground overlooking the East Branch of the Potomac River (Anacostia) on land which Dorothea persuaded its owner, Thomas Blagden, to sell for this purpose. The act authorized the Secretary of the Interior to purchase the land and attend to its erection and furnishing under the direction of the President.

At Dorothea's solicitation, Fillmore named Doctor Charles H. Nichols as its Superintendent, a post he held from 1852 to 1877.

Oct. 1, 1852

My Dear Miss Dix,

I have perused and herewith return Dr. Nichols' letter. He certainly writes like a man of sense, and I trust that his employment will give entire satisfaction.

I have also read and herewith return the letter on *"Spiritual Manifestations."* The writer is evidently a full believer but I see nothing in what he has communicated at all miraculous. The mystery evidently consists in the *belief* that the spirit is there. Whether it be so or not, seems impossible to determine.

But these "speaking" spirits are evidently a great improvement on the writing, and prove—if there be any thing in it—that epistles are not the only means of communicating with the *spirit land*, and that the advantages of this new science are to be equally open to the learned and the unlearned, to the wise and the ignorant.

But enough of this folly and humbug. Let us turn again to the assylum [*sic*]. You ask when I am at leisure. Never! But nevertheless I will be happy to see you on any day after 12, except Tuesdays and Wednesdays; they being reception and cabinet days.

I perceive that you never tire in well doing. Your active mind is always engaged, and your vigilant attention neglects nothing.

May Heaven bless you for what you have done and preserve you long as a blessing to others.

I am your friend.

MILLARD FILLMORE

◄§ 21. To DOROTHEA DIX

Fillmore's eulogy of Dorothea is warm and tender.

Sunday Morning, Oct. 3 [1852]

My Dear Miss Dix,

I have perused and herewith return the notes which you were so kind as to send me.

That poetic address to you from the *Intelligencer* is beautiful because it is true. It contains Sentiments which have often passed through my mind, and I presume the minds of all others, who have witnessed the happy combination of feminine delicacy, and softness of manner, which are at once the grace and charm of your sex, united with a disinterested and unselfish devotion to the happiness of others, which form the prominent traits of your character. With a sympathy as unbounded as human suffering; industry that never tires, and an energy that never flags, you have for years pursued your Heaven-born mission; and I say without flattery that you have accomplished more for the relief of suffering humanity than any other living man or woman. May God prosper and sustain you, for "nations shall rise up and call you blessed."

Do not fear that your notes are ever unwelcome. I felt a little disappointed at not seeing you yesterday. I approve of all you do or propose to do in reference to the assylum [sic]; and had you called I should have proposed a ride after dinner to look at the sites out east.

But "the church-going bell" admonishes me to close. What a quiet, sabbath-like stillness pervades the atmosphere. The restless busy city is hushed in silence, and all nature seems reverently mute on this holy day. It is really the sabbath of the Lord. Do you not feel it?

Heaven Bless you. Adieu!

Yours sincerely,
MILLARD FILLMORE

⋙ 22. To DOROTHEA DIX

Dorothea made occasional trips to Trenton and Baltimore during the summer and fall of 1852 when her bill and her work on the Washington asylum were quiescent.

Fillmore was prepared to send his carriage (a magnificent piece of workmanship, presented to him in the name of Mrs. Fillmore by supporters in New York City) to meet Dorothea at the Washington depot upon her return from an unidentified journey.

It would appear that Fillmore wished to discuss an appeal

against the appointment of Doctor Nichols by Doctor Thomas
Miller, a prominent Washington physician, and founder of
the Washington Medical Association and proponent of the
hospital.

Washington Oct. 21, 1852

My Dear Miss Dix,

Mrs. Fillmore is suffering from an ague in the face and not able to write, and she therefore desires me to address you and request you on your return to the city to call and spend a few days with us. We shall both be happy to see you, and at this moment we have no one staying with us. Please let me know the time of your arrival and my carriage will meet you at the depot.

Dr. Miller has been to see me and protests very strongly against *"importing"* a physician to take charge of the hospital. He claims much merit, and for aught I know, truly, in having procured the passage of the law, and desires the appointment of governing or consulting physician.

He is evidently much displeased at the selection which has been made, and manifestly suspects that it has been done through your influence. I therefore think it is proper that you should be advised of this fact before you return.

Mrs. Fillmore joins me in cordial regards to yourself; and

I remain sincerely and truly yours,
MILLARD FILLMORE

◄§ 23. To DOROTHEA DIX

Fillmore acknowledges correspondence he had received
from Dorothea while she was out of the city. The letters to
which he refers are missing.

Washington, Dec. 9, 1852

My Dear Miss Dix,

I thank you for the enclosed slips and agreeably to your request herewith return them.

Your kind note of the 6th and 7th came to hand this morning, and I am gratified to perceive that Dr. M[iller] has not disturbed your peace of mind. We are all well. Hope to have the pleasure of seeing you on your return. I am ever, Truly, your friend

MILLARD FILLMORE

24. To DOROTHEA DIX

Fillmore acknowledges communications from Dorothea, and notes that he is looking into the cause of an unwholesome odor (from the Potomac Canal?) to which she alludes. Dorothea's papers are missing.

Washington
Jan'y. 20, 1853

My Dear Miss Dix,

I herewith return Mr. Bell's private letter, and have filed the other two in favor of Mr. [Fuller?] as consul.

I thank you for your favor of yesterday and have directed an investigation into the causes of the unwhol[e]some odor to which you allude.

This is, indeed, a charming day, but I have only seen it from my window. It is now 4 and I must take my accustomed walk.

But whether walking or working, I am

Truly yours,
MILLARD FILLMORE

 ◆§ 25. To Dorothea Dix

Fillmore advises Dorothea that he does not have access to the Geological Report *written by David Dale Owen, Geologist of the United States.*

Washington, Feb'y. 19, 1853.

My Dear Miss Dix,
  On enquiring I learn that the work of Mr. Owen of which you desired a copy, is a report to Congress and printed and distributed under its authority. I regret therefore to say that I have no power to comply with your request, or I should do so with great pleasure.
  This is with me a very busy time or I should have written you before, but I am ever, truly yours,

             Millard Fillmore

 ◆§ 26. To Dorothea Dix

Fillmore obtained a copy of the Geological Report, *and presents it to Dorothea.*

Feb'y. 23, 1853

My Dear Miss Dix,
  After writing you the other day I learned that I could obtain a copy of Mr. Owen's *Geological Report* at the Land office, which I procured and take great pleasure in presenting it to you.

            Truly your friend
            Millard Fillmore

5

Tragedies and Adjustments

1853–1854

The eighteen months following Fillmore's retirement from office were marked by tragedy for him and disappointments for Dorothea.

Abigail died a few weeks after moving from the White House, and her sorrowing family muddled through the readjustment in their old homestead in Buffalo. Just over a year later Abby was stricken by cholera, and expired just after her father and brother reached her bedside. Basically a family-centered man, Fillmore reeled under these blows.

Dorothea shared the tragedies, and on several occasions was virtually reduced to begging for evidence that Fillmore had survived the shock and remained physically well. Meanwhile, she suffered two emotional shocks: a sudden and seemingly irrefutable report that Fillmore was about to remarry, and the defeat, after seven years of labor, of her federal land grant for the indigent insane.

❧§ 25. To MILLARD FILLMORE

With her land grant lost or deferred by Congress for another year, Dorothea sought rest and relief from her labor amid old friends in Philadelphia. She prescribed a similar therapy for Fillmore.

Abigail, who had been unwell for some weeks, became seriously ill after attending the inaugural of President Franklin Pierce, where she may have suffered a chill. She was confined to the Fillmore suite in the Willard Hotel.

Washington Irving, who stood by Abigail during the inaugural, recalled her exposure and discomfort:

> *I almost think poor Mrs. Fillmore must have received her death-warrant while standing by my side on the marble terrace of the capitol, exposed to the chilly wind and snow, listening to the inaugural speech of her husband's successor [in a letter to Robert C. Winthrop quoted in Severance, op. cit., II, iv].*

Plans the Fillmores had made to visit the South (neither had been south of Richmond) were discarded, and awaiting Abigail's recovery, they delayed from day to day their departure for Buffalo.

Phila., March 21st, 1853

Dear Sir and Friend,

With Dr. and Mrs. Hare, and surrounded by those who are substantially friendly to you, and supporters of, and firm to you politically; and who are sincere and cordial, I cannot but wish you were in this city, rather than in Washington where disinterested friendship and honest opinions are not the prevailing characteristics in general society, or in political cliques.

I trust that Mrs. Fillmore's strength of constitution has

surmounted the force of an alarming and dangerous malady—
and hope that her recovery will be rapid and complete.

Dr. and Mrs. Hare desire that, should you come to Philadelphia, when they are here, they may have the opportunity of testifying their esteem by personal attentions to yourself and family.

I am not sufficiently well to venture on forming any definite plans for pursuing my usual labors, but have made the first advance in remedial means for securing recovery, in leaving Washington, and putting aside with resolution all regrets of past disappointments, in the failure of Congress to complete my wishes in relation to the Bill for the Insane.

Your successor does not appear likely to find his rest on beds of Rose leaves,—nor to breathe in a Garden of Paradise. Station brings surely little but access [?] of burthening cares, and serious responsibilities. Few Statesmen could employ the Legend of your Seal, "Be Just, and fear not," for very few consider the ways of Justice, or ponder the paths which conduct to the Temple of Truth.

With sincere respect and friendly regards, I am yours Sir cordially,

D. L. DIX

Dorothea enclosed a clipping from a Louisville newspaper which promised a warm reception for Fillmore and his entourage during his projected visit to the South.

MILLARD FILLMORE.—We want to see Millard Fillmore —the man who, with characteristic modesty, attributes all the glory of his administration to "the wisdom, harmony, fidelity, and ability of his associates"—the gentle man whom the ladies call handsome, and becoming the Chair with exceeding éclat —the personage whom many will delight to honor with their supreme suffrages in 1856.

The people of Louisville will welcome the late President to their city, and give him a reception worthy of his reputation. His southern tour will be one triumphal procession from Washington around to Buffalo. The inhabitants of this Western Valley will not be outdone in their expressions and exhibitions of admiration, by any attentions which New Yorkers paid him and his councilors at the opening celebration of their great railroad in the spring of fifty-one.

May all the members of his Cabinet accompany himself and family, in the tour which Mr. Webster once attempted, but failed to accomplish owing to declining health [*Louisville Courier,* undated].

[Miss D. L. Dix, March 21, Rec'd. 21, 1853]
[Rec.d and ans'd, March 22]

ᴗᴥ§ 26. To MILLARD FILLMORE

Learning from Fillmore that Abigail's condition had worsened, Dorothea offered her help if it were needed. Fillmore's letter of March 22 is missing.

Phila., March 23d [1853]

My dear Sir and Friend,

Yours of the 22d has just been brought in by "the Carrier," and I assure you I am at once grieved and disappointed by the account it contains of Mrs. Fillmore's health at the time of your writing. I had received on Saturday evening a letter from a friend which gave more encouraging account than your note which had decided my departure from Washington;—and on Monday, a second letter was still more satisfactory. I deeply regret the severe trial and inconveniences to which you are subjected; but most, I sympathize in your anxiety. I am satisfied that my presence could not be of essential advantage to

Mrs. Fillmore, and therefore do not propose coming on, but I cannot be just to my own feelings except I express my willingness to do so, should it seem at any time desirable.

Dr. and Mrs. Hare unite with myself in expressions of hope for Mrs. Fillmore's speedy recovery,—and sympathy with you both under your present pain and solicitudes.

Dr. Hare says again, "express to the President my highest esteem and regard," and in this Mrs. Hare joins. Come as soon as possible to this city, where so many will hasten to surround you with comforts not procurable in Washington.

With respect and sincerity your assured friend,

D. L. Dix

I am occupied with the Hospitals and kindred plans.
[Miss D. L. Dix, March 23, Rec'd. 1853.]

27. To Millard Fillmore

Abigail died during the morning of March 30.
After receiving the details from Doctor Nichols, Dorothea expressed her sorrow in a few poignant lines.
Burial was made in Forest Lawn Cemetery in Buffalo.

Phila., April 2d [1853]

My dear Sir and Friend—

I will not increase your trouble by attempts to direct your disturbed thoughts to sources of consolation. It belongs to friendship to be silent, and grieve with the wounded spirit,— and wait till the troubled heart rallies somewhat from the paralysis of sorrow before language can express the methods of consolation, or present the arguments which assist in recovering from a great bereavement.

If I remain silent after this brief reference to the true sorrow I bear in your behalf, it will be from the conviction that at present, all modes of expressing sympathy would fall worthless from the pen,—and that at a later time your own good heart, and sound mind will gather such helps to resignation—and calmness as will suffice for every want of your life.

Our Father bless you and keep you.

Your assured friend,
D. L. Dix

Do not feel it necessary to reply to these lines. I send a letter I had from Dr. Nichols in evidence of his remembrance of and sympathy with you.

[Dr. Nichols and Miss Dix, Rec'd. April 8, 1853.]

◄§ 28. To MILLARD FILLMORE

Receiving no response from Fillmore, Dorothea wrote again from Baltimore, seeking reassurance that he was physically well.

Baltimore, May 15th, 1853

My dear Sir and Friend,

I have forborne writing for many weeks however anxious to hear more accurately of your health than through the unreliable medium of the public journals. I am aware that it is not reasonable to expect many lines in return for the thousand questions a sympathizing friendship is eager to propose, and I shall endeavour to be satisfied with the simple reference to your physical health.

I hardly know if it would most console or disturb you to learn how large and wide is the sympathy which is manifested for you and your children. No day passes that I do not hear you named with consideration, respect and interest. You are confirmed in the minds, and rooted in the hearts of your friends; and your prosperity, peace and happiness will continue to them subjects of a concern by no means common in measure or duration.

I shall be greatly obliged if you incline to send a line to my address in Philadelphia next week,—to acquaint me of what I can learn only upon authority from yourself. Are you strong and free from disabling illness?

Your friend with respectful regard,

D. L. Dix

At present all is safe and well with the Hospital at Washington.

[Miss D. L. Dix, May 15, Rec'd. 18, 1853. Ans'd May 22.]

⊷§ 27. To DOROTHEA DIX

Fillmore assured Dorothea that he and his son and daughter were in good health and were prepared to resume housekeeping in their old residence.

"But it does not seem like home," he lamented. "The light of the house is gone; and I can never hope to enjoy life again as I have heretofore."

Buffalo, May 22, 1853

My Dear Miss Dix,

I have your kind note from Baltimore of the 15th inst. and feel grateful for the solicitude which it manifests for the welfare of myself and family. I should have acknowledged your repeated acts of kindness both before and since my painful bereavement, but for the fact that I took a severe cold soon after I arrived in this city, from which I suffered for two or three weeks, and when I recovered from that I really felt too depressed in spirits to attempt to write.

For three weeks past I have been much occupied in fitting up my old residence, preparatory to house-keeping, in which work my good children have rendered me every assistance which I could expect or desire; and I am happy now to inform you, that we have removed into the house, and are once more all together, and in the enjoyment of excellent health.

But it does not seem like home. The light of the house is gone; and I can never hope to enjoy life again as I have heretofore. But I will not dwell upon this painful subject.

I am happy to hear that all is well with the hospital at Washington; and I need not assure you that I shall always be happy to hear of your health and prosperity, and ever pray that your life may be spared for the sake not only of yourself and friends, but of those objects of charity, who are so deeply indebted to you for your disinterested labors in their behalf.

I am your friend
MILLARD FILLMORE

§ 29. To MILLARD FILLMORE

Rallying her spirits, Dorothea sailed for Nova Scotia in June. After reviewing the cords that bound her to Fillmore, she surveyed her plans for hospitals in the Maritime Provinces and made an evaluation of the effects of a proposed policy of free trade between the United States and Canada. A reciprocity treaty was ratified the following year.

St. John's, Newfoundland
June 28th, 1853

My dear Sir and Friend,

While I do not mean to burthen you with letters; neither can I remain long and altogether silent. Allowed to regard you as a friend; for some time a member of your family and a participant in its quiet cheerful influences and pleasures; bound to you by ever-remembered obligations in connection with

Hospital affairs; sympathizing in your varied anxieties and trials, I cannot omit sometimes to pause on long distant journeyings in remote places, and say a few words by the pen.

It was a great comfort to learn before leaving Philadelphia that you had rallied from the indisposition which had for a time weakened your usually sound health. Many, many whom you will never know, have with sincere sympathy entered into your grief, and have prayed fervently that you might find your strength to be equal to your day of trouble. Many returned devout thanksgivings that your life had been prolonged, when boding[?] fears had fallen on the mind, sustained by the journals reporting your illness[?]. May God bless you ever!

I arrived here from Sydney, Cape Breton, on Tuesday, and if the weather is fine, I shall sail for Harbour Grace on Saturday, returning thither after a time, and not proceeding to Labrador this season. I do not know how long my services may seem to be needed on this Island and the Provinces, but now suppose I shall reach the States by August. Affairs for the construction of a Hospital for the Insane here, look well, and I imagine that patient endeavour will soon be followed by good results. In Nova Scotia I have given a plan for building, to be commenced at once.

The accounts which are circulated in the public journals in the States, concerning the difficulties on the Fishing Stations are greatly exaggerated, in fact they seem to parties *here* to be almost nominal. Free-trade is earnestly desired by all the Provinces, and to secure this with the States, I think they yield to the temptation of urging grievances which do not exist to any serious extent, in order to effect a compromise, opening for them so real advantages. Maine and Massachusetts would certainly, for a time, suffer loss; the one through the lumber-trade, the other by her fisheries, but I shall leave wiser minds to settle these questions. The waters round Newfoundland employ 25,000 British subjects, and those fishermen are thus the Apprentices from which is derived the force and power of the English Navy. My letter address is Boston.

With sincere respect and regard, I am your friend

D. L. DIX

Kind regards to Mr. Powers Fillmore and to Miss Fillmore if you please.

[Miss D. L. Dix, June 28; Rec'd. July, 1853; Ans'd. Aug't. 5.]

⇜§ 28. To DOROTHEA DIX

Before retiring from the Presidency Fillmore had decided not to return to his law practice. In his judgment jousting with lawyers for fees would degrade the office that he symbolized. He could not discard the mantle of office like a suit of clothes; it entailed a continuing trust.

Making the decision and living with it, however, were quite different. He was soon bored and restless. A widower at fifty-three, in good health and with no young children requiring parental care, he seemed to have no place to look except backward.

Buffalo, Augt. 5, 1853

My Dear Miss Dix,

Your kind letter of the 28th of June, dated at St. John's, New Foundland, came to hand some days since, and I could not but exclaim that wherever misery found an abode you were sure to follow it and minister to its wants and relieve its sufferings—else what could have sent you to that distant and inhospitable shore. But you are fulfilling a holy mission and May God speed you in your noble enterprises. I shall ever hear of your success with delight and to know that your charitable and self-sacrificing efforts are appreciated by the world is a source of sincere gratification to me.

But what can I say of myself. Nothing—absolutely nothing. I have done nothing; I have felt no desire to do any thing. Since I recovered from the slight indisposition from which I suffered from a short time after my return, my health has been perfectly restored, but yet, I have felt no desire until within a few days to make the least mental exertion; to think was an effort, and to write was fatiguing labor. I therefore busied myself in fitting my old residence for house keeping, and dissipated thought by reading. But I felt that the indulgence of this languor of body and apathy of mind was all wrong, and for the purpose of shaking it off and again interesting myself in the affairs of this world, I went up to Cleveland last week and looked in upon the annual meeting of the American Association for the promotion of Science, and I think the journey did me good.

My son has commenced the practice of law in the city, and since my return, I have been in the daily habit of visiting his office, and for his sake, and by way of amusement, I interest myself in the various questions which present themselves, so far as to afford him my advice. While I have no design of again entering the profession, I can not perhaps find any better or more agreeable recreation than this which I am now pursuing. At all events it has the desired effect of occupying my mind with something useful to others if not beneficial to myself.

My daughter succeeds altogether beyond my expectation in house-keeping, and I should be most happy if you could in your round of labors look in upon us and see how quietly and neatly we live. My children are all I could desire and we are all well and should be grateful for the blessings we enjoy. But to me there is an aching void; a lonely solitude which none can appreciate but myself. But I did not intend to mention it, and will add no more.

Your letters are always welcome and I shall be happy to hear from you as often as may be convenient.

When I took up my pencil I intended to sketch a letter to be written out with a pen, but it is not worth it, and I hope you will pardon me for sending it in pencil.

> I am truly and sincerely
> Your friend
> MILLARD FILLMORE

◄§ 30. To MILLARD FILLMORE

Fillmore's mental depression elicited a warm and sympathetic response from Dorothea. She accepted his welfare as a personal obligation and assumed that she had a right to share his griefs.

She speculated upon the possibility of seeing him in Buffalo and sharing her recent experiences in the Maritime Provinces, a possibility which soon became a reality.

Boston, August 11th, 1853

My dear Sir and Friend,

I arrived here two days since after an eventful two months in the British Provinces and Islands, and your letter with many beside, waited my return. I thank you for writing, for though your penciled lines stir deepest sympathies of my heart, anxiety is relieved of its sharpest solicites. You say you have nothing to write of yourself, but you have said all that is important for earnest friendship to know. You speak of physical inertia and mental languor: be patient with yourself; what else could be expected under circumstances so exciting and distressing as those which lately encompassed you? That you have borne up under such a burthen of trouble is wonderful. I had faith that you would meet trial with manly firmness; that if it shook the very foundations of your strength of thought and life, it would not overthrow them. I expected the results you describe:— that you have risen but measurably from a great shock of the mental and nervous forces is all your friends could look for, and more than their fears at first permitted them to hope. I do believe it would comfort you to know somewhat of the *real* feelings of respectful and overflowing sympathy with which you have been regarded and remembered by many appreciating minds; but after all we are poor in those means of consolation which can be of avail to you.

I am glad you went to Cleveland; it was wisely considered to meet those who would there receive so much pleasure from your presence, and whose objects were so much more satisfactory than the aims of associated politicians. All you are doing and proposing seems just what you require for the gradual progress of heart and mind to a more cheerful state. As you slowly attain this, new occupations will arise. You cannot and will not cease to remember with tender affection the friends and companions of so many years of your life; but pain will be less and less associated with her memory. You will dwell on what is happiest to recall; her place cannot be filled, but your power of enjoyment and your peace will have access day by day, and though shaded, your remainder of life will have rich store of blessings, and will abound in rational satisfactions. Believe it, I shall be proved a true prophet.

I know your good daughter had capabilities which would answer all unusual demands; I rejoice that your children are devoted to you in all those relations which render your home comfortable and cheerful.

You say you did not intend to mention your individual feelings. Why should you withhold such expression from a sincere friend? Of what use is friendship indeed, if it be but an abstraction? For my part, when my friends are happy and prosperous, I feel that they do not need me, but when in affliction or adversity, I have a *right* to share their calamity and their griefs; and by sympathy at least, be a partaker of their sorrows. You say my letters are welcome. I shall then sometimes write, but amidst so busy a life, I can hardly collect my thoughts to make communications farther satisfactory than making them the evidence of unabated esteem and friendship. If I were near you, I should have a thousand things to tell you of my recent journies [sic] and voyages, but the detail on paper would be tedious.

Probably I shall be here several weeks before I finally proceed on a new quest.

If you are inclined, I shall be glad to hear from you. It is not probable that I can be in Buffalo for many hours, if at all. But I will not pass through that city without seeing you all—if my calls of duty conduct me in that direction.

Farewell my friend, God bless you always, and recollect ever.

Yours with just appreciation and sincere regards,

D. L. Dix

[Miss D. L. Dix, Aug't. 11, Rec'd. 14, 1853.]

◄§ 31. To Millard Fillmore

Dorothea details her plans for a short visit with the Fillmores in Buffalo.

New York, November 10 [1853]

Dear Sir and Friend—

I hope to reach Buffalo on Saturday November 12th and to pass Sunday there. In which event I trust I shall see yourself and family, and have much to learn and impart. I cannot now indicate my Hotel, leaving that to decide, but will, if I arrive in season, inform Miss Fillmore.

I intend to leave Utica so as not to reach Buffalo after midnight and wish not to be later than 7 P.M. As I do not know the car hours I am not able to be more definite.

I am truly your friend.

With affectionate regards to Miss Fillmore and remembrances to your son.

D. L. Dix

I may be detained at Utica, but hope otherwise.
New York, Nov'r 10th
[Miss D. L. Dix, Nov. 10, Rec'd. 12, 1853.]

◄§ 32. To Millard Fillmore

Dorothea approved of what she saw in Buffalo: Fillmore, Powers, and Abby in their comfortable home and the good-will and mutual respect which shaped their relations. She left with a desire to share more of it.

During her tour of the Canadian Maritime Provinces Dorothea's attention had been called to Sable Island, a sand spit lying ninety-five miles east of Nova Scotia, and known to generations of navigators as "the graveyard of ships." During a two-day inspection of the island a shipwreck occurred, and while providing first-aid for survivors she received a more graphic picture of the inadequacies of its lifesaving facilities than she could have anticipated.

On her return to Boston she launched a drive to build and equip lifeboats. With her usual zest she was soon extracting gifts from committees in Boston, New York, and Philadelphia. Before the end of the year she dispatched four lifeboats, a life car with mortar, cables, trucks and harnesses, and, for good measure, several hundred books for a library. The ship carry-

ing the boats was wrecked and the lifeboats were damaged, but by the following October they were repaired and delivered. Several days later the Arcadia was wrecked on the island, and the new boats were sent to the rescue. One hundred and eighty lives were saved!

Dorothea enclosed a column-length newspaper clipping from an undated New York paper containing her letter of November 2, 1853, to E. Meriam detailing her experiences on Sable Island. Meriam, in turn, forwarded it to Walter R. Jones, President of the New York Life-Saving Benevolence Association, who passed it along to the press.

It would be interesting to know in what way their mutual friend, the Reverend Doctor G. W. Hosmer, Pastor of the First Unitarian Society of Buffalo, was "a little imaginative."

Trenton, New Jersey, Nov'b. 25th, 1853

With one of your pens, my dear friend, I write to inquire after your health and to report myself. Pray in the first place let me say take care of yourself. The Country needs you, your children need you, and *we*, your friends, need you.

On reaching Utica, the morning I parted from your hospitable dwelling, I found travelling reproduced fever and exhaustion to such a degree that I paused at Utica through positive necessity, and of course did not reach New York till Saturday. Then it became necessary to proceed to this place for some Documents,—resting on Sunday. I took the cars on Monday for New York and the Steamer via New York and Fall River for Boston. I was passing upon the Boat, when Mr. Meriam, who was seeking, met me, and gave me the pleasant intelligence that Mr. W. R. Jones had himself added another boat to my fleet. This good news dissipated the fatigue which began to encroach upon my strength, and I reached Boston late the morning of Tuesday, almost forgetting an unresting night. If nothing occurs to prevent I hope for a modified quietness of a week or so at no distant time.

I cannot express the satisfaction I have had in seeing you in your own comfortable dwelling. I like the good judgment which adopted it; and the good taste which furnished it, and most of all I like to think of you there with your children, who seem so much devoted to your comfort and happiness. May our gracious Lord spare them and you. Your son would not allow me to pay the Coachman who took me to and from your house so I found pleasure in acquiting myself of that obligation by purchasing a quantity [of] Engravings which I sent to Toronto Provincial Hospital for the Insane—as a gift from one of my friends, for I did not feel at liberty to name you—in this connection.

I might hear from you at Philadelphia—291 Chestnut if you could give me a line this week, but if not the week following at Washington. I do not design imposing on you a sustained correspondence. I could offer too little in return to venture on that: but I must hear from you sometimes,—just reporting, health, occupations, etc.

Pray have you now thought good Mr. Hosmer a *little* imaginative?

Your friend
D. L. Dix

This is not the *well* written letter I promised you.
[Miss, D. L. Dix, Nov. 25; Rec'd. Dec. 2, 1853.] [Ans. Dec. 6.]

✍§ 29. To Dorothea Dix

Obviously Fillmore's spirits were rising. He was now looking outward rather than inward and taking a renewed interest in issues and events.

*His Thanksgiving guests, in addition to his father, were
Calvin Fillmore of East Aurora, and Ariel C. Harris and
Julia (Fillmore) Harris of Toledo, Ohio.*

Buffalo, Dec. 6, 1853

My Dear Miss Dix,

Your kind favor from N.Y. reached here during my absence at Lima [N.Y.], to attend a meeting of the Trustees of
Geneva College. I feared much when you left that your health
was too feeble to justify you in pursuing your journey; and
regretted that you did not stay long enough with us to rest
yourself after so much fatigue. But it seems to be a characteristic of your benevolent heart to think only of the sufferings of
others, and never of your own.

I am gratified to perceive that your labors for the ship-
wrecked sufferers on Sable Island have been crowned with
such signal success. Until I heard your account of your hazardous voyage there, I had no idea that the place was either so
dangerous or so desolate. Since I saw you I have read a ludi-
crous account of the escape of one of those wild ponies which
you saw shipped while on the island. He seemed to spurn all
restraint, and distanced the fleetest horses.

My children are both well. We spent thanksgiving very
pleasantly. My father and uncle and my sister and her husband from Ohio were all with us and spent several days; and
had it not been for the vacant seat at our festive board which
was once filled by one so dear to us all, we should have been
happy indeed.

My Daughter goes to New York in the morning with
Judge Hall and his lady to be absent from one to two weeks. I
would go with her if I had any reasonable excuse for visiting
the city; but without some object I feel more desolate in the
busy crowd of a fashionable Hotel than at home in my library

where I can always find something to interest and instruct.

I perceive by the telegraph that Congress is organized and the message will probably be delivered today. I presume therefore that you are at Washington prepared to renew your untiring efforts for an appropriation of lands for the relief of the Insane. God grant that your disinterested labors may this time be crowned with success.

I am happy to see that Mr. Bell is reelected to the Senate; and I hope Mrs. Bell's health is fully restored. They are both excellent people, and I congratulate you upon having such reliable friends.

I perceive on looking at your letter again that it is dated at Trenton and not New York.

I read with a good deal of interest the tract which you sent me on the trial of our Saviour by Pontius Pilate. I read the Jewish view of the case to which this is a reply many years since.

My children join me in kind regards to yourself whilst I remain

Sincerely your friend
MILLARD FILLMORE

⮌§ 33. To MILLARD FILLMORE

Dorothea was again in Washington to revive her quest for the land grant. She observed some new and old sights in Washington and reported her first interview with President Pierce. Her reservations regarding his attitude toward the land grant were justified.

Edward McManus was a doorkeeper at the White House during the Presidencies of Fillmore and Pierce; Louis (?) was an attendant during the same period. Thomas Ustick Walter, a Philadelphia architect, was appointed by Fillmore to direct

the reconstruction of the Capitol. The Library of Congress in
the Capitol had burned in December of 1851 and was now
restored.

Fillmore was now reconsidering the southern tour which
he had canceled in the spring because of Abigail's death.

Washington, D.C., December 8th, '53

My dear Sir and Friend—

Yours of the 6th just received. I arrived yesterday and go
today. There will be but little done this month. And I have
desired to have the Bill introduced for the sake of securing it a
place, and then I return to complete unfinished work in Pennsylvania, New York, etc.

I had as advised an interview yesterday with the Presi-
dent(!) In the familiar doorway I encountered Edward and
Louis. My heart was so full of quickened and sad memories
that I half forgot my purpose till the "please to walk in" recalled to my thought the *realities* of the place. The old Mansion is completely remodeled, and transformed, it must be
owned much for the better. And I only regretted that the comforts (the luxuries I did not measure) of the Executive residence had not been secured to its late residents. I was seated in
a gorgeous apartment (the red and gold room) for an hour
with ample time to meditate. The President came from a
crowded reception in the Executive Office, his manner waver-
ing and hurried. I chose to detain him but a short time—referred to the Land Bill, which he said had his warmest sympathy, but he had not well considered the question of such
landed appropriations. I said shall I say to the Committee that
the cause has your interest and good will. "More than that
Miss Dix, more than that, I sincerely regretted that it had not
passed the last session. I shall be glad if it passes now; but I
really have not gone into the subject. I wish you success."

And so we parted. I, much wondering if that air of restless, half uncertainty which he wears, would not pass into that which would be more lamentable: this *entre nous*.

I thank you for your interest concerning my affairs, and, through your sympathy in my cause, interest in myself. The good opinion, the support, the affectionate regard of the wise and good are of inappreciable value. I shall try and effect all that is before me to perform; and God, I think, will surely give me strength for *His* work so long as he directs my line of duty. It is true that I pine for repose, and sometimes think I *must* have it; but new strength for every hour is given, and I proceed with that which appears to demand my care. I recall with much pleasure my *rest* beneath your roof. It was just what I needed, and has done me *so much good*. Can you send me the account of the *wild horse race* at Sable Island. I cannot conjecture who could have known any thing of this except persons quite incapable of describing it. I witnessed the whole scene and am curious to know what is said of the affair.

It is my purpose to return here about New Year's, and I shall then find myself occupied with writing for some time, and the less satisfactory duty of seeing Members, and daily meeting numbers of indifferent people, who except it please Heaven to make them unhappy enough to be pitied, have no possible hold on one's interest.

I saw Judge [James Moore] Wayne this Morning looking well, and in all respects better than usual. Mr. Bell seems in excellent health, and Mrs. Bell not ill. They are at housekeeping on 14th St. nearly opposite Willard's in a house of [Thomas Ustick] Walter's. Walter has immortalized himself. The new Library is admirable; do come and see it *sometime*. Mr. Everett is in for the Presidential race, and is really much and flatteringly attended to; *but*, the heart of the people is not with Mr. E.

I hope you will make your Southern tour as proposed later in the season, but not too late.

If you find yourself inclined to write again this month, without assuming a claim on your time, I only can say I shall have great pleasure in hearing from you. A letter addressed either 291 Chestnut St. Phila. or to Trenton, New Jersey, will be very certainly received. I have no little hesitation in suggesting occasional correspondence from a sense of inability, through primary engagements, to give in return for yours, letters of interest.

> With kind regards to Mr. [Powers Fillmore]
> and Miss Fillmore,
> I am sincerely your friend D. L. Dix.

[Miss D. L. Dix, Dec. 8; Rec'd. 10, 1853; Ans'd. Dec. 20.]

≈§ 30. To Dorothea Dix

Fillmore correctly assessed President Pierce's approach to the land grant.

With both his son and daughter away from home, Fillmore expressed his loneliness and a desire to "have a pleasant hour of your society." He was also apprehensive that Dorothea's strength might not sustain her "unremitted" labor.

In referring to the Resolution of '98, Fillmore refers to the Virginia and Kentucky Resolutions defending state rights and condemning national usurpation by the Federalist Party.

Buffalo, Dec. 20, 1853

My Dear Miss Dix,

I received your kind and welcome letter of the 6th on the 10th, and suppose you must soon be at Washington, and therefore venture to trouble you with a response, though I have really nothing to say which can in the least interest you.

I was probably misunderstood in what I said of the *wild horse* from Sable Island. The newspaper account which I read described the frolicksome pranks of one of those wild horses in this country, not on the island, which had escaped from its keepers. I regret that I have lost the paper, but I have looked for it and can not find it.

I was much interested in what you said of your call upon the President. His language seemed to leave you in great doubt, how far you might rely upon his aid, for your land bill. My inference from what you write is this, that he really and truly sympathises with the object which you have in view, but he has not fully satisfied himself, that as President he can constitutionally approve the measure. In other words that his heart and soul are with you in this benevolent object, but he fears the Resolutions of '98 are too stringent to allow him to give full vent to his sympathy. Think of this as the matter progresses and see if I am not right. If I am, he will seek to avoid the veto by having his friends defeat the measure in Congress. God grant, however, that this may not be the case.

We have had a most delightful autumn. Until three days since, neither snow nor cold weather; but now we have good winter weather and fine sleighing.

I am quite lonely and often wish that you were where I could now and then have a pleasant hour of your society. My daughter accompanied Judge Hall and lady to New York near two weeks since, and my son went after her near a week since and left me entirely alone, but I expect them home tonight. Were they here they would desire to be remembered.

Permit me again to urge you to spare yourself. Do take more rest. Your constitution can not long hold out with such unremitted labor of body and mind. I only wonder that it has endured so long. For your friends, for the holy cause in which your [*sic*] engaged, if not for yourself, do be advised and preserve your health and wasting strength.

But I can not say more. May Heaven prosper all your noble efforts to relieve the distressed and suffering, and spare your life and preserve your health is the sincere prayer of

Your friend
MILLARD FILLMORE

34. To MILLARD FILLMORE

Dorothea forwarded a clipping containing her letter to committees in Boston, New York, and Philadelphia in which she described the boats and equipment she had delivered to Sable Island. Her pride in the matter is obvious.

My dear Sir and Friend,

I send you a paragraph from the *Inquirer and Journal of Commerce*—and think you will congratulate me on the completion of my work for Sable Island.

Let me at this approach of a New Year wish you health, happiness, and a useful life; with cheerful patience to bear whatever privations are joined with present things.

Your friend, with kind remembrances and friendly wishes to your son and daughter.

D. L. DIX

12 Brevoort Place, New York
Dec. 29th, *en route* for Phila.
[Miss D. L. Dix, Dec. 29, Rec'd. 31, 1853. Ans'd. Jan'y. 6.]

35. To MILLARD FILLMORE

Dorothea insisted that Fillmore's letters were meaningful and much to be desired.

Fillmore did not serve on a board dealing with harbor limits.

Phila., 3d Jan'y. [1854]

I have just arrived here from New Jersey and New York, and thank you for a letter forwarded with others from Washington. My dear friend, why do you continually repeat that you have nothing to tell me in letter writing; is it of no moment to friends to have assurance of the well-being of those they esteem? If you have only to answer my inquiries by making out a Bulletin of health, your response will have a value which will make me repeat the same questions.

I wish you a Happy New Year—many happy years—God bless you now and always. And as the days of life on earth are measured may the seeds fall on sunny hills and green valleys where cheerful contentment and useful existences are measured.

I learnt incidentally in New York that your name is selected with that of Professor Davis [Charles Davies?] of West Point and Mr. Dix [?] for determining by survey and arbitration the Harbour limits; you may already know this.

Your counsel I will endeavour to profit from by sparing my strength so much as is possible, but it is very difficult to do this with such urgent claims ever recurring.

My love to Miss Fillmore and kind regards to your son. I am yours Sir,

sincerely in the alliance of a cordial friendship.

D. L. Dix

I expect to reach Washington by the 9th. Your conjectures respecting the President's opinions will, I do not doubt, prove correct.

[Miss D. L. Dix, Jan'y. 3; Rec'd. 6, 1854; ans'd. Jan'y. 6.]

◄§ 31. To DOROTHEA DIX

Fillmore offered Dorothea his congratulations upon the completion of the Sable Island project and extended his best wishes for the new year.

Buffalo, Jan'y. 6, 1854

My Dear Miss Dix,

Your note of the 29th ult. reached me in the stage on my way to spend the New Year with my father, and I read the enclosed slip from the Newspaper, containing your letter to the generous donors for Sable Island with a good deal of interest. I think you were very happy in selecting your names for the various objects; and I congratulate you on your success in this noble and humane enterprise. I perceive by the papers this morning that a terrible shipwreck has just occurred near Cape Sable, Nova Scotia. I send the account.

I return you many thanks for your kind wishes for the New Year, and be assured that they are all most cordially reciprocated. We are all blessed with health, and contentment. What more can be asked? But I am interrupted and can not say more, than that I received your very acceptable letter of the 3d inst. this morning.

I am
Truly and Sincerely
Your friend
MILLARD FILLMORE

Excuse errors. I can not read over.

◄§ 36. To MILLARD FILLMORE

Dorothea reported the news from Washington and expressed misgivings regarding the fate of the land grant. She

urged Fillmore to take the long postponed journey to the
South and volunteered a few suggestions. She recommended
as a suitable traveling companion John P. Kennedy, Fillmore's
Secretary of Navy. Fillmore had also considered Washington
Irving as a companion for the trip.

Jan'y. 18th [1854]

My dear Sir and Friend,

I am your debtor for a welcome note telling me just what I
desired to know, viz., that you are well, and were taking some
recreation. Abbie writes that you may go South. I cordially
desire this *if* you have satisfactory arrangements connecting
you with pleasant traveling companions. Mr. Kennedy of
Maryland would be a cheerful associate.

Do not take the ocean route, and do take care to arrange
your plans with prudence. You will do well to secure a good
white servant. I think you could hardly go without some one,
white or colored. Pray excuse my volunteer suggestions.

There is just executed a fine Bust of the Chief Justice
which is highly commended, but there is no place for it in the
capitol! Nor any where beside in Washington. I hear little said
of the President. I don't think that many persons regard him
with confidence; for my part I regard him as a person to be
pitied and should not be surprised if his health fails long before his period of official rule expires. The *land* question is
taking new phases, and either the whole public domain will be
disposed of at *random* or all Land Bills, my own included, will
be crushed; at least such are the signs at present.

But you know how unstable are all things connected with
political affairs, and it is rather bold to hazard predictions.

[James E.] Harvey, the Whig letter-writer, is dying at
Whitney's. Henry at the Smithsonian is harassed at the Institution and abroad. Nichols is hoping for an appropriation with

yet $38,000 in hand for carrying on the *whole* hospital build-
ing. I want a lot of land added to the farm—that which you
will recollect cuts in on the road of approach. I think we shall
get it, even at a large price, to avoid the proximity of a tavern
with which we are threatened. We, that is, the hospital.

The end of my paper suggests a conclusion to my note, and
I add only what you already know, that I am your assured
friend.

D. L. Dix

[Miss D. L. Dix, Jan'y. 18; Rec'd. 26/54.]

◄§ 37. To Millard Fillmore

*The lecture text forwarded by Dorothea has not been iden-
tified.*

Baltimore, Jan'y. 26th [1854]

My dear Sir and Friend,

I have read the lecture of which I send you a copy, and
think it is marked with good common sense and the result of
reflection. Will you give me your opinion of the views it presents, at your leisure.

Your friend, cordially

D. L. Dix

[Miss D. L. Dix, Jan'y. 26, Rec'd. 29, 1854.]

◄§ 38. To Millard Fillmore

*Wearisome delays left Dorothea rather cynical about the
behavior of politicians.*

*She advised Fillmore of a rumor purporting a possible mal-
feasance in the Treasury Department during Fillmore's Ad-*

ministration and noted the damaging effects of inflation upon the completion of the Washington mental hospital.

Her reference to James G. King in Hunts Magazine *relates to a eulogy of his public services. As a Congressman from New York, he had labored in behalf of the land-grant bill and had also contributed to the library and the landscaping of the Lunatic Asylum of New Jersey at Trenton.*

Washington City, Feb'y. 9 [1854]

My dear Sir and Friend,

I have returned here from the North but two days since, and hear nothing worth recording—as giving facts in this city. The usual assembling and dispersion of the Senate and House, with little effected through *much speaking*—the usual amount of gossip, and the usual measure of vapid conversation and idle talk. The intrigue and selfish aims are by no means less conspicuous—with all that is so poor, so mean, so worthless. One, if time be had, may find amidst all this chaff some grains of good wheat—and buried beneath the rubbish of a mountain of base metal, some traces of pure gold.

Dr. Nichols is at work asking for an appropriation which Secretary [Robert] McClelland [Secretary of the Interior] "approves" but will not recommend. You may not know that after the Bill was passed and about the time the work was commenced wages and building materials rose 25 percent. Had this not taken place the whole would have been done $41 less than the first estimates; a fact quite *novel* in the history of buildings, and I fancy quite unexampled in the annals of *public building*. Mr. [Thomas Gold?] Appleton and some others of our friends are much interested in the new Hospital. A resolution is to be introduced inquiring whether the necessities of the District and the wants of the Army and Navy require the completion of the whole original plan or extension at this period.

I feel no special encouragement concerning my Land Bill, though Senator [Solomon] Foot, who has charge of it, says it will pass the Senate and Mr. [William H.] Bissell says it will pass the House. This opinion has often been expressed before.

I hear absolutely nothing of the President; and I have had no occasion to see him.

I have a quiet word to *whisper*. It is just possible that the Department secret, connected with Mr. [Thomas] Corwin [Secretary of the Treasury in Fillmore's Cabinet], may transpire. [Simeon] Draper in New York it is true paid over more than a million of the public monies, and in consequence *failed*; but there are chances that the whole transaction may *come out*, as the saying is. I hope not, for we have more than enough unpleasant revelations connected with infidelity of public officers.

Happy are those who dwell apart from the harrowing tumults of public life! You may not be suffered to remain in quietness, but I hope you will never refuse a good to your country though it may involve many sacrifices.

Your friend with respectful regard and sincere esteem,

D. L. DIX

Have you read a notice of Mr. J. G. King in *Hunt's Magazine*, January number.

"The estimated cost of wharf, aqueduct, reservoir and other preparations for building, and of erecting and furnishing the Hospital as now commenced, was $73,000, the balance of the appropriation after the purchase of the farm and site; and the above deficit of $18,209 is $41 less than the estimated advance of 25 percent on the price of labor and materials, which occurred soon after the first estimates were made."

[Miss D. L. Dix, Feb'y. 9; Rec'd. 11, 1854. Ans'd. Feb'y. 11.]

๛ 32. To Dorothea Dix

Fillmore described some of his current reading, and expressed his apprehension lest the Kansas-Nebraska Bill of Stephen A. Douglas would revive the agitation over slavery.

He expressed his gratitude for her interest in his southern journey and her helpful suggestions.

Buffalo, Feb'y. 9, 1854

My Dear Miss Dix,

I was highly gratified to receive your kind letter of the 18th ult. and much obliged for the pamphlet which you sent, though I have found time only for a partial perusal. You may wonder that I am so much occupied; but my forenoons are generally spent in business or letter writing and my afternoons in reading history or works of science. Lately my attention has been turned more particularly to Natural History. Professor [Louis] Agassiz has been delivering a course of lectures on Geology in which I have been a good deal interested, and this morning I received from some unknown hand a whole bundle of pamphlets, mostly written by our esteemed friend, Dr. [Robert] Hare on cognate subjects from the perusal of which I anticipate much pleasure and instruction. No note accompanied them, and I tried to make out that the superscription was in your hand writing, but could not. They may be from My good friend, the Doctor himself, and if I knew they were, I should take pleasure in acknowledging the favor, but not being acquainted with his hand, I am unable to form any opinion.

I am sorry to see you write so despairingly about your bill, but from what I see and hear I am not without my apprehensions. I fear that this Nebraska bill is to open again the bitter fountains of slavery agitation, and if it does, little or nothing will be done for the good of the Country.

The prospect now is that I shall go South about the first of next month. I am greatly obliged for your advice as to a servant and have determined to follow it. Had I your experience in travelling, it would be worth something to me on this journey. But I have never been South and all will be new to me. I hope the novelty will compensate for any annoyance or inconvenience I may suffer from my ignorance of southern customs and habits.

I shall probably go to New York the last of this month where I may be detained a few days in some necessary preparations. Indeed I find no servant yet that suits me and have written Mr. Kennedy to inquire for one at Baltimore. Do you know of any one whom you could recommend.

The winter has been very gay here but in this I have taken no part. We have all been very well and as happy as we could be with the remembrance of our bereavement.

I perceive that your letter is not dated at any place, and I therefore hardly know where I should address you, but presuming that you may be at Washington I shall send it there.

With sentiments of the highest regard and esteem,

I am truly your friend
MILLARD FILLMORE

ᴥᔥ 39. To MILLARD FILLMORE

Dorothea was also critical of Senator Douglas for opening the slavery issue and attributed his decision to his inordinate ambition to reach the White House.

Her detailed suggestions for Fillmore's projected itinerary reveal her intimate knowledge of the means of travel and the problems of the traveler.

Washington, D.C., 11th Feb'y. [1854]

My dear Sir and Friend,

You were right in the conjecture that the package of Pamphlets came from your *fast* friend, Dr. Hare. And though it is evident he did not look for an acknowledgement I am sure a few lines from your hand (you he esteems as the present incarnation of Washington; and Mrs. Hare is no less your friend), would give him sincere pleasure. Speaking of some personal affairs lately at his own breakfast table, he suddenly addressed to me the inquiry if he should not call his large new Hotel built in Baltimore, "The Fillmore House,"—but not waiting my reply he added yet one can't do that for he is yet living. It was suggested that this was not a sufficient reason for seeking farther for a name less known and less popular, as many precedents existed of honoring the living as well as the departed by such evidence of esteem. We were interrupted and the subject was not resumed. I am gratified that you have heard and enjoyed the lectures of the great and good Agassiz. Your notice of engrossment of your time does not surprise me. [An] active mind does not often sink into sluggish inactivity.

Mr. Everett attracted lately a vast crowd to hear his speech on the Nebraska question. Every body seemed to enjoy his fine oratorical powers except that fine specimen of a great man and gentleman, Senator [Stephen A.] Douglas, who discovered in the advertisements of a newspaper somewhat more to his taste and the level of his mind. But the Judge already sees himself in the *White House,* and demeans himself like the tom-tit, which fancied itself an Eagle.

Adieu my dear Sir.

Peace be with you. Yours with respect,

D. L. Dix

Mills new Hotel in Charleston is to be preferred to any other. Wiltberger's is the best in Savannah; Little choice in

Cuba or Mobile; St. Charles or Verandah in New Orleans;
  Burnet House in Cincinnati.

The best Hotels in St. Louis and Louisville, as well as in
Nashville, Tennessee, have since I was in the West been destroyed by fire.

The Wilmington Boat runs no longer, the mails being
taken by Rail Road to Charleston. Except you wish to see the
Country from Richmond inland to Charleston the least expos-
ing and *much* the most comfortable and safe route to Charleston is by Steamer from New York. If you take the *Isabel* to
Cuba, you will find it well to compute your times before setting off, as she makes her trips only once a fortnight.

Summer apparel will be needed altogether at the South,
winter garments *en route* thither. Pray excuse these items.

If I hear of a reliable body-servant, used to proper service,
I will inform you.

Does Miss Fillmore accompany you? If so remind her that
in Charleston, etc. she will meet *warm* weather.

[Miss D. L. Dix, Feb'y. 11; Rec'd. 14, 1854; Ans'd. Feb'y.
18.]

40. To Millard Fillmore

*Dorothea's report of a "department secret" and a hint of a
scandal involving Corwin in her letter of February 9 took Fillmore by surprise. He wrote immediately for details (a letter
which Dorothea seems not to have saved). She, in turn, was
upset by his alarm, and her response reflects her embarrassment and reluctance to elaborate on the rumors.*

*Lending money from the Independent Treasury at no cost
to the borrower was not uncommon, and neither Corwin nor
Draper was officially charged with misconduct.*

Fed by the gold of California, an inflationary spiral had pushed up prices and spawned luxuries and extravagance as well as speculation. A sharp, though temporary decline occurred in October of 1853—Crystal Palace stock, for example, sank from $175 to $55 in the course of several weeks, and Draper, who had been a frequent contributor to Whig campaign chests, fell a victim of his overspeculation.

Dorothea was now distressed to become the carrier of news regarding the Fillmore Administration's unwashed linen.

Albert T. Burnley was a Kentucky publisher and politician, and a close friend of General Taylor. He spent some time in Texas and Louisiana and became involved in Texas bonds. During Taylor's Presidency he came to Washington to edit the Republic, a move designed to give Taylor a favorable press there.

Washington City, Feb'y. 14th 1854

It is due to you my dear Sir and Friend to reply distinctly and without circumlocution to your inquiries respecting the Treasury question. I should prefer not to do so. I supposed you had, generally, cognizance of that affair; and therefore I shall only be able to enlighten you in part. An individual *directly* in the *service* and *confidence* of Government, and accustomed to speak and write openly to me (but not expecting me to repeat private history's of public affairs) remarked with an expression of satisfaction that he had closed some business affairs which had given him much trouble and anxiety,—after a pause added a strong remark on the infidelity of public officers—and said that Mr. Corwin had proved if not dishonest as embezzling Governmental monies—not worthy of trust in the custodial department, since he had not hesitated to lend the large amounts, which he had now seen all called in, to hazardous speculations. Mr. Draper's failure resulted from being obliged to refund either $900,000 or $1,100,000 which he had received for certain speculative business transactions *from Mr. Corwin* of the General funds—both no doubt intending the principal should be returned to the coffers, but retaining the profits drawn from the use of the same themselves, etc. This is all I have to state as *fact,* and all I heard in New York. I give it to *you, solely,* in *good faith,* and ask you not to *record me* amongst those who rehearse all they hear—for in fact I feel a little disquiet at relating this matter. Mrs. [John] Bell is often declaiming against all who have holden office—I often think saying more serious things than she really believes. However she has *steadily* held the opinion that Corwin was not reliable and that the B's [Bureaus?] were as dishonest as opportunity allowed. Your integrity is not impugned, but to me it was, those short years of your administration, ever painful to feel that you had so little *real* support from the Members of your Cabinet. That Statesman is indeed happy who can count as his friends the really honest and consistent; the true Patriots, and the men of honorable thought.

I now recollect that some time since Mrs. Bell said some very bad transactions of [Albert T.] Burnley's would be brought to light, but I did not wish to sustain conversation in that direction and it was dropped. Adieu, dear Sir, Your friend, D.L.D.

There has been no loss through the funds in Mr. Draper's hands—but the restoration caused his failure.

Please destroy this hasty letter.

[Miss D. L. Dix, Feb'y. 14; Rec'd. 14, 1854; Ans'd. Feb'y. 18.]

◈§ 41. To Millard Fillmore

*After what may have been a sleepless night over Fillmore's
alarm at the report of irregularities in the Treasury Department, Dorothea wrote a supplemental note to try to reassure
him.*

*Her advice relating to the problems involved in employing
black or white servants in the South accents the racial issue
there.*

15th Feb'y. 3 P.M.

Dear Sir,

Let me be understood—I had very few moments for writing last night. *All* the funds, drawn by Mr. Draper at Mr.
Corwin's instance, and by his authority were "restored without
loss to the Government,"—"only the Hazard." But as a consequence of calling them in in separate amounts Mr. Draper
failed.—$900,000 certainly—and I think $200,000 in addition were loaned out of the Sub-treasury to his account.

Mrs. Bell's charges upon Mr. Corwin and Mr. Burnley refer to other matters, of which I have no knowledge.

The idle and false reports spreading through society here
are so many and so monstrous that one is quite willing not to
hear them or if hearing not to repeat and perpetuate them.

Your friend,

D.L.D.

I suggested your taking on your journey a servant. Possibly
you may find this troublesome as it would also nearly or quite
double the expense of travelling. This you may or may not
regard as of any moment. I this evening heard from friends
who four weeks since left Philadelphia for Charleston, via
Baltimore, Norfolk, Weldon and the land route through.
Their representations of the great exposure and fatigue from

Weldon on has determined others who were following to take the *sea route*. By doing this you would I suppose sacrifice one of the chief objects of your journey, seeing the country, and acquainting yourself with the resources of the people, and the people themselves.

If you take a *white* servant, he will never find his place. He cannot sit at table with *you,* nor will he go with the Negroes. If you have a slave, and I could get you a first rate servant who is; you might lose him somewhere; a free Negro of character then is your only choice, if one of the right sort can be found.

◄§ 33. To Dorothea Dix

If Fillmore had written a few days earlier he would have spared Dorothea from one of the most nerve-shattering experiences of her life. For instead of receiving his denial of any plans to remarry she heard the rumor stated as a fact by trusted friends.

The Washington Star reported Fillmore's alleged plans to remarry on February 15, 1854:

> *It is stated that ex-President Fillmore is about to lead to the alter Miss Elizabeth Porter of Niagara Falls, only daughter of the late Gen. Peter B. Porter, a hero of the War of 1812, and Secretary of War under John Quincy Adams. Miss Porter is 32 years of age, and a lady of superior intellect, high cultivation and large fortune. Her brother and herself are the sole heirs of their father's great estate, including Grand [Goat] Island and other lucrative property at Niagara Falls. Miss Porter has long been a reigning belle in Western New York.*

Fillmore offered a harsh appraisal of the demagoguery in-
volved in the current debates upon the Kansas-Nebraska Bill.

Buffalo, Febr'y. 18, 1854

My Dear Miss Dix,

I thank you for your kind and frank letter respecting the
Treasury matter. Without in any way alluding to you, I shall
make an effort to find how this matter stands. It seems to me
incredible that Mr. C[orwin] should be a dishonest man in
money matters. If so I fear I shall lose all confidence in mankind. And it is a painful thought to distrust a friend.

Could I suffer myself to be annoyed at any gossip from
Washington, I should feel so at an impertinent and wholly
groundless report, originating with some foolish letter writer
in that city, that I was about to be married to Miss [Elizabeth]
Porter. I scarcely know the lady, and have never seen her but
once since my return and then only for a moment when she
called upon my daughter at the Falls last summer. The heartless trifling in such a matter, shows that the author of the
Report, was as void of the fine sensibilities belonging to an
affectionate and cultivated mind, as of the properties of a gentleman in giving it such publicity. But these letter writers have
long been a nuisance and the telegraph seems to be chiefly
employed in spreading false rumors.

I am still making preparations for my journey, and hope to
profit by your kind and wise suggestions. I have finally submitted it to Mr. Kennedy, after suggesting the inconveniences
which you mention of a white servant, to say, whether we
shall take white or black.

I have also suggested to him that perhaps we had better go
down the Mississippi and return by the Atlantic States. By
this course we shall be more likely to avoid the cholera and we

may have a quicker, more comfortable and safer journey on the River than to come up it, later in the season on our return.

I perceive that Congress has again engaged in slavery agitation, and all other business must be neglected.

Really it seems to me there is more *reckless demagogueism* [*sic*] this winter than I ever witnessed before; for I regard all this as mere bids for the Presidency, hereafter, and for presidential favor, now. May Heaven in its mercy save the country from the folly of madness and the ambition of knaves. But these are strong words, yet no stronger than I feel. Prudence however, suggests that I should be more cautious, and I should be to any but a most confidential friend.

I perceive that your bill has been up and laid over. I do hope that you are not to be again disappointed. Your patient, untiring and distinterested labors, deserve a better reward.

I am truly your friend

MILLARD FILLMORE

42. To MILLARD FILLMORE

While Dorothea had heard at least one report that Fillmore planned to marry, she dismissed it as Washington gossip. But upon entering the home of the Hares in Philadelphia she faced an alleged confirmation, said to come from Fillmore himself. The impact was devastating.

The Hares identified Isaac Newton as their informant. Newton, a Quaker, was a friend of the Hares, and possibly an acquaintance of Dorothea. In addition to being a confectioner, he owned a large land tract in Virginia, where he engaged in scientific agriculture. He had a zest for politics and seldom lacked an axe to grind. He was a Fillmore man in 1852, and would support him again in 1856. Later, he joined the Republicans in time to advise President-elect Lincoln at Springfield on appointments and to receive the office of Commissioner of Agriculture before the office was given Cabinet status.

Dorothea did not exaggerate when she labeled him a gossip. He also had his share of vanity, but there is no evidence that he was malicious.

Newton had written to Fillmore on February 11. In reporting the purchase of the Benjamin Ogle Tayloe plantation in Virginia, he also noted that Mrs. Tayloe had given him "some information concerning thy future prospects, which I was pleased to hear." He urged Fillmore to call on him when he came to Philadelphia.

Fillmore replied, indicating that he planned to stop in Philadelphia enroute to or from the South. But he seems to have offered no comment on Mrs. Tayloe's remark.

The Fillmore letter to which Dorothea refers in her conversation with Doctor and Mrs. Hare as proof that he was "too sorrowful and serious" to contemplate matrimony seems to have been destroyed as she indicates. However, she could have been alluding to his letter of February 9, in which he observed, "The winter has been gay here but in this I have taken no part. We have all been very well and as happy as we could be with the remembrance of our bereavement." If such is the case, she neglected to destroy it.

Fortunately, Fillmore did not heed Dorothea's request that he destroy her ringing defense of his honor and the evidence it contains of her emotional involvement in his life.

Phila., 20th Feb'y. [1854]

My dear Sir and Friend,—

It is difficult for me to write, and as difficult to forbear—at this time. If I am silent, I can not acquit myself *to* myself of discharging the duties which *real* rightly founded *friendship* requires. And if I write candidly, I open upon myself the charge from *you* of rudely and indelicately interposing in your affairs, and assuming a personal lead which may seem to touch on your individual rights and independence.

I must speak and take the chance of not being misinterpreted.

Some weeks since when I went to Washington, Mr. [John?] Bell's salutation was followed by a conversation having reference to yourself, and followed by "You need not look so incredulous, for I know the facts—it is from family friends that we know here in Washington that Mr. Fillmore is about to be married." I did not choose to argue such a point with people who always jump at conclusions, and I merely replied, "The story seems quite improbable judging from the character of the party named.["] I changed the subject of discussion, and not considering myself *authorized* to deny what I have not certainly believed. I have taken no notice at all of the gossip and gossippers of Washington City. It seems the whole country however thinks this a *public* question. I came here on Saturday to return today to Washington. On entering Dr. Hare's I found my friends discussing with warmth this subject. Mrs. Hare, who is a woman of great spirit and dignity, up to that hour had adopted you as a sort of Washington and "knight without fault or failing" was just yielding her opinion as I entered borne down by what was assumed incontestable evidence, *viz*, your correspondence with that weak conceited babbler, [Isaac] Newton, the confectioner!

I must admit my weakness in at once becoming very *angry* that Dr. Hare in the *first* place should condescend to receive such communication from such a man, not over much respected in this city. Next that he [Newton] should quote your letter—which I flatly and presumptuously denied, saying that while I stood in no relation which authorized me to pronounce positively upon such a question, yet that all I did know of your character and your plans made such a step absolutely impossible *at this period.* I denounced Newton as a deceiver. I did not believe *he* was as he called himself *your personal friend* and *special* confidant, and carried my point to a certain extent. I confess *to you* that I was truly vexed with you for opening your mind to a man to[o] weak and silly to be trusted—and who was so capable of injuring your *position* in this community.

If he were a friend of strong sense and discretion *who* could be *trusted,* I do not think his rank in life any reason for your withholding your regard, no not in the least. But he is no such person, and except you wish to be made ridiculous I beg you will, if you choose to make him a correspondent, say nothing you do not wish *spread abroad.*

I am exceedingly reserved, but I *for the first time since I have known you* on Saturday evening referred to your writing to me and said that I had received a letter *recently* which was too sorrowful and serious but to determine your present position. Your private letter, your business, is destroyed of course.

Dr. Hare was piqued by my declarations of disbelief in Newton's veracity, and the stern indignation with which I denounced his ridiculous vanity; and he went to him to ask if he had misunderstood him. He [Newton] *then* admitted that you had not written that you were to bring Mrs. Fillmore here in a week or so, but that you had written that you regarded him as your chief and best friend here, that you were coming on etc. But that the *other fact he had by letter* from *relatives!* He read parts of your letter to Dr. Hare, and this result of a visit to the confectioner's, intended to put him in a better light, had just the reverse for Dr. Hare is now amazed that I gravely declare I do not believe Newton your confidential friend or that you ever wrote him such letters—as he quotes.

I must add that all this *turmoil* in Dr. Hare's parlour grew out of the fact first of Dr. Hare meeting Newton on the street, who told him he had just got a letter from you and you were coming here. Dr. Hare hurried home to say to Mrs. Hare you must be written to to be their *guest*. Then Dr. Hare went out, saw this precious confidant again, who added the intelligence that you were going to be married. Returning just before I arrived Mrs. Hare's indignation was really roused by such a calumny on you.

I should have taken the matter cooly but for my displeasure at Newton's folly.

My good friend, seriously I am greatly shocked at all the abominable gossip. Nothing is sacred, no person is respected, *no one is free*. I should be sorry if after a suitable period your domestic life should not be restored so far as may be to its former experience of comfort and cheerfulness. I would not now have written except for my desire to *caution* you, or suggest caution in your correspondents.

Newton may have some good qualities, but he is greatly excited in the idea of being in your confidence—and your correspondent, and this vanity will result in more harm to you than you can easily appreciate.

If I wound you, recollect only that I would *prove* my friendship something more than a profession, if I assume to suggest, it is both a profound respect mingled with my friendliness.

Why should you write to that man "about what you might tell him now of your future prospects, but which you defer," etc. etc.

The carriage comes for me—Your friend,

D. L. Dix

Please destroy *this*.

[Miss D. L. Dix, Feb'y. 20. Rec'd. 25, 1854, ans'd. Feb'y. 26.]

43. To Millard Fillmore

On the same day that Dorothea excoriated Newton's be-
havior, Newton wrote again to Fillmore to invite him to call at
his house if he came to Philadelphia.

He then offered his version of the late-night conversation
with Doctor Hare:

I had a visit from Dr. Hare of our city last evening at a
late hour, to enquire if I had any knowledge of the rumor
of our friend Fillmore's intended marriage. I said I had no
other than what the newspapers say. When he was leaving, I thought his visit a singular one at 11 o'clock, I had
retired to bed, I said to him, is Miss Dick [Dix] in the city
now. Yes, he said. She is going to leave in the morning.
She is at my house. I thought I could understand the cause
of his visit at that late hour. Curiosity for knowledge seems
to be the order of the day. The Doctor is one of thy fast
friends [Fillmore papers, Oswego].

It is evident from Newton's question about "Miss Dick"
that her name was also linked to Fillmore.

Though no longer as incensed as she had been three days
before, Dorothea continued to seethe at the thought of New-
ton as a confidant of Fillmore.

The prescription for his possible illness during the journey
to the South is missing.

Washington

My dear sir and friend,

I wrote to you a letter on Sunday at Philadelphia. But perhaps I had better not have sent it. Only I can not help repeating, *do not write confidentially* to Newton. If you really main-

tain a familiar correspondence with him, indeed it injures you socially and politically in Philadelphia. I may have implied what I did not intend that *he* circulated originally the rumors alluded to and which was as reckless as heartless. He maintained on *your* authority seemingly, when it was spoken of and received through the Washington papers. Nothing can be imagined more utterly regardless of propriety or of truth than "the letter-writer" here, and following *en suite,* three-fourths of society.

I am grieved that the noise of that vile gossip forced its echoes to your ear—and I should not have explicitly referred to the subject if it had not chanced to meet me in such a form in the house of my friends and your friends. I was really overbalanced by their accepting just at the last moment the idea of its certainty from N[ewton]. The source offended me quite as seriously as the imputation on your dignity of character and rightness of sentiment. I never questioned your position—for I thought I had the correct measure of your understanding if not knowledge of your faithfulness to the wife of your youth to waver. But so many asserted and quoted such direct authority that I was quite amazed and very angry finally with N[ewton], perhaps unjustly too, for he would not have your letters to boast of if you did not write, and would not affect to know more than he does if he had no communication at all.

Certainly, it does not become me to direct you. But, except you throw off my faithful friendship, you will have to wear it sometimes *as* heretofore—as a severe remedy—a sort of moral fly-blister!

Do not say too much about the Corwin business. I *know* the New York transaction to be true; the rumors here of another matter, is quite likely, considering it had origin *here* in Washington, to be false. If I hear anything of consequence I will write.

The storm will retard your journey I suppose. I trust you will escape all illness. Let me give you from eminent physicians' and my own experience and observation a suggestion which I hope you will have no occasion to take advantage of practically, either for yourself or others, but which there is no harm in knowing. See slip enclosed. I have just received your last letter, and grieve still more that you are to be so annoyed by silly people.

I have much need to ask you will excuse my rapid scrawls: —I think you will. On your journey you *must* receive continual attention, and be exhausted by many wearying demands on your time, but you are a public man and the country requires that you should not sink into obscurity.

The Democrats in their quiet conversations admit that you are the only man their party need fear, if your friends take you out of your present retreat. A leading member of the Democratic Baltimore Convention said lately in public if Mr. Fillmore's party had nominated him rather than General Scott he would now have been President of the United States.

Yours Sir, respectfully, cordially, and with

steady esteem and friendliness,

D. L. Dix

[Miss D. L. Dix, Feb'y. 23, Rec'd. 25, 1854; Ans'd. Feb. 26.]

◄§ 34. To Dorothea Dix

Fillmore assured Dorothea that her letters had not offended him—on the contrary they were the evidence of a "sincere friendship."

He explained his relationship with Newton and indicated that he regarded the rumors of his marriage as malicious.

He suggested that his mind had been eased by an investigation of the Corwin-Draper affair.

His dependence upon his son and daughter is suggested by
his reluctance to be separated for several months. Powers was
now twenty-five and Abby, twenty-two. Neither had married.

Buffalo, Feby. 26, 1854

My Dear Miss Dix,

Yours of the 20th from Philadelphia and of the 23d from
Washington have this moment come to hand. I beg of you to be
assured that your letter from Philadelphia gave no offence, but
on the contrary very great satisfaction, for I considered it an
evidence of sincere friendship.

I am greatly surprised at what you say about Mr. Newton's
having aided in giving currency to the malicious and absurd
report that I was about to be married. Certainly he had nothing from me that justified even an inference of the kind. He
had been very friendly to me and had taken a great interest in
an Agricultural Bureau at Washington, and he wrote me a
letter complaining of the present Executive for not having recommended it and urging me to attend the meeting of the
United States Agricultural Society at Washington on the 22d.
inst., and said a great many flattering things of my past administration, and the prospect of my being recalled to it again.

I answered his letter explaining why I could not attend the
meeting of the Society, and not wishing to write any thing on
the other subject to which he alluded, I excused myself by
saying that I expected to pass through Philadelphia in a few
days, and should then be happy to see and converse with him.
He did not allude to that foolish report in his letter to me nor
did I in mine to him. Indeed, I am not certain that when I
wrote him I had even heard of it; for it was not published in
the paper which I take here, and I did not see it until some one
called my attention to it; and even then the report which I saw
gave no *name*, and I had not the remotest suspicion to whom it

alluded. But it has been a painful subject to me, and I am now convinced from your letter that it has been to my friends. I hope, however, that Dr. Hare and his lady have been appraised of its utter falsity, that I may be restored to their good opinion, if I suffered in their estimation from the report.

I am very anxious to know who could have started this rumor, for I can not doubt that it was entirely *malicious;* and since it has come out, Judge Hall has informed me that Mr. Corcoran told him in New York (I think in Nov. or Dec. last) that he had heard such a report, but Judge Hall knowing that there was no truth in it, and thinking it might injure my feelings to know that such a report was in circulation, did not even mention to me what he had heard until after it was published in the papers. From all these facts, I infer that the report was started some time since and was first set afloat in Washington, and I suspect a gentleman from this city, who spent some time there last fall, and who might have a selfish object in view in circulating such a report, but I have no proof and therefore say no more of him.

I am preparing for my journey south and hope to leave on Wednesday or at fartherest, Thursday, of this week; and expect to meet Mr. Kennedy, (who will be my sole companion,) either at Columbus or Cincinati [*sic*]—We shall probably spend next Sunday in Cincinati [*sic*], if no accident occurs to thwart our purposes—I am greatly obliged for your *recipe* but hope I may have no occasion to use it—As my journey is entirely one of pleasure and observation, I shall not knowingly expose myself to any epidemic or unnecessary danger.

I have received a full report of the Draper affair. No allusion is made to you, and I know not that I shall have any occasion to speak on the subject. I am surprised at it, but as it turned out, nothing was lost, but $24,000 saved to the treasury; and I am inclined to think the motive was good, but I should never have run such a risk for such a consideration. Fortunately, it resulted well. I am also happy to be informed that there is a prospect of recovering the $100,000 from those gentlemen in Ohio. If so then I suppose that all pecuniary matters connected with my administration will be made right and I shall be greatly gratified, not merely on account of the Nation but on account of Mr. Corwin; who, notwithstanding all that has been said, I think, is an honest man, but if he has a failing it is that he places too much confidence in *professed* friends, and is sometimes persuaded to yield too much to their selfish importunities. Still, perhaps I ought not to congratulate myself that this is the last, as I perceive you add, "The rumor here of another matter is *quite likely,* considering it had its origin *here* in Washington to be false." Pray may I inquire what this *other matter* is? I have no idea to what it can allude.

As the time approaches when I am to commence my journey, my children seem to be grieved at the thought of my leaving them, and I confess that I look forward to the separation with infinitely more pain than pleasure; and have been almost persuaded sometimes to give it up. But I want to see the country and think the journey may divert my mind and do me good, and that my children may be benefitted by being thrown for a little time upon their own resources. It is a hard school, but self reliance can only be acquired in this way, and if we are permitted to meet again, we may all be better for the temporary separation. But they are all that is left me of the dear, departed one and they seem doubly dear, since my affections are no longer divided, but concentrated on them alone. Still, even we must separate. Should Heaven spare their precious lives, I could not reasonably hope that they would always remain with me. Nature and the God of love have decreed otherwise, and to these, like the decrees of fate, we must submit. But I still hope for their society yet a little longer, and hope that when we do separate, it may add to their happiness if not to mine, and that they may be the better able to bear the separation for having been taught a little self reliance while I am yet within striking distance to hear and advise.

We are all in the enjoyment of health and my daughter expects a young lady to stay with her during my absence. This will relieve her somewhat from the loneliness of her situation, and as I have the most entire confidence in the *good conduct and discretion* of both my children, I shall suffer no apprehension on that account.

It would of course be agreeable for me to hear from you occasionally on my journey if convenient, but I can not promise any response, as I shall be very busy.

Truly your friend,
MILLARD FILLMORE

44. To MILLARD FILLMORE

Fillmore met John P. Kennedy at Cincinnati as planned and they steamed down the Ohio River to Louisville, where they disembarked for a pilgrimage to Clay's "shrine" at Ashland and stops at Lexington and Frankfort. Resuming their tour they moved down the Mississippi to New Orleans.

The response of the people could only have been gratifying. Crowds assembled wherever they paused, and they were dined and wined (though Fillmore drank no alcohol) in a manner befitting high office. Everywhere Fillmore was gracious and charming. He avoided controversial issues, preferring to dwell upon the ever present signs of achievement: rising cities dotting a productive countryside where a generation earlier there was only the raw frontier.

After several crowded days in New Orleans they embarked for Mobile, where Fillmore met the glamorous Madame

Octavia Walton LeVert, celebrated throughout the South for her beauty and literary talents. At Montgomery several days later he found time to address a note to her inviting her and her husband, Doctor Henry Strachey LeVert, to visit him in Buffalo. Madame LeVert, in turn, responded that she found their association an "infinite delight." She was confident they would meet again, "for I fear my heart is always near you." They did, in Paris a year later. Their correspondence continued until Fillmore's remarriage.

From Montgomery the two men traveled by rail to the Georgia border and down the Savannah River to Savannah. At Charleston they returned to the rails to reach Augusta, Atlanta, Chattanooga, and Nashville; Columbia, South Carolina, central North Carolina, Richmond, and Norfolk.

They bypassed Washington but paused at Baltimore, where the two travelers separated. Fillmore was back in Buffalo by May 23.

Meanwhile, worried that Fillmore's presence in Washington might cast him into the political cauldron, Dorothea wrote anonymously to him to advise him to avoid it. And not knowing his precise itinerary she sent similar warnings to Petersburgh, Richmond, and Norfolk, but none reached him until he arrived at New York. However, his own political instincts had forewarned him to avoid the capital.

Dorothea's friends in the Senate did not "stand fast in the ranks," a sufficient number of the Democratic senators switching sides to uphold Pierce's veto of her land-grant bill. It was a bitter blow after six years of unremitting labor. Pierce's biographer attributes his veto to his fear that passage of the bill would intensify pressures to carve up the public domain and initiate an orgy of trading and peddling at state capitals. He does not agree with Dorothea that it was dictated by Jefferson Davis (Roy F. Nichols, Franklin Pierce [1958], pp. 138–139).

The veto drew protests from Pierce's philanthropic country-men.

Washington City

20th May [1854]

This letter my excellent and valued friend will I trust find you once again in your own dwelling, restored safely after an eventful three months' absence, to the arms and affection of your children. I have not written during your "progress" through the south and west believing that the engrossing character of your journies would render the receipt of letters of mere friendly greeting rather unwelcome for the time.

Several of your true friends were anxious that you should *not* come to Washington—and this desire for your protection from mischievous partisans being reiterated in my presence—I wrote from the library three letters severally addressed without signature to Petersburgh, Richmond and Norfolk hoping one might meet your eye. Our friends in Philadelphia are greatly disappointed not to have had the opportunity of giving you dinners and exercising other hospitalities, but your stay was too short for their purposes and friendly wishes. I rejoice that you have made this tour, and at this time, rather regretting that circumstances did not favor your seeing Cuba.

I am too thankful however for your safe return to have many regrets for what has been omitted—which might have enhanced your pleasures and have multiplied your memories of these cheerful days.

I hope that *now* you believe what I so often told you, *viz.* "that you dwell in the hearts of the American people."

You have heard of the veto message, and will readily believe that I have felt a great disappointment. But should my friends stand fast in the ranks, and as yet the message is not disposed of.

I shall send you the speeches as soon as they are printed. Those of [George E.] Badger and [Albert G.] Brown of Mississippi are admirable.

The poor President! His *"conscience"* would not suffer him to make that bill a law! So he said—but all here know it was Jefferson Davis who would not suffer it.

Alas for these evil times.

Your friend,

D. L. DIX

[Miss D. L. Dix, May 20, Rec'd. 24, 1854, Ans'd. May 26.]

✒§ 35. To DOROTHEA DIX

Fillmore expressed his disappointment over the loss of Dorothea's land-grant bill through Pierce's veto, and extended his gratitude for her multiple warnings to avoid Washington. He then informed her of his plans to attend the grand opening of the Chicago and Rock Island Railroad.

A few weeks later, accompanied by Abby, he went to Chicago and joined there the "greatest Railroad Excursion of the Age," for a ride upon the new line to Rock Island. They then steamed up the Mississippi River to the Falls of St. Anthony (St. Paul) in the Minnesota Territory. Returning to Chicago, they sailed the length of Lake Michigan to view the unfinished Sault Ste. Marie Canal at the foot of Lake Superior. They returned to Buffalo on June 25.

Buffalo, May 26, 1854

My Dear Miss Dix,

Thank kind Heaven, I am again safely at home. My journey was a most pleasant one, without accident of any kind, yet very fatiguing. I had no time to write, yet I often thought of you, and sympathized most deeply in the disappointment you must have felt, after laboring so long and so patiently for the passage of your bill for the relief of the indigent Insane, to have it at last defeated by a Presidential veto. This was like dashing the cup from your parched and thirsty lips, when you were just ready to taste the cooling draft. But yet I perceive you do not wholly despair, though I confess, I see no hope during this administration. You have, however, one satisfaction of which no earthly power can deprive you, and that is a consciousness, that you have done your duty, most nobly and most disinterestedly.

I have your kind favor of the 20th, but your anonymous notes addressed to me at Petersburgh, Richmond and Norfolk were all received in New York City. I was happy, however, to perceive that your views concurred so entirely with my own. I had intended from the beginning to avoid Washington in my journey, not merely because I did not desire to mingle in party politics, but because I deemed it indelicate to visit there, especially when important political questions were under consideration. The President however, was so kind as to tender me the hospitalities of the Executive Mansion, which of course I declined.

I should have been pleased to have seen more of my personal friends both in Philadelphia and New York, but I found it was impossible, so I yielded to my destiny, hoping that at some future time, I might enjoy that pleasure.

Some six months since I promised to attend a celebration of the opening of the Chicago and Rock Island Railroad, and since my return I have been notified that it will take place on the 5th of June. I shall therefore leave with my daughter on Monday next for that place, and may go to the Falls of St. Anthony before I return.

My daughter says she owes you a letter but has so little to communicate and is so busy preparing for her journey that she desires me to excuse her and remember her most affectionately to you.

I am interrupted and can not say more, than that I am as ever,

Your Sincere friend
MILLARD FILLMORE

＊§ 45. To MILLARD FILLMORE

Despite her depression over the loss of the land-grant bill, Dorothea found pleasure in the congressional appropriation to complete the Government Hospital. She was particularly grateful to Congressman Haven of Buffalo, a former law partner of Fillmore, for steering it through the House, and to Fillmore for his assistance during its formative stages.

Washington, July 13th [1854]

My dear Sir and Friend,

I write just now for the pleasure of saying what I think you will be gratified to know, that mainly through the discreet and prompt action of Mr. [Solomon G.] Haven the appropriation for carrying forward the Hospital buildings making up the Deficit created by the ¼ advance upon wages and building materials, was carried through the House without a murmer of objection. It is not supposed the Senate will object, and the Dr. [Nichols], with accustomed alacrity presses on his work already, *through your* patronage and decision, so well begun and advanced.

The Hospital is the more likely to succeed through the failure of my Land Bill, which has now been wholly *crushed* in the Senate, Shields [Illinois], Mallory [Florida], and a few other renegades having been brought over by the President. The *price* of their forfeited honour is not shown; probably the bid for so poor a commodity was not high. I have remarked with pleasure the good spirit which has marked your progress through the South and the West. The people seem to feel more secure in the knowledge of possessing an honest man and sound Statesman, for the Nation is not burthened by such, and *here,* alas, a dreary eclipse prevails, broken only by lurid light breaking from *lower depths.* The "West End" bears the significant synonym, "the Tombs."

I shall leave this city shortly to pursue my work I trust not without success in New England for a time and in New York. I am wanting to devise some practicable plan for the sure relief of the unfriended insane throughout the States, but as yet see no way by which this can be effectually accomplished.

With love to Miss Fillmore, I am your friend, D. L. Dix [Miss D. L. Dix, July 13; Rec'd. 19; Ans'd. July 20.]

✑§ 46. To Millard Fillmore

It would appear that Dorothea forwarded press clippings relating to Fillmore prior to leaving Washington for Trenton.

Trenton, N. Jersey, July 22nd [1854]
My dear Sir and Friend,

Though you are not specially given to dwelling upon evidences and demonstrations of your own popularity, your friends have pleasure in often noting facts which show the tone of public sentiment.

I wish your health may not suffer under the prevailing heat of this hot summer.

I left Washington a day since rather sooner than I proposed for I clearly saw that nothing more remained for me to do.

With sincere esteem I am your friend

D. L. DIX

[Miss D. L. Dix, July 22; Ans'd. 1854.]

36. TO DOROTHEA DIX

A short tribute to Dorothea.

Buffalo, July 24, 1854

My Dear Miss Dix,

I was made happy a few days since on my return from Brooklin [*sic*] to find your favor of the 13th.

I am indeed gratified to hear that the appropriation has been made for carrying out the plan of the Hospital at Washington; and it adds something to the pleasure to learn that it has been obtained through the exertions of my own Representative. This is something gained but I sympathise with you most deeply in the loss of your land Bill. I am happy to perceive however, that no defeat discourages you in your good work. If one effort fails, you immediately fly to another. Few could do this. Most people are discouraged by defeat, but it only seems to add new vigor to your untiring energies. May Heaven reward you for all your labors and all your sacrifices.

I am quietly at home again enjoying the society of my children, but taking no part in politics. Merely looking on to see the strife; and wondering that I could ever have been so much interested in it.

Should your journeys of mercy lead you this way, I need not say that we should all be very happy to see you.

Your sincere friend

MILLARD FILLMORE

⇜§ 47. To Millard Fillmore

On July 25 Abby had driven to East Aurora to visit her grandfather and help him get settled in a new house. She had been ill a few days earlier, but after a strenuous day had retired in good spirits. During the night she was stricken by what was diagnosed as cholera. Fillmore and Powers were summoned from Buffalo, but by the time they arrived she was unconscious. She died several hours later, scarcely twelve hours after the seizure.

Fillmore was disconsolate. Almost immediately after her funeral, in company with Powers he left Buffalo to seek privacy with old friends and relatives near Moravia. Beyond a formal notification of her death, he could not bring himself to consider correspondence.

Dorothea's anguish is recorded in her touching expression of her sorrow.

Trenton, July 27, 1854

My much esteemed and valued Friend,

I have just learned of your most grievous loss. I pray that you may be sustained, comforted under this great sorrow, so sudden, so unlooked for. I have no words of consolation. I can weep for you; I can *be silent;* yet if this expression seems unseasonable, forget it.

I could not but join my sorrowful regrets to your deep mourning.

My affectionate regards to your Son. God spare you to each other, and both to the world.

Your friend,
D. L. Dix

I beseech you take care of your health.

[Miss D. L. Dix, July 27; Rec'd. Aug. 1 at Moravia, 1854; Ans'd. by Obituary notice, Aug. 2.]

ᵛ❧ 48. To MILLARD FILLMORE

Dorothea's tender letter reveals a deep affection which
would not permit her to remain silent in the face of Fillmore's
personal tragedy. His suffering was obviously her suffering.
She had waited four days without any word from him.

Trenton, Sunday Eve'g, July 30th [1854]

My Friend,

I cannot be silent. I know that your heart will but echo the
words of the afflicted of old, "Miserable Comforters are you
all." But when the soul really mourns with those who are "in
the shadow of a great affliction," utter silence cannot be borne.
I *must* tell you again and again that your grief is also the grief
of those who hold you in the sacred bonds of an established
friendship. I have sat by you and yours, and broken the bread
at your table; I have made one of a happy family circle, and
then and there measured the grace and beauty of domestic
affections. I have allowed myself to become attached to and
interested in and for all. And now that two have gone to the
other home, the good wife and mother, with her heart filled
with all wifely and maternal love; the devoted, gentle, good
and beautiful daughter, the "little girl" of the mother's fond
regard; who than myself can draw nearer and keep with you,
and recall the solid worth of those treasures you have been
required to give to that other life wherein, after a time, we all
shall enter. Death has no victory when the good depart: they
have gone to a higher state; yet they are not very far removed;
they may possibly draw near to bless those who are made so
lonely by their departure.

My dear, good friend, be comforted. Alas, alas, how poor
and vain are these words: they console only for a moment. I

mourn that they will not still your sighs, nor lighten the burthen of your mighty grief.

Bear with me at least; I find comfort in writing; though all my words will fail to infuse any balm of consolation into your heart.

Your friend, D. L. Dix

[Miss D. L. Dix, July 30th; Rec'd. Aug't. 2, 1854.]

◄§ 49. To Millard Fillmore

On August 2 Dorothea received the formal announcement of Abby's death. It was scarcely the word of reassurance she begged for, but better than no response. In her search for a means to console him she turned to the treasures of literature.

Trenton, N. Jersey, just from
Phila., August 2nd
[1854]

An enclosure just received from Buffalo via Washington, which I acknowledge with tears and thanks. My excellent friend, would to God I could console, or even comfort you.

It is under trials like this which bows your head, that one feels too certainly that friendship holds no balm for healing such wounds as lacerate your heart. That you will not sink beneath accumulated calamities I feel confident. But I cannot bear to think of you as suffering. I cannot bear to know that you are suffering, and that so far from consoling, my very letters may disturb you. The Baron von Humboldt writing to his friend, Madam Stein says, "When the heart has been already shaken by a great grief, we rouse from a new sorrow with profound impression of the instability of all outward sources of happiness. Gradually submission and rationality return worthy of our intellectual part [?]. Henceforth incapable of really joyful expressions, the thought with chastened melancholy dwells upon the virtues of the departed, and yet we learn to turn to the outward, and calmly resume our duties, and take part in the concerns of life.

"Our beloved abide in our hearts; we consecrate to the virtues of the departed the most precious of our thoughts; our real life is hidden; and we have a fountain of consolation that is invisible to the world."

We will not despair; for God is with us, we will not falter for the great work of our life is incomplete. Thus the bereaved reason with themselves; and in time quietness comes, and possibly tranquility.

My excellent friend, may you be sustained and blessed.

I am yours with sympathy, D. L. Dix

[Miss D. L. Dix, Aug't. 2, Rec'd. 8, 1854 at Skaneateles.]

◄§ 50. To MILLARD FILLMORE

"I cannot be silent. . . . I must mourn with you."

Trenton, N. Jersey
Aug. 6th '54

My excellent Friend,

I may seem very forgetful of the common usages of social intercourse that now I write so frequently; but with every sympathy within me quickened to acute life by your sorrows, I *cannot* be silent. I have said I feel powerless to comfort you, but *I must mourn with you;* and while tears fall, I find a growing anxiety for your own health.

Recollect, I hear nothing of you through any certain sources: What I gather from the newspapers only distresses

me, and much as it may seem to ask that any friend or friendship should at this sorrowful time be remembered, I must
claim so much for my own release from a painful solicitude, as
to have a line to tell me how you are, and also Powers. May he
be spared to you, and may you both be spared to all.

Our fair and good; now a glorified Angel has left a precious legacy for our comfort and *instruction* too. Should you
like me to write my impressions of her character? I have
feared as the idea has repeatedly returned to me, that I should
omit much that was excellent through my want of more intimate acquaintance; yet I think I observed and could define
more correctly than some who have already written.

My friendly regards to Powers of whose grief I too take
part.

Your friend,

D. L. DIX

I have been of late a good deal indisposed, and now by
order of my physician am in my room chiefly, which explains
being stationary here.

[Miss D. L. Dix, Aug't. 6, Rec'd. 10, 1854; Ans'd. Aug't. 10.]

§51. To MILLARD FILLMORE

*"I allow myself to hope for the relief friendly solicitude
craves of having a few words from you."*

7th August—Trenton [1854]
Looking over lately the works of Jeremy Taylor I noted the
following passage:

> The word friend is of large signification; and means all
> relations and societies, and whatsoever is not an enemy;

but by friendship I suppose is meant the greatest love and usefulness, and the most open communication, and the noblest sufferings, and the most exemplar faithfulness, and the severest truth, and the heartiest counsel, and the greatest union of minds of which good men and women are capable.

Friendship is the allay of our sorrows; the ease of our infirmities; the sanctuary of our calamities; the counselor of our doubts; the repose of our minds; the emission of our thoughts; the exercise of our meditations Though I love my friend because he is worthy, yet he is not worthy if I can do him no good, or if he can do me no good. He only is fit to be chosen for a friend who can fulfill the offices for which friendship is excellent.

And I may add to Taylor's remarks, Bacon's definition of Friendship:

Peace in the affections; counsel in judgment, and assistance when necessary—the heart, the head, the hand— sympathy, judgment, help.

It is a true remark of Lord Verulam that the benefit of friendship in communicating our minds to others is that by this sorrows grow less and joys greater. And indeed sorrow, "like a divided stream; loses itself in other channels; and joy acquires by reflected rays added brightness."

You see my friend, that I try to believe that in the sincerity, discretion and stedfastness of my friendship, you must find some little resource: Broken and imperfect as is our intercourse, I still believe that your mind would feel a greater intensity of solitude if you did not perceive the sincerity of that tender sympathy which now moves the hearts of your tried friends. Be comforted I beseech you: Garner up your strength, and search out now how you may so dispose of time as its heaviness shall not corrode your mental facilities, and weaken their powers.

The *past* has infinite good for you: You dwell on the excellencies of those who were precious to your heart, and when the sharpness of a first anguish has subsided, you will feel, not that you have lost the jewels of your household, but that though removed from your gaze, and their lustre no longer reflected by the outward light, yet are they bestowed in an imperishable casket; safely holden by one who hereafter will conduct you to where your treasures are laid up in Heaven; in the world of mind, and where the indestructible soul rises to a nobler than its earthly life.

Farewell my good friend. Preserve yourself; for the world cannot spare you.

Your friend,
D. L. Dix

I am aware that you are in Cayuga County, but I do not know if you are to remain some time, and so address letters to you in Buffalo. I allow myself to hope for the relief friendly solicitude craves of having a few words from you. In your unhappiness you will not be willing others should suffer when their anxiety can be relieved.

[Miss D. L. Dix, Aug't. 7, Rec'd. 11 at Skaneateles, 1854.]

⟜§ 52. To MILLARD FILLMORE

Dorothea seems to have canceled all of her activities to await Fillmore's reply. She could not accept silence and the frustration of rejection.

"My very heart is aching for you . . ."
After almost two weeks of waiting she received a response;
possibly a newspaper clipping.

Trenton, August 8th [1854]

My dear friend,

Affection is requiring, and friendship at times becomes arrogant. Even so it is now with myself—persuasion, which allows me to imagine I might possibly afford you some little comfort if I were less distant from you. It seems when acts are repelling; when words are disquieting, *silent* expression can be borne. Yet this possible influence cannot be exercised. I sit here alone in my room, and think of you. I am writing powerless to cheer your broken heart.

Just now comes a letter. It is your writing on the envelope, and from this I extract the assurance I fain would have in declared words; you are not absolutely ill, or you would not have written even the address. The post-mark I cannot well make out, but at a venture send this messenger of regard, a token that my very heart is aching for you, that you have not at any time this sad week past been out of my thoughts.

I thank you for the printed pages.

God bless you, Good bye,

D. L. Dix

I have received (via Washington) a letter, and an enclosed printed sheet: alas, our fair and good!

Mr. Haven, that excellent man writing of you to me says "my heart aches; I dare not write to him." Dr. Hare says with eyes overflowing with tears, "I will not venture to write, but God knows my heart is grieved for him."

[Miss D. L. Dix, Aug't. 8, Rec'd. 10, 1854; Ans'd. Aug't. 10.]

~§ 53. To MILLARD FILLMORE

Dorothea at last received a few lines from Fillmore.

"It has been a great comfort, though fraught with deep sadness."

Her descriptive account of an accident while enroute from Trenton to Washington is illustrative of the perils of railroad transportation.

Trenton, New Jersey
August 12th [1854]

Through the gracious mercy of God I live to fulfil as I hope the office of consoler and friend to those whose sorrows are known to me, or of those who are bound very closely by a sincere friendship. I reached here last night, and received this message, your letter, anxiously looked for. I thank you for writing; I thank my dear friend for making this effort for my sake. It has been a great comfort, though fraught with deep sadness. I only want you to tell me that you are but bodily ill. Don't try to write a line more. No one, least of all myself, can ask letters of reply now. But indeed it is needful to know you are but ill in your room; if that is shared, I hardly expect more.

I will tell you of myself; and then you will wonder that I live to write now. On Wednesday, finding myself stronger than of late, and very anxious to secure something for the benefit of the Hospital at Washington, which I only could do; and considering too that the institution is to be opened in October or November, I went on, making the journey in one day, taking the express train ¼ before 1 P.M. from Philadelphia, whither I had gone at an earlier hour.

All went securely, till we had passed the Wilmington station as far as the switch which regulates the two tracks to Baltimore and Newcastle:

[Omitted here is Dorothea Dix's sketch of the tracks involved.]

The train was at full speed; the switch tender, a new hand, became confused, uncertain which train was coming. And prepared for the Newcastle, he discovered that it was the express for Baltimore; tried to change, failed at *half* the distance, and our train, destined for destruction, rushed on; and in one moment Engine, Tender, Mail Car, Express Car, Baggage Car, and the Passenger cars were a mass of ruins.

It is certainly a miracle that not one passenger was hurt, so as to be at all disabled. The Engineer was killed—he had been on duty only that day, having taken the place of one killed on the same road belonging to the same Train, the day before. Thrice men had been killed on three successive days on the same road, on the same line. It seems quite *incredible* that under circumstances like those on Wednesday, every passenger had but been killed, and yet not one was harmed.

A force came in twenty minutes from Wilmington, consisting of 150 men (from the works), and in three hours' hard labor so cleared and repaired the tracks that the trains due passed, and an extra, taking up those belonging to our train conveyed them onward!

I was one day in Washington, and returned here on Friday evening too much indisposed to proceed, as I had intended, to New York. I shall remain here probably for a week or ten days, till quite well, comparatively, with present disability.

My good friend, I have written all this about myself, not that I suppose it of any importance to you, but simply for the moment to engage your thought. Write to me again soon or not as you feel inclined. The only argument I urge is one quite too selfish to be pressed again so importunatly [*sic*] as when 1 last wrote.

Adieu, God bless and keep you now and always,

Stedfastly your friend,

D. L. Dix

[Miss D. L. Dix, Aug't. 12; Rec'd. 15, 1854.]

◄§ 54. To MILLARD FILLMORE

"*. . . As I had sat long with unused pen, pondering what I could suggest to you and Powers . . . to stimulate your minds to action.*"

Sunday Morning

[Aug. 13, 1854]

Peace be with you, my good friend, and indwelling trust that the bitterness of this present hour shall pass away, and that softened memories shall gradually take the place of keen griefs.

This day is sultry, and Nature seems to faint under the morbid languor of a debilitating heat. The mind partakes of this influence which affects so sensible the physical condition.

"They also serve, who only *stand,* and *wait.*" This thought of Milton occurred to me just now as I had sat long with unused pen, pondering what I could suggest to you and Powers as an object of action of sufficient consequence to stimulate your minds to action, and call you off, beyond, and out of yourselves, to think and do. All will come *in time,* but I dread the effect on you both of such grief as this you now struggle with. Still I can suggest nothing. Wherever you go, whatever you do, and propose to do, still you will bear with you the heart-grief. And so dear friend, you will just get on for the present, day by day, and not determine on any present fixed plan. In the autumn perhaps, you will go to Europe, and so occupy the winter in seeing what is most worthy of study and observation in the old civilized world.

I throw out the suggestion vaguely. You ought not certainly to go to your house in Buffalo, unless you have some companionable, judicious female friend or friends, who can make a present home residence comfortable in its general arrangements. None can fill the void created there, but you will strengthen yourself to bear the changed lot, I am sure. Your mind will recover its balance gradually, and in this confidence I find relief from a great solicitude on your behalf.

Farewell. If you think fit, offer my sincere regards to your son.

Stedfastly your friend,

D. L. DIX

[Miss D. L. Dix, Aug't. 12 Rec'd. 16, 1854.]

⊷§ 55. To MILLARD FILLMORE

Though she continued to dwell upon Fillmore's grief, Dorothea's spirits are obviously rising, and her tone is optimistic and reassuring.

Sunday P.M.,

Trenton, N.J.,

August

I trust that this day will not pass without having procured for you, my excellent friend, something of composure and a measure of peace. The memory of the past, wrote one who like yourself had tasted deep at the fountain of bitter waters, "The memory of the past hath in it an infinite virtue; for even if it reproduce painful feelings, it also affords an inexpressible enjoyment. When we lose what has been, as it were, the moving principle of the best part of our affections, a new epoch of life begins. All enjoyments are shared with a graver temper; all comforts minister to a calmer, more subdued life of the heart and mind. Happily, there is something in man that he can hold fast to if he will, and over which fate has no power. No well balanced mind can abandon itself unreservedly to an existence of grief, but gradually returns to its daily duties, and renders to mankind its share of influence or of labor." "The good sacrifice themselves to the necessities of society, and so are through a reflected action, in their turn, blessed."

My excellent friend, if because you are bereft of what was most precious and lovely, the joy of your heart, and the light of your eyes, you are deeply afflicted, still in this very greatness of affliction are you blessed; for you had a great treasure, now safely bestowed in Heaven, beyond the touch of mortal woe, and whose virtues you can ever contemplate in review of the past, as a most consoling subject. True your own loss is the greater, as was the object of your paternal love most lovely; but so much the greater abstractly is the measure of your consolation.

I tell you what I have before said, my friend. I do not write expecting response or that I shall open to your afflicted soul any spring of refreshment in this dreary waste. But the good Lord will grant you strength from above, now that human help fails, and the best friends are but "miserable comforters."

Farewell, your friend,
Sincerely,
D. L. Dix

[Miss D. L. Dix, Aug't. 20; Rec'd. 22, 1854.]

ᴥ§ 56. To MILLARD FILLMORE

Between August 20 and 26 Dorothea went to Boston; on August 25 she "very suddenly" decided upon a trip to Europe. She offers no explanation. Disappointment attending the defeat of the land-grant bill, the lack of a definite plan for a resumption of her work in the states, delicate health, the offer of a free passage and stateroom by the officials of the Arctic, and Fillmore's gradual recovery from his mental depression may have all been contributing factors. She inadvertently referred to the Arctic as the Baltic. Eight days later she was on her way.

Boston, Aug. 26th [1854]

My excellent Friend,

Yesterday very suddenly I was induced to consent to sail next week for Europe, by the *Baltic.*

I am not ill, but really exhausted, and must take a rest from my long uninterrupted labors. I cannot go without expressing for you every good wish, and trust your present sorrows will be timely mitigated; how, or where or when, no one can now foresee or suggest. This I feel confident in: You will endeavor to bear your great affliction patiently, and as a man and Christian should. I go tonight to the country and on Monday to New York; then to Philadelphia and to Trenton on Thursday and Friday.

Friday night to New York to sail on Saturday. I trust I may before departure learn how you are.

Your friend, very sincerely, with kind regard to Powers.

D. L. DIX

I do not know how long I shall remain abroad; nor does it seem needful to determine any period of return.

[Miss D. L. Dix, Aug't. 26, Rec'd. 28, 1854.]

⌘ 37. To Dorothea Dix

Fillmore prays that she will have a safe journey and return reinvigorated.

". . . but I feel that life has little left for me. My good son, only, of all my little family remains."

Buffalo, Aug't. 29, 1854

My Dear Miss Dix,

I was greatly surprised yesterday to learn from your short note of the 26th from Boston, that you were to sail next week for Europe. You do not state the object of your visit nor how long you intend to be absent. But I infer that your object is to recruit your strength, and if so I can not but approve of your resolution. Considering your apparently frail constitution and incessant labors, I am surprised that you have held out so long. But God has blessed your good work and sustained you through all trials. My sincere prayer is that He may continue to do so, and that you may return again to your native country—which owes you such a debt of gratitude—reinvigorated, and in the full enjoyment of all this world can give.

I hope when you return to feel in better spirits, but I feel that life has little left for me. My good son, only, of all my little family remains. I have none other now to sympathise with me in grief or rejoice with me in prosperity; and my dwelling, once so cheerfully [sic] and happy, is now dark and desolate. But I do not mean to grieve; much less complain. Heaven has blessed me many years, and has now withdrawn these precious jewels from my sight and taken them home, to wean me from this world and tempt me to my celestial abode. I must, at any rate, soon follow, and I hope that I may there again be united to those who have gone before, and who were so dear to me here. But pardon me, I did not mean to speak of

this. But merely to answer your inquiry after my health, by assuring you that it is very good and that of my son is also. We
are yet in our old residence and expect to remain there this
winter.

May Heaven prosper you in your journey and may you
return safe and reinvigorated to the arms of your friends in
America is the sincere prayer of

Your friend,
MILLARD FILLMORE

6

Rendezvous in Europe

1854–1856

eemingly at loose ends after the defeat of her land-grant bill in Washington Dorothea was off to Europe —this despite her continuing concern for Fillmore's melancholy. She left in September of 1854 with the hope that he and Powers would follow her and find peace and renewed hope in the scenes of the Old World. But in this she was disappointed, for a time.

Despite her previous statements about need for a rest, she did not look upon a European trip as a rest or a sight-seeing excursion for herself. She was searching for new fields of conquest. She was in England for only a short time before taking a look at the plight of the insane in England and Ireland. She found a greater challenge in Scotland and the Island of Jersey, where the care of the insane seemed to ask for her attention.

Later she interceded with the Pope to lift standards in the Papal States and traveled to Turkey, Russia, and Scandinavia to observe practices there.

Meanwhile, Fillmore had second thoughts about Europe.

With his eye on a possible nomination for the Presidency in 1856, his removal from the welter of politics would be timely, and he embarked in May of 1855. He, of course, was not unaware of Dorothea's presence there.

Learning of his arrival in England Dorothea contacted him in London, and they met there, and again, in Switzerland and Paris. Fillmore's tour took him from Scotland to Italy and from Berlin to Paris. During his residence in Italy in February he was nominated for President by the American party, a political outgrowth of the nativist Know-Nothing movement, and he returned the following summer in time for the campaign.

Dorothea reached New York early in October, 1856.

⋙ 57. To MILLARD FILLMORE

". . . but your friends honour and love you—and she whom you have called a true friend."

A passage on the Arctic offered attractions unknown at the time of Dorothea Dix's previous crossing eighteen years before. The Arctic and its three sister ships of the Collins Line had been designed to destroy the almost complete Cunard monopoly on steam navigation between New York and Liverpool. In 1836 three or four weeks were required for a crossing under sail. By the late 1840s Cunard steamships had repeatedly broken their own records to reduce the time to an incredible eleven days. But E. K. Collins' sidewheeler Pacific did it in nine days in 1851, and the Collins Line was soon carrying more passengers on this route than Cunard. Speed was costly, however, and only substantial subsidies provided by Collins' adept lobbying in Washington kept the project afloat. In February of 1852 he had dispatched the Baltic to the Potomac, where he dined and wined more than two thousand notables, including President Fillmore and members of the Cabinet,

*House, and Senate. Later the same year Congress increased
his annual subsidy from $385,000 to $853,000.*

*Collins' gesture to Dorothea came in the wake of her well-
publicized campaign to provide Sable Island with lifesaving
facilities.*

*But Collins' luck ran out when two of his ships went down
in the Atlantic within the space of a year and a half. The first
of these was the Arctic, which was lost in a collision off Newfoundland on the return trip following Dorothea's passage to
Liverpool with a loss of more than four hundred lives. Hence
her reluctance in her letter of December 26, 1854, to advise
Fillmore to make the Atlantic crossing.*

Narrows, Steamer Arctic; Sept. 2nd [1854]
Pilot just going off.

Yours received. My excellent friend I am distressed as I
think of your deep grief; and yet I have great confidence you
will *bear* your great trials well.

I have only time to say you do not speak rightly when you
say you are alone. Your dearest and best are gone, but your
friends honour and love you—and she whom you have called
a true friend.

Is it right to say you are alone when sincere attachment
through just and high appreciation of your character binds one
steadily to you[?] Your joys and your griefs are *shared* by
your friends. You are not desolate of these.

I am not ill but much exhausted and am compelled to rest.

Adieu,

The boat is parting from New York.

[Miss D. L. Dix, Sept. 2d; Rec'd. 5, 1854.]

☙ 58. To MILLARD FILLMORE

*From the Arctic Dorothea again bade Fillmore adieu. She
lingered briefly upon her distress at leaving him while he was
in anguish, but her focus was upon the future, and she repeatedly urged him to follow her to Europe: "Come at once."*

*As a final incentive, possibly hoping that it might tip
the balance, she drafted a letter of introduction to William
Rathbone at Green Bank, Liverpool, her host on her earlier
trip.*

*"Dear Sir and Friend," it read, "I have the honor of intro-
ducing to your acquaintance, the Honorable Millard Fillmore,
ex-President of the United States; and I am sure in this I perceive a gratification to both parties; since good men, and sound
patriots stand on common ground"* [*Fillmore papers, Oswego;
enclosed in her letter of September 10*].

Steamer Arctic, at Sea
September 10th [1854], 8 days out

My dear Sir and Friend,

I write now, ready to forward on arriving at Liverpool (if
our voyage shall be so far prospered), a few lines hoping I may
influence you to leave the United States for the coming winter, and *with Powers certainly*,—pass the cold and dreary
months approaching, in France and Italy. This I feel persuaded is the wisest course for you both and I think no time
will ever arrive when you will so surely find the change and
novelty of travelling so useful, and so easy. Do come at once. I
shall not expect to hear from you by letter, but should you feel
inclined to write, address me at London, care of Messrs.
George Peabody and Co., Bankers.

I have made no plans, my health not allowing any defined

purposes of effort. Nor have I fixed on any settled period of return. More tired and worn than ill, I shall try to adapt my movements and occupations to such ends as shall restore me to active capacity for better usefulness than at present.

I cannot write farewell without referring to your present afflicted state which deeply distresses me. I know that I can say nothing that will assuage your anguish. I know I cannot with deep words of sympathy hope to console you; but I have faith in your own ever regulated mind, and look for the time when you will be able to possess your life long grief, without this now-keen anguish. Your dear wife, your sweet daughter fair and good, you will yet meet again: the life towards which we all are tending opens the way, I fully believe to a happy reunion with those who are precious to the heart here. In those words of Jesus, "Where I am there shall ye be also," I find the clear idea of recognition of and restoration to the beloved ones who precede us to the higher world.

My excellent friend, may you be strengthened, may you bear this burthen of life—patiently; and a calmer time will come.

Your friend, steadfastly,
D. L. Dɪx

Think well of the European plan. It will be useful both to yourself and Powers.

I have not been able to write what I proposed concerning your departed [a tribute to Abby], but shall do so. Allow me to make a suggestion with tenderness and gentleness.

You will in due time erect a Monument to the memory of both your departed ones; let *this* or *these* be quite *simple, durable,* and not costly, but take the fund which you would so apply, as a gift to constitute a permanent fund aiding some charity,—as a widow's and orphan's Asylum, or any thing you choose;—thus establishing, in their name, a memorial more beautiful and really perpetuating, than the costliest mausoleum. This would stand as a precedent, presenting an example others may wisely imitate. Excuse the directness of this suggestion.

[Miss D. L. Dix, Sept. 10; Rec'd. October 1, 1854; Ans'd. Oct. 3.]

৶§ 59. To MILLARD FILLMORE

Three days after her arrival at the Rathbone estate Dorothea was again active.

She continued to press Fillmore to make the voyage and offered several suggestions pertaining to his accommodations and travel.

Liverpool, Sept. 16th [1854]

The *Arctic* arrived here after a *very* pleasant and safe passage of little more than ten days leaving New York on the 2d at noon and making the Northern Light on the Coast of Ireland at 2 o'clock on Tuesday morning, the 12th, rounding the Giant's Causeway at 6 and 7 A.M.

I still counsel you to make the voyage if nothing special hinders. It will do both you and Powers good. If you come take rooms at the Adelphi, in Liverpool, and rest there, it being a point whence you can make a number of pleasant excursions; assuring a sort of rest before proceeding to London.

I remain here a fortnight till after the meeting of the British Association for the Advancement of Science; then shall visit the Public Institutions in England and Scotland, and probably proceed to the Continent some time in November if I do not return; which is hardly probable. I am just going to see a Hospital and have as much as I can do at present in Lancashire.

Your friend, cordially,

D. L. DIX

≈§ 38. TO DOROTHEA DIX

Fillmore decided against a European tour at this time. With a touch of self-pity, he noted that he had originally considered the trip with Abby in mind. Now he would have too many reminders of her absence.

Buffalo, Oct. 3, 1854

My Dear Miss Dix,

I was greatly gratified to learn from your letter, written at sea, but closed at Liverpool, that you had arrived safely in England. I hope your journey may be the means of recruiting your health, but I fear from your communication that you are about to engage in your usual labors in that country. Your benevolent heart is too powerful for your weak frame. Let me entreat you to spare yourself. You require rest. Your travels should be for recreation, not for business. Your whole soul has been devoted to the unfortunate. For their sake, if not for your own, you should endeavor to renovate your health. There is a time for all things, and this is the time to renew your strength for the labors which you will have to perform after your return.

I do not think I shall visit Europe; at any rate, not at present. My Dear Daughter was extremely anxious to go, and to gratify her, I had consented to undertake the journey; but her untimely death, has taken away all inducements. Indeed, I think the journey at this time would be positively painful. I could enjoy nothing. The more agreeable the journey, the deeper would be my regret that she could not share it with me. Every pleasure would be tinged with melancholy and every joy with a secret sorrow. I could not endure it. I must wait until time has somewhat softened my grief, and obliterated the remembrance of those dear ones which I shall see no more on this side of the grave.

Nothing new has transpired in regard to myself. My son enjoys good health but is much depressed in spirits. He is, however, engaged in his profession and is gradually regaining his wonted cheerfulness.

I spend most of my time in reading history and the current literature of the day. I do this for the purpose of keeping my mind occupied.

With my best wishes for your health and happiness and safe return to your native land which owes you so much,

I remain
Your sincere Friend
MILLARD FILLMORE

◄§ 60. To MILLARD FILLMORE

Since her previous letter Dorothea had spent a month in Ireland, where she found the countryside more beautiful than England. She was saddened by the poverty and misery of the people, but was unwilling to make the United States their sanctuary. "Alas for the people of that Emerald Isle," she confided to Ann Heath. "They are sorely degraded by a thousand causes; and we reap the curse of a vicious population sent over to people our now fast corrupted and over burthened country" [December 8, 1854, Harvard College Library].

Finding the Rathbones and their friends at Green Bank an attraction, she gave up any thought of passing the winter on the Continent. In fact travel without an objective, even a

visitation of institutions for the insane, without a means to initiate reforms, left her cold. She was almost haughty in rejecting Ann's suggestion that she tour prisons in Italy. She declared herself "amused" at the proposal. It had not occurred to her to see "those places of so many bitter *memories and horrid sufferings. What should I gain? . . . Where I do visit prisons it is where I have before me a* rational *object and a clear purpose"* [Ibid].

Harriet Beecher Stowe in the wake of her sensational Uncle Tom's Cabin had visited England and Scotland the previous year in response to invitations from Scottish antislavery societies. Her arrival touched off an ovation which followed her from Liverpool to Scotland, and Scotland to London. In addition to the costs, which were met by these philanthropic societies, she accepted a "penny subscription" from the Liverpool Negroes' Friend Society which had been converted into 130 gold sovereigns, and in Edinburgh, 1,000 gold sovereigns on a silver salver, also collected in pennies from the poor. The fastidious Dorothea found such a "personal relief fund" extremely distasteful.

Unfortunately she does not offer an evaluation of Mrs. Stowe's literary classic in her correspondence. With her firsthand knowledge of the South and a wide acquaintance with southern leaders, her assessment of the work could have scarcely been favorable.

Instead of the Continent Dorothea turned to Scotland, and finding that private institutions for the insane needed immediate reform, she could not resist the challenge. *"I am confident that this move is to rest with me,"* she advised Ann, *"and that the sooner I address myself to this work of humanity, the sooner will my conscience cease to suggest effort, or rebuke inaction"* [February 26, 1855]. And to Mrs. Rathbone she added, *"It is not a self-indulging and indulgent pursuit. . . . I have here at all events 'passed the Rubicon' and retreat is not to be thought of."* [*February 20, 1855, quoted in Tiffany, p. 234.*]

She visited the indigent insane in Scotland and publicized her findings. Then, learning of a plan to block her proposals, she raced to London for an interview with the Home Secretary just hours before her adversary made his appearance. As a result of her intense activity a Royal Commission was appointed to inquire into the condition of the insane asylums and the existing state of the law in reference to lunatics and lunatic asylums in Scotland. Historians are agreed that she hastened reform in that country.

Liverpool, Eng'd., Decb'r. 26th, 1854

My dear Sir and Friend—

You will be much surprised to get another letter from me dated from this point—the facts and causes will follow.

After the Sessions of the British Scientific Association were over in September, I visited some of the Public Institutions in England, near this place, and next proceeded to Wales and Ireland, seeing there all Hospitals and Literary Institutions, etc. not returning here till the early part of November. While here prosecuting some important and interesting investigations, my strength gave way, and a low fever, with consequent debility has till now kept me mainly subject to care and rest. I am so far recovered as to be prepared to go forth after the first of January for Scotland, and intend to follow (more leisurely indeed) the same course of observation and inquiry as attracted and engaged me in Ireland.

I have avoided the Continent this Winter altogether, in the belief that I should not find either in France or Italy the climate or the means of care which my health requires, a climate no better than that to be found in England, and with such limited means of comfort as offered no inducement for *mere* curiosity's sake to adventure upon such enterprizes. Here I am gratified in the midst of highly cultivated society, and have the means of much useful acquisition. Here I *learn,* abroad on the Continent, I should *see.* You will approve my decision in remaining here and appreciate the distinction between intellectual attainment, and the gratification of observing the works which genius has immortalized in works of Art.

I on the whole am glad that you have remained in America. The hazards of the ocean, so painfully illustrated this year have forever silenced me in imposing any and all voyages to friends. I cannot assume so grave responsibility any more.

You read of course the record of misery the terrible War in the Crimea produces. I am horror-struck at the carnage, the varied consequent suffering, and multiplied disasters by sea and land, which have made distressingly memorable the past year. And then not only is the seat of war the scene of distress but the whole people here at home suffer unmeasured misery through suspense and by actual bereavement. I look with anxiety on the results too which are hidden now in the future—the facts revealed by Hospital records during the past thirty years in France are but indicative of what is to fall on this country, through the effects of present trouble affecting mental and physical health.

I read no American newspapers, and am content to remain ignorant upon all political questions till a time comes when we may hope for some wholesome change in our National Government. I have such entire distrust, such contempt for the present Administration, that the less informed I am on its proceedings, the more is my mental quiet increased or assured. The English are disposed to discuss American Policy, and I am sorry that conclusions are not always nor often now such as redound to our credit. I avoid the subject as far as possible.

The slavery question I positively ignore. Mrs. Stowe's absurd career here, has really for the time produced the most mistaken and often absurd notions of America and American life. I trust she will henceforth practice more discretion, and be content, like Kossuth here, to live quietly in her own House on the contributions of her disciples, and the penny contributions of the multitude. I have been really mortified to find an American taking collections, as a *personal relief fund*, in Ireland, Scotland and England, under such influences as those used by Mrs. Stowe. I am afraid I hardly excuse this sort of pauperism.

I must conclude my letter, my excellent friend, with sincerest wishes for your health, your peace, your comfort. I think of your great trials with sincere sympathy, and I trust that as time interposes its gradually softening and healing influences you will be able to seek and find sources of comfort and enjoyment which will give to life some aspects of peaceful enjoyment. I trust Powers is in a measure restored to cheerfulness. The losses you have both sustained cannot fully be repaired, but some thing may be newly gained, taking away the keen sense of solitude and bereavement.

I am stedfastly your friend.

D. L. Dix

The season here has been mild. I recollect frost but twice this year in England; and though snow has fallen it melted as it touched the ground. The fields and lawns are as freshly green as in May with us; the birds are as cheerful in their flight and songs. I have abundance of five or six sort of *flowers* from the open gardens, and the varieties of evergreens shrubs contribute to the delusion which gathers over one, that the winter season is not at hand. Rain falls daily, either in light showers or in abundance. The humidity of the climate is not pleasant; and yet the people as a race, look, and are well.

It is not easy for an American to become accustomed to the miserable subjection and dependence of the lower classes upon those who possess wealth, and hold the high positions secured either by rank or official station. Yet *we* are learning these foreign distinctions already in New York and elsewhere. [Miss D. L. Dix, Dec'r. 26. Rec'd. Jan'y. 21.]

৵§ 61. To MILLARD FILLMORE

Though Fillmore had rejected the possibility of a European tour in October of 1854, he reconsidered a few months later. Politics seems to have been the preponderant influence.

The American party (Know-Nothing party), one of the recurring nativist movements of the nineteenth century, had arisen as a backlash to the massive immigration of Irish and Germans after 1847. Its rapid growth stemmed from its secrecy (members uniformly responded to inquiries relating to it with an "I know nothing"), the seeming threat of Catholicism to American freedoms, the competition of foreigners with native workers for jobs, the increase of mob violence in the cities, and the exploitation of immigrants by corrupt politicians. In the elections of 1854 the party carried Massachusetts, Delaware, and Pennsylvania, and showed surprising strength in other states including New York. It offered the possibility of enlisting moderates from both the Whig and Democratic parties in the North and South, and thereby combating sectionalism.

Fillmore was a logical choice as the party's nominee for President despite his freedom from nativist proclivities. After some urging from his friends he quietly took the oath of membership in the secret society and drafted a letter to Isaac Newton for limited circulation among the Fillmore coterie. He noted the "corrupting influence" of the competition for the foreign vote, which converted elections into an "unmeaning

*mockery." Immigrants, he insisted, were entitled to a refuge
from the oppressions of Europe and the equal protection of
the law, but officeholding should be reserved to those who had
been "reared in a free country" [January 3, 1855, Fillmore
Papers, Vol. II, pp. 347–348].*

*Fillmore declined an invitation to accompany Doctor and
Madame LeVert to Europe and turned instead to John P. Kennedy and W. W. Corcoran, the Washington banker, who had
accompanied him to White Sulphur Springs in 1851. Finding
that they could not join him at the outset, he finally accompanied Henry E. Davies, a long-time friend, and sailed on the
Atlantic in late May.*

*The moment the ship weighed anchor Fillmore was freed
from taking a position upon divisive issues. He might now
ignore Abolitionism, the Kansas-Nebraska controversy, and
even nativism. Traveling about Europe would obviously draw
attention to himself; and it would require no commitments.
Meanwhile, time might clarify his ultimate position.*

*If Dorothea's presence in Europe affected his decision, he
did not reveal it. But it remains an interesting speculation.*

Green Bank, Liverpool
June 12th, 1855

To the Honorable Millard Fillmore
My dear Sir and Friend,

Taking up the *Times* just now I remarked the announcement of your arrival in London—as I suppose by the last
steamer; and I would not be latest amongst your American
friends in congratulations upon your safe passage and arrival in
our common *Fatherland*, the country of our ancestors. I did
not know you were coming, though I have constantly hoped
that at this interesting and eventful period of European affairs,
you might, with your son, be induced to cross the ocean and

explore scenes and look upon people which present new phases of society, and create as well as stimulate new subjects of thought. I am really glad you are in safety (I hope in health), and here.

For myself, I left Scotland in April, journeying gradually through Northumberland; but in Yorkshire at York, became ill from fatigue and lack of *working* strength, and last week found myself so far reestablished, that my Physicians allowed me to join my dear friends here, where I shall remain probably a week or ten days longer. Allow me to repeat good wishes, and that I am yours, with esteem and with stedfast friendship,

D. L. DIX

[Miss D. L. Dix, June 12, 1855; Rec'd. and Ans'd. at London, June 14.]

◄§ 39. To DOROTHEA DIX

Fillmore immediately answered Dorothea's letter and expressed a desire to see her while they were in England.

The injury to his eyes became chronic, and he suffered from it for several years.

Fenton's Hotel [London]
June 14, 1855

My Dear Miss Dix,

I have this moment received your kind note of the 12th inst. and am gratified to hear that your health has so much improved. I enquired for you at Liverpool and here but could learn nothing definite and feared you had left the country. I hope now to have the pleasure of meeting you before I leave England. My present intention is to leave here about the 27th inst. for the North by way of York and Edinburgh, returning through Glasgow, etc.

I owe you many apologies for not answering your last kind letter, but I had this journey under consideration, and delayed writing that I might inform you if I was coming, but the matter remained open for causes which I can not now explain until finally when I decided to come I left immediately.

I took a severe cold just before leaving New York which has so affected my eyes that I have been unable to read or write much since, but they are gradually improving.

I have been exceedingly busy in seeing what I could in and about London, but the calls which society makes upon me are a serious interruption, and the late hours injurious to my eyes. I shall escape from here as soon as possible.

I am, as ever, truly and sincerely
your friend
MILLARD FILLMORE

✍§ 62. To MILLARD FILLMORE

Having received no reply to her letter of June 12th, Dorothea again dispatched a note of welcome. She continued to assume that Powers Fillmore had accompanied his father.

Green Bank, Liverpool
June 22d, 1855

I cannot refuse my dear Sir, to *repeat* my communication to you, congratulating you on your safe arrival in England; and I do this with the less hesitation as my first note may not have found you as addressed at Fenton's Hotel, St. James Street.

I sincerely hope no untoward circumstances may interfere with your plans to travel while in Europe. I infer that your health must be good, and that your son is with you. I have been seriously ill, but have so far recovered since I left York as to propose resuming my journies [sic] and objects of engagement in July.

        With all good wishes, very cordially your friend,

                                D. L. Dix

At William Rathbone's, Esquire

[Miss D. L. Dix, June 22, 1855, Rec'd. June 23d at Fenton's, Ans'd. July [June] 23.]

≪§ 63. To Millard Fillmore

Just after posting her previous letter, Dorothea received Fillmore's note of June 14. Fearful that she might not see him in England, she asked for his itinerary on the Continent, but, meanwhile, she hoped that their plans might be altered to permit a meeting in London.

While she was in Scotland her attention had been drawn to the Island of Jersey where, she learned, contractors responsible for the care of insane persons transported their wards to avoid English regulations. In July she went to the island and conferred with the Governor, and before leaving had the satisfaction of seeing the principal offender arraigned. She also helped to select the site for an insane asylum. As it turned out, it required another thirteen years to complete the structure. But she returned to England triumphant.

                        Green Bank, near Liverpool
                    at William Rathbone's, Esquire
                      Friday Morning, June 22 [1855]

My dear friend,

    Yours of the 14th just received. I was most thankful to hear from you. What you say of the state of your eyes gives me much concern; pray be careful.

    I should like to know, if not intrusive, what are your plans for the Continent. You propose going over the ground I have transversed in Scotland and England. I greatly fear I shall quite miss seeing you; that is, if you leave London as you now propose on the 27th. My present design is to leave this place *for London* on the 2d of July, *enroute* for Southampton and the Channel Islands, where I go (but *this* is a point of reserve, not now to be announced) to secure the removal of some insane persons in great distress, whose miseries were accidently (providentially) revealed to me. My success I think depends much on great prudence in this movement. I intended after I secured the Royal Commission on Lunacy for Scotland, to have proceeded directly to the Continent, but the Commissioners desired I should meet the full Board at Edinburgh, and I returned to Scotland for that purpose. Since then I was detained 4 weeks in Yorkshire, and have been here three weeks.

Just let me have a line to say if your northern journey will be possibly delayed, but do not injure your eyes by too much use. I sent a note yesterday to you by Mr. Morgan, not being fully sure of your address, and thinking the first might miss. You are not going to the United States *immediately* from Liverpool I take it.

Cordially and stedfastly your friend,

D. L. Dix

[Received June 23 at Fenton's. Answered July [June] 23.]

40. To Dorothea Dix

Fillmore changed his itinerary so as to be in London for a Fourth of July celebration. He hoped that it would also enable him to see Dorothea prior to her departure for Southampton and the Island of Jersey.

Fenton's Hotel
London, June 23, 1855

My Dear Miss Dix,

Your two notes of yesterday have this moment come to hand, and I hasten to say that I should feel much disappointed not to see you while here; and I think instead of going to Scotland or Ireland now, I will go to Wales and return here on the 3d of July, as I am engaged to dine with Mr. Peabody on the 4th at the Star and Garter, Richmond Hill. This, I hope, will enable me to see you here at that time. Please write me where you will stop and how long remain in town.

I have just returned from the Isle of Wight, etc., and am engaged to go out and therefore have only time to say,—what you very well know already—that I am truly your friend

MILLARD FILLMORE

P.S. I am sorry to say that I am yet suffering from my eyes.

64. To MILLARD FILLMORE

Dorothea juggled her timetable and confirmed their proposed meeting in London, but she failed to convert Fillmore's plans for an excursion to Wales into a stopover at Green Bank. Her disappointment is suggested by the feeling of expectancy which runs through her letter.

Green Bank, Liverpool
June 25th, 1855

My dear Sir and Friend,

I received yours this morning. My plans are as follows: To leave Liverpool on Monday, the 2d, either in the morning (9½) or the P.M. (3½) train for London direct. I have written to take rooms at the Hotel, 22 Dover St., Piccadilly, where

I have friends. If none there are vacant, I shall go to the hotel in Hanover Square. These are neither distant from St. James Street, and have decided me. Time in London is, as you have already discovered, at a premium. If I knew that it would fall in with your plans and choice to come to Liverpool I would wait here till the 3d, and go hence to London on that day. A journey there at the same time, would afford some leisure for communication, *en route,* but I do not know whether you take in Liverpool.

I could introduce you here to pleasant friends. Should you come or go (on your way to or from Wales) by Liverpool, please let me know, and at what time, as I can arrange accordingly.

I shall not be in London this time longer than the 5th or 6th of July unless something *very* special requires it. I feel urged to Jersey as after the next month I can do nothing for the insane of that island through official influences in London, the present year. If I *do not hear from you again,* I shall still adhere to my plan of proceeding to London on Monday *the 2d.*

Green Bank, the seat of William Rathbone, Esquire, is three miles from Liverpool, or three from the Adelphi Hotel. I should much like you to see the place, if it is in your way to come from Wales for London by Liverpool.

The *shortest* note to me is sufficient; spare your eyes.

Your friend stedfastly,
D. L. Dix

[Miss D. L. Dix, June 25, 1855. Rec'd. July 3 at 12 M. Fenton's. Ans'd. July 3.]

⤙ 65. To Millard Fillmore

To avoid a last-moment confusion over time and place,
Dorothea detailed her possible movements in London.

[Liverpool]
Sunday, July 1st, 1855

My dear Sir and Friend,

It does sometimes occur that one, of a sudden, has so many objects, even of urgent need, crowding together, as to be on the point of giving up in despair, and sitting passive till the whirlwind passes.

I cannot detain you by details. I have been unexpectedly long for some sufferers for Newfoundland, and I *cannot* I believe leave Liverpool for London sooner than Tuesday Morning at 9½. I hope to be in London at 4½. I have by a sudden death in a family in Dover Street lost the rooms I expected to have secured there, and it is always a *question where one can go without a long previous notice,* in Hotels and Lodging Houses at the "full London season." (I selected that hotel having there some English friends resident just now.) So I *take* my chance. I may get in at Dover Street, 22 Piccadilly, or not; that is yet to prove. But I shall send a note to you, *if* I fail there. I know your time must be filled; mine is also much crowded, but I *cannot* give up the great gratification of seeing you and conversing with you before each again sets forward on a different course of travel.

I have thought it *just possible* that you might return from Wales via Liverpool, rather than probably. I send this forward to meet your arrival, and report myself.

Your friend stedfastedly,
D. L. Dix

I should be glad if it falls in with your convenience to find a line telling me of either your engaged hours or disengaged that I may fix mine so that I shall not miss your call; this letter rather sent to the care of the Proprietor of the Dover Street Hotel—enclosed will be kept by him till I arrive at a little past 4 or 5 P.M. All this suggestion grows out of unavoidably limited time in a place one is hardly enough acquainted with to hold fast on any aims and plans.

[Rec'd. July 3 at 12 M. at Fenton's; Ans'd. July 3.]

ᕯᔧ 41. To Dorothea Dix

Fillmore was preparing to call at six. If he did not deviate from his schedule, they had but a brief hour and one-half.

The following day Fillmore was the guest of honor of George Peabody, the wealthy American merchant, banker, and philanthropist, at his annual Fourth of July dinner at the Star and Garter. It was a gala affair with more than 250 American and English guests.

Unknown, it would appear, to Peabody, Dorothea was one of the ladies invited to sit behind a screen where they might listen unseen to the proceedings (in the Victorian Age, women were sometimes permitted to observe male festivities if they remained out of sight). From the Island of Jersey the following week she wrote to Peabody to express her approval of the sentiments which reverberated from the banquet hall.

The presence of her "esteemed countrymen," and in particular "of one, who is honored not less in the retirement of private life than he was honorable and valued as the Chief Magistrate of the United States, 'the just man,' whom one of his most determined political opponents declared in the United States Senate 'to be above corruption or any unjust act' " [July

7, 1855, Fillmore papers, Oswego] assured her a higher satis-faction than he would have supposed.

Without her knowledge Peabody forwarded the letter to Fillmore with the explanation: "I received the enclosed note this morning from the celebrated Miss Dix who it seems was behind the screen on the 4th. Hand it to Mr. Davies for perusal and return it to me" [July 17, 1855, Fillmore papers, Oswego].

Fillmore may have considered Peabody's comment gratui-tous. In any event, instead of returning it, he placed it in his valise and eventually filed it with his papers.

It would appear that the paths of the two travelers did not cross again until autumn. Returning from Jersey Dorothea ac-companied Mr. and Mrs. Rathbone to Switzerland, while Fill-more toured England, Scotland, and Ireland. In London he and the venerable Martin Van Buren, the first two ex-Presi-dents to visit England, appeared together in the gallery of the House of Commons. Fillmore attended the opera with Pea-body, visited Westminster Abby, and was presented to Queen Victoria at the Court of St. James. He declined an honorary degree from Oxford University with the explanation that his education did not warrant it.

Joining Corcoran, who had just arrived in England, he crossed the channel to Paris where he viewed the International Exposition and was presented to Emperor Napoleon III. Late in August he and Corcoran (Davies was then in Germany) proceeded to Brussels and Cologne, and thence up the Rhine to Switzerland and Geneva. At Freiburg in Switzerland in September he and Dorothea met again, but no details have survived.

Fenton's Hotel
St. James Street
Thursday 12 M., July 3, 1855.

My Dear Miss Dix,

I have just arrived from Cambridge and find your note of the 25th ult. and 1st inst. and as I am engaged to dine out at 7½ I shall venture to call on you at 6.

I am in great haste
Truly your friend
MILLARD FILLMORE

◆§ 66. TO MILLARD FILLMORE

When her stay in Switzerland was prolonged by the illness of Mr. Rathbone, Dorothea gave up hopes of reaching Paris to rejoin Fillmore; but she planned to keep in touch with his movements through mutual acquaintances.

Vevey [Switzerland]
Oct. 1 [1855]

My dear Sir and Friend,

My sojourn here by reason of the slow convalescence of two friends who have been dangerously ill, has been prolonged beyond the time I anticipated when I saw you at Freyburg; and I now see no chance of reaching Paris much earlier than the 14th or 15th of this month. I therefore enclose my notes which I hold in reserve as furnished by a friend resident in Egypt, and which I put into your possession to copy or make notes from. I may need them again, and therefore will thank you to enclose them for me should you arrive at and leave Paris previously to my coming. Mr. James Demming of New York and Mr. Wainwright will know of my arrival, and also I shall send a line to your Banker, so I shall not fail to know how you are in health. I should be sorry that you should go to Egypt without considering whether your eyes which have now for so many months been affected may not suffer *there* more seriously. I have only time to express what you already know, the stedfast friendship and esteem with which I am yours,

D. L. D.

[Miss D. L. Dix, Oct 1. Rec'd. 18, Ans'd. Oct. 19.]

ᴥ§ 67. To Millard Fillmore

Dorothea had hoped to find Fillmore in Paris upon her arrival there but was disappointed. He received her note in Amsterdam.

Paris, 14th Oct. [1855]
Hotel de la Paix, Salon No. 3
Rue de la Paix

My dear Sir and Friend,

I arrived with my friends, the Rathbone's of Liverpool, from Switzerland yesterday, and probably leave for London on Thursday or Friday of this week. I should be happy to see you, if your leisure allows. But in Paris as elsewhere you will have numerous engagements. I am almost sure I shall not return to the United States before the Spring, in either May or June.

I hope should you not have arrived at this date you will receive a package which I forwarded from Geneva, containing notes for assisting a journey to Egypt. Let me hear your plans when they are determined.

My address here you have. In London it is care of George Peabody and Company, Old Broad Street, Bankers.

With all and every good wish I am yours stedfastly as a sincere friend.

D. L. DIX

[Miss D. L. Dix, Oct. 14, 1855; Rec'd. at Amsterdam, Oct. 27.]

❧ 42. To DOROTHEA DIX

From Switzerland, Fillmore had proceeded to Munich, Regensburg, and Vienna; thence to Prague, Dresden, Magdeburg, and Berlin.

Berlin, Oct. 19th, 1855

My Dear Miss Dix,

Your kind note enclosing a memorandum for a tour in Egypt (which I herewith return), came to hand last evening. I have copied most of it, but find I shall not reach Paris until you might want it.

I shall go in a day or two to Hamburgh, Hanover, Bremen, Dusseldorf, and Amsterdam (where I may be addressed) and thence to the Hague, Antwerp and Paris.

Mr. Corcoran leaves me here for Paris. I have not time to say more than that I am ever truly yours

MILLARD FILLMORE

❧ 68. To MILLARD FILLMORE

After returning to England with the Rathbones, Dorothea prepared to set out upon a more ambitious tour of the Continent.

During the first week in November she was in Paris, and in time to welcome Fillmore when he arrived from Brussels. It

*was their third European meeting. This time it was not so
hurried.*

London, Sunday [Oct. 28?, 1855]

My valued Friend,

I have no idea where you now are, nor what your plans are
likely to embrace for the Winter, but I cannot forbear urging
you to seek some reliable pleasant companions for your remaining months in the ~~Eastern Hemisphere~~ Europe.

I arrived in England from Switzerland via France last
week, and now have arranged to revisit France (which I
merely crossed) part of Germany and Holland with Dr. [Jo-
seph] and Mrs. Parrish of Philadelphia to see the charitable
and humane Institutions of those Countries. I shall leave London if Dr. Parrish is sufficiently recovered from an indisposition, which now seems slight, on Wednesday the 31st. It is
a little doubtful which route is taken. We may or not go to
Paris first.

I hope to learn of your health and plans.

With a thousand good wishes I am cordially your friend,

D. L. DIX

[Miss Dix, Rec'd. at Paris Nov. 9 [1855].]

⋖§ 69. To MILLARD FILLMORE

*Dorothea reminded Fillmore that he was no longer Presi-
dent, and that it was more proper etiquette for him to call on
her than for her to call on him!*

*Fillmore left Paris on November 14 in company with two
Buffalo friends, Doctor Thomas M. Foote and Elam R. Jewett,
who had recently joined him. Foote took more interest in jour-
nalism and politics than in medicine. He was one of Fillmore's
most trusted advisers and had been given two foreign assign-*

ments during the latter's tenure of office. Jewett and Foote
were publishers of the Commercial Advertiser, *the Fillmore*
political organ in Buffalo.

They toured the Riviera en route to Italy, and arrived in
Rome in late December. During a month's visit there Fillmore
was presented to Pope Pius IX, but not without misgivings
over its possible political repercussions back home. "To kneel
and kiss the hand of the Pope, if not his foot," was to invite
political disaster, but the ordeal was not required. The Pope
received him sitting, "neither offering hand or foot for saluta-
tion" [Fillmore to S. G. Haven, January 22, 1856, Fillmore
papers, Buffalo, quoted in Rayback, p. 400].

Fillmore spent most of February in Naples, where he
learned of his nomination for President by the American party.
He enjoyed the hospitality of at least one family among the
local gentry and received a reluctant farewell from his uniden-
tified hostess:

> *I deplore the time was too short to see you oftener, but*
> *it has been sufficient to appreciate you and give you all my*
> *affections. My thoughts and my heart will follow you*
> *everywhere. . . . Do not forget me. . . . Your leaving*
> *Naples is distressing to me, and it is more distressing I can*
> *not express my deep feeling for you in your own language*
> *[February 27, 1856, Naples, Fillmore papers, Oswego].*

Paris [Nov. 9, 1855]

My dear Sir and Friend,

I recollect I had not the civility to say I should be glad to
see you at the Hotel de Lille et d'Albion, should your leisure
allow you to call at any of my unseasonable disengaged hours,
for example, tomorrow A.M. from 9 to 10. You are not now
President of the United States, and I suppose etiquette and

usages of society will hardly allow my calling at your drawing room; and where you receive *parties* of your friends, gentlemen and ladies, but not ladies unattended. I have been all day at Charenton, and am much tired, but I must tell you that if you visit Egypt this year the present month is *the* time for ascending the Nile, which has full banks, and can be traversed at no time so well, nor in fact without difficulty. I hope you will go.

Your friend,
D. L. Dix

Friday Evening, 7½.
[Rec'd. Nov. 10, 1855.]

◂§ 43. To Dorothea Dix

Dorothea's letter of February 5 and the one written in Rome are missing.

Separating from his companions who proceeded to Egypt, Fillmore returned to Rome in March and toured Florence, Bologna, and Venice in April. At Venice he received official notification of his nomination from the Committee of the convention. He also learned that Andrew Jackson Donelson, nephew and formerly private secretary of Andrew Jackson, had been selected as his running mate.

He was back in Paris in May, and on May 21 dispatched his acceptance of the nomination. He subscribed to the principles enunciated in the declaration of the National Council in Philadelphia, but his focus was upon the Whigs who might be drawn into the movement if they were convinced that it arose out of public necessity to cope with disunion.

Dorothea meanwhile remained in Paris for a few weeks following Fillmore's departure for Italy. Then in January, traveling alone, she proceeded to Italy by way of Marseilles to Naples and Rome, inspecting hospitals for the insane rather than works of art. At Rome she found facilities for the insane deplorable and took her case to Cardinal Antonelli, and finally to the Pope. She noted, "The appeal to the Pope involved care, patience, time and negotiation" [Quoted in Tiffany, p. 288]. But he listened and thanked her for her intervention. She was gratified later to receive word that a site had been designated for a hospital and that preliminary steps had been taken to erect an asylum on the most approved plan.

In March Dorothea was in Florence, Genoa, and Turin. Then, accepting what she considered to be a "call" to Constantinople, she crossed the Mediterranean by way of Trieste, Corfu, Athens, and Smyrna. She paused at the English military hospital at Scutari to inquire for Florence Nightingale, only to learn that she was at Balaklava. She arrived at Constantinople on April 10.

Naples, Feb'y. 13, 1856.

My Dear Miss Dix,

Your kind note of the 5th inst. reached me last evening, and another from Rome was more than two weeks in reaching this point. Fearing therefore that you may leave before you can receive this, I hasten to say, that I have concluded to remain here some 10 days or two weeks longer, and then go to Rome and spend the Holy week there or go direct to Florence. My travelling companions have gone and I am alone, resting quietly for my eyes.

I appreciate fully the good sense and sound discretion of all you have said on behalf of your friend. In all that adorns the female character, she has no parallel but yourself, and I concur in all she has said.

But I shall still hope to have the pleasure of meeting you at Rome or Florence. I intend to go on to Bologna, Venice etc. as soon as the opening Spring will render travel agreeable in that latitude.

> I am, in great haste,
> Truly your friend
> MILLARD FILLMORE

⌇§ 70. To MILLARD FILLMORE

Leaving Constantinople on April 30 Dorothea traveled up the Danube River to Vienna. Continuing northward by way of Prague and Hamburg she circled the Baltic Sea, visiting St. Petersburg, Sweden, Norway, Denmark, Holland, and Belgium before returning to France and England.

> Belgrade, Upper Danube
> May 1st, 1856

I learnt in Constantinople that probably you would be in England sometime this month, and in the idea that a letter may possibly reach you before you embark for the United States I wish to express good wishes for your safe voyage and auspicious return to the country which expects you. I have thought it best to defer my return voyage for a short time, perhaps two months or three.

In visiting Constantinople I have found the Turkish hospitals much better than I had expected; and the Greek and Armenian with some things so good that one is astonished to see others *very bad*. This is the more striking in contrast with the Moslem Institutions. Altogether there is much in Stamboul and its vast suburbs to interest a visitor for one or two weeks, but the aspects of society are so semi-barbarous that one would not desire to reside in a place where the feelings are so pained by witnessing ignorance and degradation. Nothing can be finer than the situation at Constantinople. It is to be regretted that you did not embrace this Eastern Empire of Europe in your tour. I have thought you would possibly yet visit St. Petersburgh if your time allows.

I will not trouble you now with comments upon past or present affairs, either general or special.

I hope to hear of your entire prosperity and health, and that all your life is prosperous.

I shall not write again. Indeed I regard the fact doubtful of this hasty page coming to your hand.

Your sincere and stedfast friend,
D. L. Dix

[Miss D. L. Dix, May 1. Rec'd. June 3, 1856; Ans'd. June 7.]

⳥§ 44. To Dorothea Dix

Finding no communications from Dorothea after May 1, and not aware of her movements after leaving Belgrade, Fillmore bade her farewell and prepared to board a Liverpool steamer for home.

Brunswick Hotel
Jermyn [?] St. London
Sat. June 7, 1856

My Dear Miss Dix,

I have but a moment to say that I received your kind and welcome note of May 1st from Belgrade just as I was leaving Paris. I arrived here night before last, and have taken my passage in the Atlantic for the 11th inst. and shall go to Liverpool *via* Manchester.

I hoped to meet you here and to have had the pleasure of your company on the voyage, but have inquired for you in vain. May Heaven bless you is the sincere prayer of your friend

MILLARD FILLMORE

๙§ 71. To MILLARD FILLMORE

Three months after Fillmore's return Dorothea disembarked at New York and prepared to return to her work after an absence of two years.

The letter to which she refers would appear to be Fillmore's from London on June 7.

Trenton, N. Jersey
Oct. 8th, 1856

My dear Sir and Friend,

I have pleasure even at this late time in acknowledging your letter received long indeed after date, following my return from Russia and Norway. I can hardly suppose your mind sufficiently free at this time to enter with interest on details of my travels through the Kingdoms of Europe, and limit myself to the announcement of safe arrival in my own country by the Baltic after a passage more than usually favorable at this season.

I trust your health is good, but am not without a little uneasiness as regards your sight, since I do not imagine the conditions of recovery as laid down by Oculists consulted are likely to be observed. *Rest* at least you have not had of late.

I go tomorrow to Philadelphia, 291 Chestnut Street, and after a time to New York and New England.

With all friendly wishes for your best prosperity, I am your friend, sincerely

D. L. DIX

[Miss Dix, Oct. 8, Rec'd. 9, 1856; Ans'd. Oct. 9.]

7

Rejection and
Acceptance

1856–1858

illmore returned from Europe in late June of 1856 to become absorbed immediately in the Presidential campaign as the nominee of the American party and a remnant of the Whig party. In the absence of modern techniques to sample public opinion, it would appear that he envisioned a possible victory, either in the Electoral College or the House of Representatives.

Returning from Europe in October Dorothea found the raucous campaign of the unlettered nativists distasteful, and she regretted Fillmore's involvement. But out of loyalty to him she hoped for his success.

Following his defeat Fillmore withdrew from politics, and for a time considered a position in business. But it did not materialize, and he lived in retirement. By contrast, Dorothea resumed her campaign in the states to provide asylums, and thereby take the insane out of almshouses and jails. She became more absorbed in her work, if such were possible.

Their correspondence continued but they found less to

write about. Meanwhile, Fillmore's almost chance acquaintance (it was arranged by mutual friends) with Caroline McIntosh led to their marriage on February 11, 1858. He had made no mention of her to Miss Dix.

After waiting for several months for his letter or an announcement, and receiving none, Dorothea asked whether her congratulations would be acceptable. Their correspondence was thereby resumed—but on a more limited basis.

◄§ 45. To DOROTHEA DIX

When Fillmore arrived in New York on the night of June 22 his partisans were on hand to greet him. Delegations of Know-Nothings from the New York area crowded the docks and cascaded rockets illuminated the sky. A fifty-cannon salute added exuberance to his welcome. A committee of the Common Council presented him with the keys to the city, and he responded with a plea for unity—it would be the watchword of his campaign:

> *If there be those either North or South who desire an administration for the North as against the South, or for the South as against the North, they are not the men who should give their suffrages to me. For my own part, I know only my country, my whole country, and nothing but my country* [Fillmore at Home, *Buffalo, 1856, p. 4*].

His trip from New York to Buffalo, spread over a full week, was a triumphal procession from beginning to end. He made at least twenty-seven appearances before large and enthusiastic audiences, the whole suggesting spontaneity rather than a preconceived plan. His responses offered scarcely a hint of his connection with Know-Nothingism. At Newburgh he affirmed, "I have no hostility to foreigners. . . . Having witnessed their deplorable condition in the old country, God forbid I should add to their sufferings by refusing them an asylum in this" [Ibid. *p. 12*].

Fillmore also denied a dislike for any religious creed, but he declared he would oppose the use of religion for political purposes. *"Religion and politics should not be mingled"* [Ibid. *p. 12*].

Everywhere he decried sectionalism. At Albany, using words he may have regretted later, he asserted that their southern brethren would not submit to a Republican President and Vice President chosen by the exclusive suffrage of the North. *"Therefore you must see that if this sectional party succeeds, it leads inevitably to the destruction of this beautiful fabric reared by our forefathers"* [Fillmore Papers, *Vol. II, p. 21*].

Republicans seized upon this statement to charge that Fillmore was justifying southern secession. Though he refuted the charge, he did not silence it.

While Fillmore was en route from England the Republican party nominated John C. Frémont, the romantic hero of western explorations, but neophyte politician, and the Democrats chose the veteran politician and diplomat, James Buchanan. Their actions set up a three-way race for the Presidency.

Fillmore's welcome home to Dorothea was warm: *"Will you not visit Buffalo?"*

Buffalo, Oct. 9, 1856.

My Dear Miss Dix,

I have this moment received your favor of the 8th and congratulate you most sincerely upon your safe arrival in your native land. I have looked long and anxiously for your safe return, and hoped to have the pleasure of meeting you; but you do not speak of coming this way.

I am, as you must see, involved in the presidential contest and therefore a prisoner of State. I can not therefore hope to see you unless you come here. Will you not visit Buffalo? If you do please to advise me of your intention in advance, and come directly to my house. I am not in a situation to entertain, but I can give you a cordial welcome and comfortable accommodations.

I should be happy of an opportunity to talk over your rambles in the East. You went farther and saw much more than I did; and I should profit by your observations.

I am very well except my eyes—they are better but I have to favor them—*as much as I can!*

I am of course very busy, but not too busy to see you.

I am as ever
Sincerely your friend
MILLARD FILLMORE

◆§ 72. To MILLARD FILLMORE

Despite her reservations regarding the influx of Irish immigrants, Dorothea was not happy with the American party. Its appeal to the fears and prejudices of the masses, its grass-roots leadership and anti-intellectualism, and its background of secrecy left her embarrassed and uncomfortable. Like thousands of her countrymen she found fanatical Free Soil Republicanism, the Democratic party with its southern orientation, and the American party with its roots in Know-Nothingism almost equally distasteful.

Boston, Oct'r. 19th, 1856

My dear Sir and Friend,

I have your letter of the 9th and would have written sooner if I could have seen a little clearer my engagements in the measures consuming time. I do not think it *expedient* to visit Western New York at present, though to communicate to you information relating to Russia, Sweden and Turkey would certainly be very satisfactory, as you express a wish to know through conversation the results of my observations. I fear you would desire to learn more than the limits of time I could spend in the [conversation] referred to allowed me to reach. I am much concerned that your eyes still afflict you, and fear that the too long delay in adopting remedial means will confirm the malady, if it is not already chronic.

It is now all too late to offer opinions respecting the Presidential nominations. If I could really have sped to you the voice of the guardian Angel I would have urged a different course than has been adopted, but the course of great events has an impulse beyond our ordinary sway.

God keep you my friend, and, if a prayer would hallow your life, mine would invoke on your existence every good.

Your friend stedfastly,
D. L. Dix

[D. L. Dix, Oct. 19. Rec'd. 21, 1856.]

◄§ 73. To Millard Fillmore

At this late date Dorothea doubted that Fillmore was a member of the Know-Nothings. She decided to ask him, hoping that his answer would be in the negative.

She was not alone in this wish. Many of his old Whig friends who would have supported him as a Whig and, possibly, as a Republican, could not stomach Know-Nothingism.

28 Sumner St.
Boston, Oct. 22d [1856]

Honorable Millard Fillmore
My dear Sir and Friend,

I wish to make an inquiry which you may not find it your pleasure to answer and I therefore promise that except you choose to acknowledge this letter I shall not think it any discourtesy or unfriendliness if it be passed by.

I would, for strong reasons affecting the views of certain of your most valuable political friends, know whether you are a Member of the "Order of Know Nothings." Whether in your own House previously to your departure from America for Europe you summarily joined that party informally or formally? And if any persons were authorized to declare you a member at the Convention in Philadelphia?

I am not a declamatory politician, but many discussions occur in my presence and a quiet word or two now and then might not be useless. Only I should much like a higher authority than my own *opinion* on this question.

Hoping you are well, and not much harassed by the present aspect of affairs I am as always stedfastly your friend,

D. L. Dix

[Miss D. L. Dix, Oct. 22. Rec'd. 29, 1856; Ans'd. Oct. 30.]

◄§ 46. To Dorothea Dix

Despite his reliance upon Dorothea's discretion, Fillmore took the precaution of writing "Private" at the top of his sheet. His reply to her question may be his most candid explanation of his connection with Know-Nothingism. He too disliked its secrecy, and was hesitant to become involved. But with the lure of the Presidency inviting him he swallowed his pride and took the plunge, since it seemed to offer the only means of

*piecing together a national party and the only vehicle which
might carry him into the Presidency.*

*The account of his initiation in his own house agrees with
a reminiscence of a member of the local council of the order.
(See T. C. White to Andrew Langdon, December 8, 1898,
Fillmore papers, Buffalo.)*

In accepting the American party nomination Fillmore
clung to the hope that he could count upon the support of
Whigs who were resisting the stampede to Republicanism. If
the election had been held a year earlier his logic might have
been sound, but continuing violence in Kansas, where Free
Soil men and proslavery adherents were resorting to violence
rather than ballots to gain control of the territorial government,
polarized the Whigs, northern members moving into the Republican camp and southern, into the Democratic fold. The
latter looked kindly upon the Democratic sponsored Kansas-
Nebraska Act, since it had opened the door in Kansas to
slavery, where it had been previously excluded by the Missouri
Compromise of 1820.

Thus Fillmore's southern supporters asked reassurances
that he would not seek the repeal of the Kansas-Nebraska Act,
while his northern followers asked him to repudiate it and
reaffirm the Missouri Compromise, which had restricted
slavery in territories north of the 36° 30' line. There was no
middle position, and Fillmore could only speak in the broad-
est and most meaningless generalities.

His position deteriorated further in May. In the course of
twenty-four hours, the savage caning of Charles Sumner by
Preston S. Brooks in the Senate Chamber at Washington and
the cold-blooded murder of five proslavery men in Kansas by
John Brown and his posse in retribution for the sacking of
the Free Soil town of Lawrence by a proslavery marshal converted thousands of doubters into Republicans.

Even the American party was not immune as the national and local councils split upon the issue of free soil. Bolters who soon found a niche in the Republican party included Senator Henry Wilson of Massachusetts and former Governor Nathaniel Banks, also of Massachusetts; the latter would soon become Speaker of the House of Representatives.

Diehard Whigs from North and South gathered in Philadelphia on September 17 to add their voices to the Fillmore cause. It was but a skeleton of the party's earlier conventions, but it enlisted a cluster of older leaders who refused to abandon their traditional orientation. Edward Bates, later to be Lincoln's Attorney General, served as Chairman, and Alexander H. H. Stuart and William A. Graham, former members of Fillmore's Cabinet, ex-Governor Washington Hunt of New York, and Francis Granger, President Harrison's Postmaster General, lent their prestige to the proceedings. "Nothing but Fillmore's election," Bates insisted, could subdue the mad factions of the time, and restore peace and harmony to a distracted people. "And my prayer to God is that he will bless the Nation by enabling us to place at its head a man of moderation, order and peace. We cannot command success, but we can deserve it" [Bates to Fillmore, September 24, 1856, Fillmore papers, Oswego]. The nomination, coming as it did, from men who were both national leaders and old associates lifted Fillmore's spirits, and he accepted it with the "strongest emotions of gratitude and pride" [Fillmore to Bates, October 1, 1856, Fillmore papers, Oswego].

Private   Buffalo, N. Y. Oct. 30, 1856

My Dear Miss Dix,
    Your kind favor of the 22d. came to hand yesterday, inquiring—if I read a-right—"whether I am a member of the

'Order of Know Nothings,' and whether in my own house, previously to my departure from America for Europe, I summarily joined that party, informally or formally, and if any persons were authorized to declare me a member at the convention in Philadelphia?"

In answer to all which permit me to say, frankly; that when I saw the Whig party demoralized, and efforts made to convert it, at the North, into a sectional, abolition party, I advised my friends to unite with the American or Know Nothing party, and maintain a national organization in favor of the *Union*. Many did, and I was often pressed to follow my own advice and give the influence of my name to the party; which I was reluctant to do; mainly, because I had withdrawn from politics, and did not like the secrecy of the Order; but I finally overcame my scruples and at a council in my own house, previously to my departure for Europe, I was initiated into the order and became a member, and am one now. While I did not intend to take any public or active part I neither sought secrecy nor to give publicity to the fact of my membership. No one was authorized to proclaim me such at the Philadelphia convention, though several members of that convention knew me to be a member. I suppose, indeed, the fact was generally known, as it had been announced in the papers. I believe this is a full answer to your inquiries; but I have not time to say more than to express my sincere regret that I am not likely to have the pleasure of meeting you this fall.

I hope soon to have more rest for my eyes, which I am not able to favor as I desire.

I am in great haste,
Truly and Sincerely, Your friend
Millard Fillmore

◆§ 74. To Millard Fillmore

Dorothea does not indicate the source of her information regarding John P. Kennedy's alleged "embarrassment." The noted author and former Secretary of the Navy in Fillmore's Cabinet was in Europe from the spring of 1856 until mid-October—just a few days after Dorothea's return. He approved of Fillmore's nomination by the American party and wrote to him from London (Fillmore was then in Italy) urging him to accept. It would appear that he conferred with Fillmore in London just before the latter's departure for the United States to urge him to act, not knowing that Fillmore had accepted a few weeks earlier.

Upon his arrival in the United States Kennedy immediately enlisted his services in Fillmore's behalf, still confident that he would come out on top. (See Kennedy to Fillmore, May 31, 1856, and October 18, 1856, Fillmore papers, Oswego.) Thus there seems to have been no misunderstanding.

Dorothea expressed her gratification and satisfaction with Fillmore's explanation of his association with Know-Nothingism. But between the lines it is evident that she was encountering many criticisms of Fillmore from her friends and professional associates.

Boston, Nov. 3d, 1856

My dear Sir and Friend,

I have your letter of the 30th for which I beg you to receive my sincere thanks, the more fully expressed from the sense I have of your generous confidence and your courtesy in replying to inquiries which might wear the aspect of pressing upon *personal reserves*. I felt as I wrote almost rebuked but you cannot think how much I have wished to know the *facts* of your position in relation with your friends, and your former supporters. I am quite satisfied had I read but one phrase of your letter, viz, *"it was in the papers at the time."* Of course, if your alliance with the American or Know Nothing Party was a fact before the Public, you could not have misguided your friend Mr. Kennedy nor embarrassed his proceedings. I do not care so much for controlling the opinions of my friends as *knowing* that they are *quite* true to high and honorable principles. This position my judgment had given you, and I could not bear to believe that you could waver from the exactent [*sic*] simplicity of integrity.

I consider your communication confidential, and having only to be reassured in my own convictions of your rightness and uprightness, I do not intend to discuss the subject with others.

I am much concerned that you suffer from your weakness of sight, and beg you will use the care so imperatively necessary to preserve you from total loss of vision.

You surely could have no time for talking over European affairs, and ranging from Italy, Turkey, Hungary, Austria, Prussia, Russia, Norway, etc., if I were in your vicinity. So you should not deceive yourself in the idea that this would be realized if I were travelling in Western New York towards Toronto.

God keep you for [the] good of our Country.

Your friend stedfastly,

D. L. Dix

[Miss D. L. Dix, Nov. 3, Rec'd. 5, 1856; Ans'd. Nov. 5.]

✍§ 47. To Dorothea Dix

Fillmore carried only Maryland. The popular vote in the thirty states was: Buchanan 1,838,169, Frémont 1,341,264; Fillmore 874,534.

From hindsight Fillmore's defeat comes as no surprise. Candidate of a splinter group which lacked prestige, newspapers, money, and experience in politics, and had a penchant for antagonizing the public, he had to attract thousands of voters who had traditionally supported the Whigs. But the Republican crusade enlisted so many of these voters in the North that Fillmore ran a poor third there. Meanwhile, in the South the specter of a "Black Republican" victory frightened many Whigs into the ranks of the Democrats—albeit reluctantly—as the lesser evil. It is worth noting that Fillmore ran a close second in four southern states. He might have won them had not voters closed ranks at the last moment to defeat Frémont. Success in those states would have thrown the election into the House of Representatives.

During the campaign Fillmore's record as Congressman and President was minutely inspected, and he was besieged by inquiries to clarify his position.

From the South: Did his support of the right of petition in Congress in 1838 indicate that he favored abolition? As President, why did he pardon "slave stealers"? If elected, would he favor the restoration of the Missouri Compromise line? would he sign a bill emancipating slaves in the District of Columbia?

And from the North: As President, would he support the extension of slavery into territories now free? Because of his oath as a Know-Nothing would he proscribe a Roman Catholic on account of his religion?

Obviously, he could not satisfy one correspondent without antagonizing another. Therefore he said almost nothing.

Despite his many handicaps, however, a corps of almost forgotten volunteers worked early and late to sustain him. Hundreds of correspondents testified to their support, and most remained optimistic until the closing days of the contest.

Worthy of particular mention are Solomon G. Haven and Anna Ella Carroll. Haven, a former law partner of Fillmore and currently the Congressman from the Buffalo district, headed the Washington organization and worked tirelessly to coordinate the state and local councils. His identification with Fillmore's campaign probably defeated his own bid for reelection and terminated his promising political career.

The glamorous and imperious Miss Carroll, a member of a distinguished Maryland family and daughter of Governor Thomas King Carroll, entered the fray as a ghost writer and self-designated strategist for Fillmore. Despite a constant struggle to find money she ground out a prodigious quantity of press releases in which she trumpeted the virtues of Fillmore and warned of the menace of Catholicism. Her Great American Battle or the Contest between Christianity and Political Romanism, *"a Book for Every True American!" became the Bible of the party.*

Fillmore seems to have left almost no record of his own hopes and doubts, but his composure did not fail him during or after the election.

Buffalo, N. Y., Nov. 5, 1856

My Dear Miss Dix,

The election is over and I am defeated; yet I feel no regret, but a sincere satisfaction that I am relieved from all apprehension of being again called to the laborious and thankless task of administering this government at the risk of losing what little reputation I now possess. I therefore ask no condolence from my friends but rather their congratulations. Let us hope that the government may be so administered for 4 years to come as to allay this dangerous, growing hostility between the

North and the South, and restore that cordial Union, so necessary to our peace and prosperity.

I have your favor of the 3d but regret to say that there are some few words which I am unable to decypher [sic]. This is my fault and not yours; but from what I can read, I infer that you do not approve of the American Party, nor of my becoming a member of it. That is a point which I shall not attempt to argue with you on paper, but when we meet I shall be happy to do so. I will only say now, that if you understand the whole subject, and after a deliberate consideration of it, have come to the conclusion that it is wrong, I should distrust my own opinion, and doubt the propriety of my position. For I regard you—as I ever have—as my Mentor, more likely to be right from that intuitive knowledge peculiar to the elevated mind of our intelligent and refined female, than man is, with all his boasted powers of reasoning. But of this let us talk when we meet, if that pleasure is ever accorded to us.

But there is one thing in your letter which I think I read aright, but do not understand. You say "If your alliance with the American Know Nothing party was a fact before the public—you could not have *misguided* your friend, Mr. Kennedy, nor *embarrassed his* proceedings."

What Mr. Kennedy do you refer to and what *embarrassment* of his proceedings? I confess all this is perfectly enigmatical to me. I was not aware that he pretended that I had *misguided* him or that he was *embarrassed* by my position. Be so kind as to explain.

If, as I now suppose, the election has gone for Mr. Buchannan [sic] by the people, I shall be relieved from all further annoyance and responsibility after a few days, and should you go west or visit Toronto, I hope you will not fail to accept the hospitalities of my humble residence during your stay in

Buffalo. Be assured that I shall be most happy to see you; and talk over your European travels.

I am truly yours
MILLARD FILLMORE

◄§ 75. To MILLARD FILLMORE

Dorothea offers her post mortem on the campaign. She would have urged him, if she had had the opportunity, to decline the nomination and to wait.

The months of separation in Europe and at home had not dimmed her sense of responsibility for his welfare. She asked for his promise to safeguard his eyes and recommended that he find a home in the vicinity of New York, where he would find life more challenging.

Boston, Nov. 8th, 1856

My dear Friend,

I have your letter answering mine of the 3d. First, I can not condole with such a man as you on loss of Official Station; it is the Country which is to be commisserated [*sic*], which by a series of unexampled blunders has now produced a crisis which the most discerning and calm judging minds consider to be perilous beyond all former example. The masses are too ignorant, the educated too busy, too self-seeking or too procrastinating to heed the real facts of our National position. I cannot properly express opinions upon subjects which 1 have had neither the time nor the opportunity of properly studying or reflecting upon. My sympathies have been from the first, with the American party: whether this had been the fact or not my confidence in your rectitude of purpose would have been steady and firm. If I *could* have communicated to you in Europe, one earnest word of entreaty, when you rec'd. the news of your nomination, it would have besought you to decline it *un-*

der the *then* existing state of parties; though such a prayer might have been unavailing. I felt that a refusal then might make a *future* election certain. Perhaps I was mistaken; but hope for the salvation of the Country nurtured that opinion. One cannot but wonder how little men do to accomplish the idea of their own highest perception. More than ¾ the votes cast for *Fremont* were given not because Fremont was approved, but solely because it was supposed his position at this time might enable his supporters to carry out aims not assured in the platform of the "American Party." Mr. Fremont was not the man the *sense* of the people approved. I have heard hundreds say that if Mr. Fillmore occupied the place on which Mr. Fremont stood he would be elected over all opposition for he was the man of the *real* choice. This I believe.

But my friend, you ask a question I cannot fully answer on paper. "What Mr. Kennedy I mean?" "Who I referred to in my letter?" Of course, no other than your Secretary of the Navy; and who was *said* to have your confidence, *"to be the exponent of your private opinions; on your own authority,"* and to have been left to *act* for you during your absence. It was advanced at a large dinner that Mr. Kennedy had been *deceived* by *you* concerning the *Know Nothing* Membership; that with him, you stood on *one* proposed basis, on another secretly with the Know Nothings. Now many things might have been said of you, which if not advantageous I should have heeded little and never debated, but I *could not* hear your probity, your truthfulness, your upright career questioned, and I put a rather direct and peremptory question to the parties, requiring of them *evidence* that you had deceived Mr. Kennedy or any other person. I cannot go here upon details, but it was enough for my purpose to know that you had not linked yourself furtively with intriguers or done any thing in secret. If the newspapers recorded your course, Mr. Kennedy could not have been deceived. I did not believe it at any moment, only there are times when one feels that there is advantage in seeing one's strongest column of faith receive new support from without. I should like to converse with you on these subjects, as well as on the more cheerful topics of European affairs, but I repeat what I have already written in a former letter, a visit in Buffalo would I think be inexpedient if not absolutely indiscreet.

Affairs connected with some ill-established public Institutions, seem likely to keep me here for ten days or a fortnight longer. I trust now, you will take care of your eyes: promise me that you will; and that nothing shall interfere with this duty to yourself and to your friends. I trust whatever plans you may have for the disposition of your time, however you may dispose of your future, you will first have considered that your eyes have been long neglected, and that you cannot with impunity allow the malady to exist without curative treatment. I rather hope you will finally determine to reside in or near the City of New York. I think you may find more there to occupy your mind, and higher means of being useful to the public, than elsewhere.

I have written hurriedly and I am afraid not satisfactorily, but if you read clearly, that in simplicity of faith and sincerity I am your friend, as heretofore, I shall not think my pen ill employed.

God bless you,
D. L. Dix

[Miss D. L. Dix, Nov. 8, Rec'd. 11, 1856.]

76. To Millard Fillmore

It is obvious that Dorothea was trying to stir Fillmore into action. He did not heed her suggestion to visit Cuba.

Unknown to her at the time, Fillmore made a trip to New York where he conferred with his banker and met callers. They may have been only a few miles or hours apart.

Boston, Nov'b. 26th [1856]

My dear Sir and Friend,

My few lines to you have been so hurried, I have been so exceedingly occupied both mentally and in time, that you, as all my correspondents, have had much reason for believing themselves quite neglected; and my special friends may have felt that general objects and the pursuits of my *Vocation* are allowed to be too engrossing. It is not easy to meet the wishes and expectations of these and to satisfy at the same time my sense of duty towards the unfortunate who claim my cares. Amidst many occupations however I have thought of the weary exciting days you must have spent during the past summer, and though I know your equanimity is not easily disturbed, the political state of our Country has been such that no good man, or sincere patriot, could witness with calmness the agitating scenes which have been presented. It is not a little singular to observe how suddenly the election excitements have subsided. Our busy, money-making, and excitable people, from the hour of casting their votes seem to forget that greedy politicians, and wordy demagogues have ruled *them* and made them *their* tools for selfish and narrow ends. Thus it is with the masses. The more rational and reflecting are anxious and silent: past mistakes can not be rectified; present clear-sightedness will not reverse the wheels of time, and give opportunity for repeating past acts, with the aid of a clearer understanding. The regrets in many quarters are sincere; not that Fremont has been less fortunate than Buchanan, but that Fillmore is not to be the next President of the United States. I have not attempted to plunge into the turbid stream of circumstances out of which the *present* has emerged, and which was at its full height during my absence, but I have learned enough to convince me that our people need to *suffer* in order to bring them to such reflection as shall regulate national affairs with such prudence as shall assure security.

My friend, as you will now have time at your disposal, I wish to know first of all if you are taking *care* to use all possible means for the recovery of your eyes; the complaint must become chronic if you allow the affection to go on without adopting prescribed remedies.

By the way, shall you not probably visit Cuba this winter? I think that Island would present much to interest your mind and occupy time. There are singular social aspects in those Islands, so near to our southern shores, worth the note of intelligent minds.

I have been unexpectedly detained here in New England, and only now begin to hope I may get on to New York by Thursday of next week. I can not ask you to use your eyes for my gratification, but if without effort, you can say how you are, addressing your letter care of Charles L. Francis Esq., Bookseller, Broadway, New York, I shall be gratified, and obliged. So late as the season now is I do not think I shall visit the Canadas. My own people have also present claims, more time consuming than I had counted on.

My general letter address is under enclosure to Dr. Buttolph, State Hospital, Trenton, New Jersey, but I shall not task your hand, only as a long-tried friend must expect to hear of your welfare occasionally.

Yours with esteem and *just* appreciation,

D. L. Dix

[D. L. Dix, Nov. 26, Rec'd, Dec. 5, 1856, Ans'd. Dec. 17.]

❧ 77. To Millard Fillmore

Dorothea seems to have limited her travels to the Boston area for several months after her return from Europe. But she now turned to New York State for an investigation of the insane in almshouses. She made Buffalo a priority, and hoped that she might see Fillmore the following week.

She learned of Fillmore's visit to New York in a Boston newspaper.

291 Chestnut St.
Phila.
Dec'b. 16th, 1856

My dear Sir and Friend,

I arrived here last evening by the late Express Train, called by some affairs of the State Hospital, and return to New York on Friday. Very unexpectedly to myself, I find my duty to the poor insane will call me to the western part of the State next week. I now intend proceeding on Monday to Albany and Utica, and on Wednesday to Rochester or possibly at once to Buffalo.

I prefer that my proposed investigation of the Alms housing, of which I get *very* bad accounts, should not be known and anticipated. I am informed on reliable authority, that there are now more than *one hundred* of these afflicted persons in *chains* in the Western districts.

My plan is to go to Mr. H[osmer]'s in Niagara Street, and ask him, and perhaps some other gentlemen, to go at the same time as myself to the Alms House of Buffalo. You asked if I should at any time visit your city to inform you in anticipation. I trust you will not be absent, for I should be much gratified to see you during my short sojourn in your city. I learn by the journals of the day that you have recently visited New York

City, and hope the journey was promotive of your health and pleasure.

I have so little supposed that you are distressed at the result of the late elections that I have had no motive for expressing sympathy that the Country is the losing party, not you; and this fact is felt by most reflecting minds, and by all your friends, of whom there are a "great company." The respect and regard in which you are holden by vast numbers who lamented that you were not the Anti-Slavery candidate is really remarkable; and if because you did not forswear yourself like Fremont, and utter promises vague and silly as he did, you had not the best good of the Country at heart. Men for the most part are influenced by feelings, stimulated by passing accidents, not by reason and substantial facts. I am sorry for the result of the present vote only for the Union, which will suffer through the senseless course the people in majority have taken. God spare us disgrace, and the punishment deserved under such a headlong career of folly.

I shall not write to Mr. and Mrs. Hosmer that I am coming at this time, having a special invitation for all times. I should really prefer going to the Hotel, but think it on the whole best not.

Your friend with esteem[?]

D. L. Dix

[Miss D. L. Dix, Dec. 16; Rec'd. 19, 1856; Ans'd Dec. 22.]

ᴥᔥ 48. To Dorothea Dix

Fillmore's observation that he had delayed writing in order to rest his eyes seems to have been more of an excuse than an explantion. He had been actively engaged in post-election correspondence and preparations for his trip to New York.

Miss Rhoda Fuller's family, lifelong friends of both Fill-
more and Abigail in Cayuga County, lived at this time in
Skaneateles. Fillmore and Powers had found seclusion in their
home immediately after Abby's death. The Fullers volunteered
Rhoda's services and Fillmore engaged her as a hostess and
housekeeper (if she was a cousin, she was a distant one). Fill-
more's widowed sister, Olive Johnson, resided in Dexter,
Michigan.

Buffalo, N.Y. Dec. 17, 1856

My Dear Miss Dix,

Since the election I have been trying to favor my eyes;
hence my neglect of your kind favor of the 26th ult. from Boston. I learn by a paragraph in the paper that you were recently
in New York, like a ministering angel as you are, devoting
yourself to the alleviation of the sufferings of the unfortunate.
Your favor arrived here during my absence in New York, and
I presume you arrived there the day after I left—Thursday,
Nov. 6th [Dec. 8]. I should have been most happy to have
met you; and had I known you were coming would have staid
a day longer for that purpose.

My eyes are better—quite well when I do not use them.
But I regret to say that My Cousin's eyes,—Miss Fuller—are
now suffering from weakness so that she can not read to me,
but my sister and Judge Hall's daughter are with me, and they
kindly supply that deficiency. So I am not wholly without occupation or amusement, and I am happy to add that my spirits
are good and my health perfect.

I did think I would go to Cuba, but the dread of seasick-
ness, and the want of a pleasant travelling companion, have
finally induced me to give it up, and I shall probably spend the
winter in Buffalo.

You must pardon this short note and believe me, as I ever am

Your sincere friend
MILLARD FILLMORE

*§ 49. To DOROTHEA DIX

Fillmore prepares to welcome Dorothea in Buffalo.
His letter reached her in Utica, where she was inspecting the state asylum there.

Buffalo, Dec. 22, 1856

My Dear Miss Dix,

I have your favor of the 16th by which I am happy to hear that we may soon expect to see you here. I write, therefore, merely to say that I shall be most happy to extend to you the hospitalities of my house during your stay in Buffalo. I have hesitated a little about giving this invitation, as I am expecting some of my relatives from the West to spend the holidays with me, and if they should come, we might not be able to make you as comfortable as I could desire, but be assured, you shall be *welcome,* and I shall be most happy to see you.

Sincerely your friend
MILLARD FILLMORE

*§ 78. To MILLARD FILLMORE

Despite her desire to see Fillmore, Dorothea does not overlook proprieties appropriate to her sex. "I acknowledge your friendly offer of the hospitalities of your house, but am clearly of opinion that I should decline a visit with you for the present."

Utica, Dec'b. 25th [1856]

My dear Sir and Friend,

I received your two letters, the one in New York, that of
more recent date here last evening, and am glad that your
kindred are both residents in your house and guests at your fire
side. I am glad too, that your eyes are giving you improved
sight. God grant you continued health and wide usefulness.

It is my intention to arrive in Buffalo in A.M. of Saturday
next if possible, probably by some evening train. If very late I
shall go to the Hotel, if early to Mr. Hosmer's. I acknowledge
your friendly offer of the hospitalities of your house, but am
clearly of opinion that I should decline a visit with you for the
present. I may perhaps take tea with your sister on Sunday
evening. I shall not remain in Buffalo longer than Monday or
Tuesday I believe.

Sincerely and stedfastly your friend,

D. L. DIX

[Dec. 25; Rec'd. 28, 1856.]

✍§ 79. To MILLARD FILLMORE

*Fillmore entertained Dorothea, but beyond the few com-
ments in her letter no other details have been found.*

*She made an inspection of Buffalo's insane (she found
conditions unsatisfactory), and then continued her junket as
far as Toronto. Her swing through Buffalo, Toronto, Syracuse,
and Utica had consumed little more than a week.*

*She was now awaiting in Albany a vote in the legislature
on the creation of mental hospitals in western and eastern
New York.*

Onondaga, January 4th [1857]

My dear Sir and Friend,

A few leisure moments allows me time to write and give expression to the pleasure I have enjoyed in seeing you so well and comfortable in your own cherished home. The harassing and unsettled scenes of the past six months have passed and left you as usual, serene and self-possessed, unhurt and un-burthened. I am almost tempted to complain of you as not quite kind in your friendship towards me, or rather not quite faithful to your knowledge of its sincerity, in never having told me how fortunate and happy you are in possessing the services and society of your pleasing young relative, Miss Fuller. I should have felt much comforted in the knowledge that your house was brightened by the presence of that sweet-voiced, sweet-mannered woman. I trust the disability of weak sight under which she now suffers will be removed. The privation of a free use of the eyes must be very great, and hourly missed.

I did not return to Buffalo from Toronto, as seemed possible when I took leave of friends there, on account of increasingly inclement weather for the prosecution of the objects I had proposed to accomplish this winter and abridged time for making practical use of the facts collected during visits to the Poor Houses of Western and Central New York. I am deeply pained as much as disappointed in the results of investigations: the want of system, prudent expenditure of funds, and humane care of the poor, the sick, the aged, the insane and the helpless are astonishing when the intelligence and ability of communities are considered.

Delavan House, Albany, 19th Jan. [1857]

I had written the preceding pages of this letter my dear friend when interruptions obliged me to place aside the paper, and till this date I have been too much occupied to resume the pen and add a brief conclusion.

I think the Bill already introduced for establishing two Hospitals, one in Eastern, the other in Western New York will pass the Senate without difficulty; there will be opposition in the House, but I think not so much as to defeat the measure. That which is of at least equal importance is yet to be considered and matured, *viz.*, revision of the Pauper Laws, and exact and searching review of the System on which the State Prisons and County Jails and Penitentiaries are conducted. New York is disgraced by its Penal Institutions as well as by the Administration of its Charitable Houses. They are with rare exceptions schools and Nurseries of Crime and Vice. But this unwelcome topic may be dismissed. At least it is not necessary to place before my friends what I must make present to my own thoughts and the subject for my own consideration.

I shall not remain constantly here; it is not necessary, but intend seeing other of the public Institutions from time to time as opportunity offers. My letter address will uniformly be Trenton, New Jersey, whence, wherever I may be, letters will be forwarded. But I am *socially,* so poor a correspondent that I feel no obligation rests upon my friends to sustain written communication. And if all goes well with them, I do not urge frequent writing. In prosperity they do not need my sympathy; in trouble I have a right to share their afflictions.

You will not reply to this note of course as an act of courtesy; that is not necessary. But if your eyes are strong and your inclination prompts, I need not say, what you must know, that I have always pleasure in receiving your letters.

Your friend, appreciatingly, and with stedfast regard,

D. L. DIX

[Miss D. L. Dix, Jan'y. 4 & 19, Rec'd. 26, 1857, Ans'd. Feb. 2d.]

50. To Dorothea Dix

Fillmore makes a rather tardy explanation of Miss Fuller, and adds an eloquent testimonial to the worth of Dorothea's ministrations.

Buffalo, N.Y. Feby, 2d, 1857

My Dear Miss Dix,

Were all my friends as considerate of my eyes as you are they would soon be well. But knowing your kind indulgence, I have delayed answering your very welcome letter, commenced at Onondaga on the 4th and finished at Albany on the 19th ult. which came duly to hand. Since then, I have heard of you at New York, and suppose you may now be at Trenton.

I was much disappointed that you did not return and stay with us. Miss Fuller understood you to say that you would do so, but I did not. I concluded, however, that she was right and we looked for you with a good deal of anxiety; and I went the next day to Doctor Hosmer's to know if he had heard from you. I need hardly add that you have a just appreciation of Miss Fuller. I had lived in her father's family; and so had my wife, and she seems to me like a sister or a daughter, and has been every thing that I would ask or hope for, under existing circumstances, and she seemed to take a strong liking to you, and often expressed her regret that you did not return, and that she had so little opportunity to converse with you while you were here. I hope when you come again you will make my house your home.

I am sorry to hear so unfavorable a report from our Eleemosynary establishments in this State; but sincerely hope that you may not be disappointed in your anticipations of legislative aid for the relief of their unfortunate inmates. Alas, they will never know how much they are indebted to you for any comforts which they may hereafter enjoy. Your efforts are so disinterested, so quiet and unostentatious, that even the outside-reading world, knows but little of the sacrifices you make and the amount of misery which you relieve, but the poor benighted objects of your compassion and benevolence can know much less, most of them absolutely nothing. Your only reward must be in an approving conscience, and the unselfish consciousness that you have mitigated the sufferings and contributed to the happiness of the most wretched of the human race. May God add his blessing to your noble charities, and untiring efforts.

My Sister is now with me and Miss Fuller has a niece visiting her, so that we are not without agreeable society, and I avail myself of their eyes to relieve mine in reading. Having finished Macaulay's History of England,—the best which I ever read—I am now reviewing my travels in Europe (with my guide-books) for the purpose of impressing more distinctly upon my memory what I saw. I find this very agreeable, but it would add much to the pleasure if I had some one who had travelled over the same ground, to join me in the review.

I find that the severe cold winds affect my eyes, and I am consequently compelled to keep too much within doors. I do not get as much exercise as I could desire.

I am as ever,
Your sincere Friend
MILLARD FILLMORE

◄§ 80. To MILLARD FILLMORE

Dorothea's apprehension of sectional agitation is revealed in her apparent willingness to accept the Dred Scott decision, the bête noire of Abolitionists and Free Soilers.

Time had not dimmed her indignation at President Pierce's veto of the land-grant bill.

Just a few days before Mrs. Harris invited Dorothea to her home in Albany she had extended an invitation to Fillmore to come to Albany and participate in the capital's social season and meet old friends. He declined. But a few weeks later she renewed her proposal, and added that in addition to other incentives she wished him to meet their friend, Mrs. Caroline McIntosh, who lived alone in the spacious Schuyler mansion amidst all of the elegance wealth could supply. When Fillmore left the invitation dangling, she wrote a third time, setting the date for March 10.

This time he did not dissent. He went to Albany the day before Dorothea dispatched her letter from Harrisburg. And there he met the future Mrs. Fillmore.

Mrs. Harris described Caroline as "not the least interesting part of the whole setting; a very bright little body, with unfailing resources in her own cheerful temperament and cultivated mind. But in spite of all this, she finds herself very lonely at times, alone in that great house."

Her enticing picture of the petite Mrs. McIntosh was not lost upon the chivalrous ex-President; nor perhaps were her references to her more worldly possessions.

Caroline Carmichael McIntosh was the daughter of Charles Carmichael and Tempe (Blachly) Carmichael of Morristown, New Jersey. Her husband, Ezekiel McIntosh, acquired a fortune as a builder of the Mohawk and Hudson Railroad between Albany and Schenectady, and in speculations in other railroad securities. He died shortly after he and Mrs. McIntosh had returned from a tour of Europe. They had no children.

Whether an assent instead of a refusal by Dorothea to Mrs. Harris' invitation would have altered the latter's recommendations to Fillmore regarding marriage remains an interesting speculation.

Harrisburg, Pa., March 11th [1857]

My dear friend,

Amidst many and crowding occupations I have from time to time intended writing to you at once acknowledging your last letter, and repeating inquiries after the state of your eyes, as well as confirming friendly relations. It must be admitted these last suffer on all hands, and those who stand in the positions of near and valued friendship rest on the faith of stedfastness rather than the knowledge which is the growth of daily expression or act. I sent you yesterday a paper written last summer by Dr. Hare for a Pennsylvania Journal, and which the editor did not regard as suited in its style to the popular reader—in as much as the majority of readers do not care for that which is more than superficial, and do not want to be troubled with argument. And in our *rushing* Country there are few who ever remember the *recent past,* fewer yet who go back forty or fifty years.

Our good friend the Dr. stands fast as your ally, come what may, and regards with great indignation the course affairs have taken. Mr. Buchanan's first stroke of policy has surprised many and gratified more, if indeed the judgment of the Supreme Court on the Dred Scott Case, and which was *arranged* to come before the Nation on the advent of the new Administration, shall prove as designed, a quietus to all political wranglers on the Slave question.

I see Mr. Pierce is presented with *Service* of *Plate* by the City of Savannah, for what *service done* on his part [?]. One seems to see inscribed on it Judas the Younger.

I was last week in Albany, and believe my efforts there were not without use: here in Pennsylvania I think my objects will be effected. At Albany I spent a week at the Executive Mansion, excepting the hours from 10 A.M. to 3 P.M. which were measured in the State Library. Governor [John A.] King seems to be acceptable to all parties *thus far*. He sustains him-self with ease, courtesy and amenity in the Executive Cham-ber as well as in his own Mansion as Host and representative of the State's Authority.

I shall always get safely any letters addressed to me at Trenton, New Jersey, whence all packets are forwarded as I find convenient.

Your friend cordially at all times
and seasons and under all aspects of life.

D. L. Dix

Mrs. [Ira] Harris whom I saw at your house in Washington called to see me in Albany, and courteously invited me to her home, but I could not accept her hospitality.

[Miss D. L. Dix, March 11, Rec'd. 20, 1857; Ans'd. April 17.]

◄§ 51. To Dorothea Dix

Fillmore, like Dorothea, was increasingly critical of politi-cians and political morality.

He makes no mention of meeting Mrs. McIntosh during his visit in Albany.

Buffalo, April 17, 1857

My Dear Miss Dix,

I owe you many thanks for your favor of the 11th ult. and also for the copy of Dr. Hare's manuscript which I perused with great pleasure. But I fear the Doctor, like myself, is a little too independent to suit these degenerate times. He does not pander to the prevailing fanaticism, or approve of the brib-ery and corruption which now disgrace our legislative Halls. But let us do our duty, stand by the right, and hope for the best. Should you see the Doctor, please to make my grateful acknowledgements to him for the favor, and assure him that I appreciate it as highly as if it had been given to the public through the press.

I was in Albany last month for a few days, but you had left before I reached there, which I sincerely regretted. I saw little of Gov. King, but all that I did see impressed me very favorably. He is certainly so great an improvement upon our last governor [Myron H. Clark], that every body seems to be satisfied. I am sorry to hear however, that no appropriations are likely to be made for Lunatic Assylums [sic]. The excuse is, that the state is too poor, but this is not so if economy be used in other matters. But the danger is that what is given to the *Insane* will be taken from the harpies and bloodsuckers who now hang around the Capitol and feed upon corruption.

My eyes feel better as the weather grows warmer, and I hope with proper care, they may soon be restored. But I am so constantly tempted to read or write, that I know not how to refrain; and I intend to go to New York next week mainly to give rest to my eyes. May I not hope to have the pleasure of meeting you there? I shall stop at the St. Nicholas; and if you should be in the city I hope you will let me know your address.

I know you must be exceedingly busy in your angelic mission, but I hope you will take time to give yourself rest. You can not endure this constant activity and intense thought forever, You must have relaxation. And that may be best taken in quiet social enjoyment. I hope I shall see you.

I am, as ever,
Truly and Sincerely
Your friend
MILLARD FILLMORE

⋙ 81. To Millard Fillmore

Dorothea had worked hard and long at Harrisburg, and was now confident that the legislature would pass her bill and that Governor Pollock would sign it. As her work expanded, her social life shrank and her letters became shorter.

Harrisburg
April 17th, 1857

My dear Sir and Friend,

I have written to you but twice for a long time, and indeed lacking leisure for anything beyond brief expressions of stedfast friendliness, a friendliness which you cannot ever question; it has hardly seemed worth-while taking your time to break an envelope for no more important reading.

I have believed it possible that you might have made a voyage to the West Indies of which at one time I think you entertained the idea, but had you left Buffalo I almost think I, busy as I am, should have had notice of the fact through public prints.

My Bill here has passed the House without division; is reported favorably from the Committee of Finance to the Senate, and I hope to see it in the hands of Governor [James] Pollock before the end of the month.

I have had of late very fatiguing journies [*sic*], but all affairs are going well, so I bear the extra pressure on mind and physical energies without quite giving out.

I must conclude with all best wishes for your comfort and health.

Your friend,
D. L. Dix

I trust your eyes are less painful; indeed well advanced to perfect cure.

[Miss D. L. Dix, April 17, Rec'd. 19, 1857; Ans'd. May 11.]

⚬§ 82. To Millard Fillmore

Dorothea continues to await legislative action in Albany and Harrisburg, but trusts that she may get away in time to see Fillmore in New York.

She invites him to inspect the New Jersey Asylum at Trenton, "the best hospital in the United States."

Philadelphia, April 21 [1857]

I received your letter of the 17th, my dear Sir, last Evening forwarded by my friend Dr. Buttolph with other letters from Trenton. I regret to have left Albany before your visit there, and also that it is not probable I shall be in New York before you will have returned from your visit. Still, should your stay be extended or your journey there delayed, I may have the pleasure of seeing both yourself and other friends. Social life is almost obliterated from my ordinary experience; and this unavoidably. Yet I admit the force and the correctness of your proposition, that it will be not only wise, but really obligatory to modify my present use of strength and time. I may become this summer rather more an idler, and perhaps on my less rapid journeys or occasional places of rest I may have the enjoyment of meeting some of my friends on their summer recreations. However, this may be, I frame no very definite plans. Mr. [Joseph B.] Varnum wrote me that the Hospital Bills would *certainly* pass, and I have felt more the necessity of my presence in Pennsylvania than in New York, in that I do not know with precision what has been done here at the close of the session. You are right in your views of corrupt legislation. *Honesty* in political life is a *myth;* abuses increase and multiply in our Country; yet your observations in Europe, must have proved that integrity in the administration of Governments is as little understood and practised in the Eastern [Europe] as in the Western Hemisphere.

Mr. Pierce seems to be wandering from place to place rather restlessly, and must experience much chagrin at the rapid falling off of his Washington *friends.*

It just occurs to me that it is possible while in New York, you may incline to look for a day into the *best* Hospital in the United States at Trenton. If so, I can assure you in advance of Dr. B's very respectful and cordial welcome, and of the capacity of the House for exercise of a liberal Hospitality.

I will not task your eyes by longer writing, nor your ingenuity in decyphering my hieroglyphics; but adding all good wishes to the expression of sincere friendship, remaining steadily and consistently your friend, take leave.

D. L. Dix

[Miss D. L. Dix, April 21, 1857; Ans'd. May 11; Rec'd. at N.Y., April 26.]

☙§ 83. To Millard Fillmore

From Harrisburg Dorothea observed that her bill had not won passage in the New York legislature, and dissatisfied with what she considered to be a failure of leadership, she exploded, "This year it was Mr. Spenser's measure, next year I claim it for mine."

She reported an encouraging item in western Virginia: a movement to nominate Fillmore in 1860.

Harrisburg, April 27th [1857]

My dear Sir and Friend,

Believing that recreation rather than business took you to New York, I have inferred that the rough weather we have lately experienced may have delayed your journey, and that you may be now at the St. Nicholas. I cannot but feel anxiety at the weakness of sight now so long lingering as to threaten an established infirmity, and hope you will adopt all possible caution to secure improvement.

In regard to the loss of the Hospital Bill, I certainly feel unqualified surprise. I had constantly received letters from the Members of the House and Senators, expressing such unqualified confidence in the passage of the Bill, that it seemed mere waste of time for me to return to Albany. It passed the Senate and *to the third* reading in the *House* without objection, and one could not reasonably expect that any peril threatened its final consideration. I felt that the necessity for these new Institutions was so absolute that it appeared needless to add arguments to support self evident facts. However, I will next year take the subject up without *sharing* responsibility. This year it was Mr. Spenser's [Mark Spencer] measure; next year I claim it for mine.

I trust your visit in New York will be not only pleasant but beneficial in all respects, and extended for some weeks. By the way I see you are renominated in Western Virginia for the Presidency in 1860, or perhaps I should say proposed for renomination. How cloudy is our political horizon! And how many difficulties impend which wear a present unpropitious aspect.

"Be just, and fear not," the simple, sage-like motto of one of my friends is a sentiment full of instruction, and suggestive of a course clearly embraced by a small minority in our very busy world.

I will not task your eyes with too severe use, but letting them trace the final characters which repeat that I am your friend. Add farewell. Good-wishes, D. L. Dix

[Miss D. L. Dix, April 27. Rec'd. 29, 1857; ans'd. May 11.]

◄§ 52. To Dorothea Dix

Fillmore found that his trip to New York placed a greater strain on his eyes than his usual activities at home but he planned, nevertheless, to make a trip to Indiana, Michigan, and Ohio to visit his brothers and sisters.

He describes a visit with his aging father and speculates upon his responsibilities. He leaves unmentioned that he was considering a position with a railroad or insurance company. None, however, materialized. (See Henry E. Davies to N. K. Hall, April, 17, 1857, Fillmore Papers, Oswego.)

Buffalo, May 11, 1857.

My Dear Miss Dix,

Your kind and welcome notes of April 17th–21st and 27th all reached me at New York, whence I returned on the 1st inst. And since my return my eyes have been taxed to their utmost endurance with some business matters and the letters which had accumulated during my absence. I am happy however to say that I think they are gradually and steadily improving, and I do not despair of their final recovery. But the least imprudence or improper exposure injures them, and I am therefore exceedingly careful; going out but little and neither reading nor writing by candlelight.

It was to avoid the temptation to read or write that I went to New York. I had business to be sure, but that I could have delayed, or possibly have accomplished by correspondence, but I thought absence from my books and the chilly atmosphere of Buffalo at this uncomfortable season might benefit my eyes. But I soon found that I suffered from the dust of travelling, and from the strong lights which I was compelled to endure at the Hotels. I therefore returned and am enduring the sharp atmosphere of Buffalo, caused by the ice which yet lingers in Lake Erie. I do not recollect that it has ever remained so late before, but as yet it gives no immediate signs of departure. I have, however, concluded to leave the ice if that will not leave me, and intend to go West this week to visit my friends in Indiana, Ohio and Michigan: and be absent some three weeks.

I visited my good old Father yesterday—or rather on Saturday—and found him enjoying his usual good health, with the exception of a slight lameness in one knee caused by being thrown from his carriage recently, and he was apparently as cheerful and happy as he was 40 years ago. But still I can see that he has nearly reached "that bourne whence no traveller returns," and I can only hope that the rest of his journey may be as happy as that has been which is passed; and that my life may be spared to perform the last sad offices of filial affection to his mortal remains when his immortal spirit shall seek its congenial resting place in the society of those which have gone before it.

But I must close with my best wishes for your health and happiness. Adieu!

Yours Sincerely
MILLARD FILLMORE

84. To MILLARD FILLMORE

Dorothea again turned to the "shaded facts of our political condition," and found little to recommend.

She was searching for sites in Pennsylvania for a school for imbecile children and a new hospital for the insane.

Trenton, N. Jersey, June 3d, '57

My dear Sir and Friend,

I received your letter announcing your proposed journey West, from which I infer you may, by this time, have returned; I certainly trust having derived benefit to your sight. It impresses me with anxiety that this affection of the optic nerve still lingers, and seems rather to have assumed a chronic form. I am much dissatisfied with the results of past treatment, or not-treatment; do you feel assured that your case is understood? And have all the cares and remedies been employed which are available? Consider that now four or five years have glided away without essential change, except indeed for the worse.

Please excuse my dwelling on this subject, but I feel deep concern that you endure so great privations as are consequent on this malady.

You hear the news of the day through the newspapers and conversation, and no doubt reflect on the shaded facts of our political condition. I do not like to contemplate our future; it is most sad to see the vanishing integrity of those who occupy places of trust and represent the sovereignty of the Nation. I am not disposed to judge in a depreciating spirit, but with best endeavors to regard the lives and acts of most of our public men as actuated by high and honorable motives; as ruled by noble sentiments and sound patriotism. I can not force myself to believe what I desire. My much engaged life hinders my dwelling deeply or long on these things, and at the same time most of my engagements require me to see a good deal of those whose course as politicians and statesmen (miscalled), I can not approve. The best antidote to the mental discomfort which unpleasant subjects create is the constant endeavor to be more rightly and usefully occupied oneself. It is a great mischief to one's own dignity of character and simple right thought to dwell upon the defects of other persons in idea, or to make them the theme of conversation. Dr. Channing used to say that subjects not people should afford the text to conversation; and in the main, he was right. We do not improve ourselves by dwelling on the defects of others.

I do not recollect if I told you how well your Protégé, Dr. Nichols, is doing in the Institution in the District—all affairs there are successful and prosperous; thanks to you, who sustained and sanctioned primary movements. I have lately been occupied in selecting a suitable farm for the school for Imbecile children, whose interests I successfully moved with the Legislature of Penna. last winter. And next week I propose going to Pittsburgh to join the Commissioners in selecting a farm for the new Hospital for the insane and in reconciling some dissentions [sic] which have disturbed the Board. They have agreed to accept my arbitration. Whether after this I shall proceed into Ohio and return towards New England via New York, I can not now determine. My letters follow me from Trenton; this being the most convenient place for first receipt of the same.

I must not forget while I exhort the care of your eyes; that reading my letters is not a remedy, but the reverse. I trust better accounts of yourself when I hear again, and am stedfastly,

Your friend,

D. L. Dix

[Miss D. L. Dix, June 3d. Rec'd. 8, 1857, Ans'd., Aug't. 31.]

⇜§ 85. To Millard Fillmore

Dorothea continued her work in Pennsylvania despite the heat of the summer.

She notes the passing of former Secretary of the Navy and friend of the insane, James C. Dobbin of North Carolina, and the death of Governor Marcy of New York.

Buchanan's home was Wheatland, near Lancaster, Pennsylvania.

Pittsburgh, August 10th [1857]

My valued Friend,

The last account I have of you through the public prints refer to your suffering from the malady so long affecting your eyes, and creates a sufficient reason for not tasking your sight by frequent writing. I had hoped your late journey west would have assisted other remedial means, and that you would have really been able to tell me something satisfactory in this regard.

I have been much occupied both in Eastern and Western Pennsylvania, and though well, find the summer weather here becoming oppressive. I hope for release from these cares soon, and to see the work I came to commence and quicken really advanced. I suppose Powers and others who read from time to time give you the summaries of European news; to all these details you will refer with more interest from having been abroad and seen much which gives the key to the political and social states of the Eastern Hemisphere [Europe], [where] affairs stand pretty much as usual.

I observe the decease of good Mr. [James C.] Dobbin of North Carolina, following soon on that of the Ex-Secretary of State [William L. Marcy]. Mr. Buchanan is now at the Bedford Springs, a favorite summer resort of Pennsylvanians, but for the tired, declining President nothing bears an aspect so attractive as Wheatlands. Position attained, has fewer charms than coveted elevation.

I will not task your sight by much writing, but wishing you all possible good, joined with rational enjoyment, add that I am your friend,

D. L. DIX

[Miss Dix, Aug't. 10, Rec'd. 26, 1857, Ans'd. Aug't. 31.]

◄§ 53. To DOROTHEA DIX

Fillmore's courtship of Mrs. McIntosh was undoubtedly taking its toll upon his correspondence; but he made no reference to it.

He had spent a few days at Saratoga early in August while en route to Montreal, where he had attended the annual meeting of the American Association for the Advancement of Science.

Fillmore was justifiably upset by the panic of 1857. It fell heavily upon railroad securities in which he had invested most of his savings.

Spiritualism was currently sweeping the nation. Fillmore was skeptical of its tenets. Taking its inspiration from Emanuel Swedenborg, the eighteenth-century scientist and mystic, Spiritualism found a popular appeal through the Fox sisters' spirit-rappings in western New York. The cult of Spiritualism enrolled several hundred thousand Americans by the 1850s, and dozens of mediums were purporting communications with spirits of the dead.

Buffalo, Aug't. 31, 1857

My Dear Miss Dix,

It is a great while since I have written you, and I feel a pang of remorse at my neglect. I have two of your kind letters unanswered, the last of which came to hand during my absence at Montreal. But in truth my life is now so retired and quiet, that I have nothing to say. I fancied that it might benefit my eyes to take a journey, if I could do so, without encountering too much heat and dust, and I went to Montreal. I was very careful and very fortunate and my eyes are much improved. They had suffered much from an imprudent exposure on the 4th of July which prevented me from attending Gov. Marcy's funeral.

Just at present my private affairs occupy my attention. All money matters seem to be in a state of confusion, and though I have but little, I fear that is in jeopardy. Our banks are failing and all Rail Road securities seem to be discredited. But I wait calmly to see the result, thanking God, for health and strength, to provide for myself. All I lack is good eyes, and I trust they will soon be well.

I met my old Friend Dr. Hare at Montreal and was glad to see him. I am sorry he is so much absorbed in Spiritualism, but if I had his faith I should doubtless do as he does. But I must say, though I have taken some pains to inform myself, I have never seen the first evidence of the interposition of Spirits; but yet this hallucination, if hallucination it be, is spreading astonishingly, and is likely to work a great revolution. Is it a truth or but an epidemic of the mind? Time and investigation must settle this.

Will you not come West this summer? I should be most happy to see you, as I am ever

Your sincere Friend
MILLARD FILLMORE

◄§ 86. To MILLARD FILLMORE

Dorothea had recently returned to Boston after seven strenuous months in Pennsylvania, where she had successfully

guided appropriations through the legislature and handled ad-
ministrative details for the state's new asylums.

But, once again, she had jeopardized her health.

Boston, Oct. 4th, 1857

My dear Sir and Friend,

I have been slow in acknowledging your last kind letter, through various engagements of time and thought. Yet this would not have been the fact, either if I had supposed you needed any written affirmation of my friendship and esteem, or if you could have doubted my sympathy under the annoying circumstances growing out of the late commercial disasters and consequent embarrassments of the financial affairs of most institutions.

I can only hope you will not experience serious losses, so as to require of you undue use of your eyes while they continue to demand special care, and suffer under daily use. It is hoped in Boston that the worst days are over.

Saco, Maine, Oct. 16

A sudden interruption has delayed my concluding this letter commenced almost the first of the month. And subsequent disability through a very severe seizure of illness in the form of fever and influenza has put a stop to all present and proposed employments, till now that I am again convalescent. I am gathering up the broken threads of engagements, and making up interrupted correspondence.

The chief theme of conversation of epistolary communication and of silent thought is the very disastrous and really distressing condition of commercial affairs and of all business relations. Thousands, rich and independent, today are relentlessly impoverished in our land, and one does not see where the evil is to be stayed.

It has seemed to me singular that there have been no

minds so experienced and vigorous, so sagacious and compre-
hensive in idea as to have proposed some saving measures to
hinder these terrible results, falling most injuriously on all, but
most fatally on the laboring classes.

My good friend, I will not task your sight to read long
letters. I only add the expression of sincere friendly wishes for
your exemption from these calamities in any really oppressive
degree.

My cordial friendliness and esteem, which I hope will ever
remain unbroken.

Your friend,
D. L. Dix

My good friend Dr. Nichols is to marry Miss Maury,
daughter of the late Ex-Mayor of Washington [John Walker
Maury] next month.

[Miss D. L. Dix, Rec'd. Oct. 18, 1857, Oct. 4 and 16, Ans'd.
Nov. 7.]

◅§ 54. To Dorothea Dix

*There was no hint in Fillmore's letters to Dorothea that he
and Caroline McIntosh were considering marriage.*

*Shortly after their first meeting in March, Fillmore intro-
duced the subject. Caroline indicated a willingness to listen.
But for a time extraneous matters got into the way of romance.
Where would they live? Both were attached to their homes and
community. Would she move to Buffalo or he, to Albany; or
would some other residence be a reasonable compromise? How
would her property be managed, including her life-interest in
the historic Schuyler Mansion? Her acknowledgment that "her
judgment and inclination [were] at war" was not reassuring to
her suitor. (See Caroline McIntosh to Millard Fillmore, July*

25, 1857, Fillmore papers, Oswego.) *Facing a stalemate, she urged him to go to Saratoga, "and write me from there, when you can come [to her home in Albany], that something definite and satisfactory can be done"* [Ibid.]. *Ira Harris intervened with a proposal that Fillmore and Caroline accompany him and Mrs. Harris to Montreal, where they would find time for conversation; but his mediation fell stillborn.*

Eventually, however, the high-strung Caroline agreed to move to Buffalo, and Fillmore purchased the elegant Hollister house on Niagara Square to receive her. Several months before the wedding they signed a pre-nuptial contract—Fillmore might manage, but not dispose of, her property.

The fifty-two-year-old widow and the fifty-eight-year-old widower were married in the "Hamilton Room" of the Schuyler Mansion on February 11, 1858, where Alexander Hamilton had married Betsey Schuyler seventy-seven years earlier. They set up housekeeping there while their home in Buffalo was readied for occupancy.

The Panic of 1857 still cast a dark shadow over the nation's economy. Fillmore expresses concern for the welfare of the poor, but his slumping railroad bonds had less relevance for his peace of mind than they had had a year before.

He could not face up to informing Dorothea of his decision to remarry, and though he was aware that rumors were appearing in the press and that the wedding would be reported in the newspapers, he sent no announcement to her.

Buffalo, Nov. 7, 1857

My Dear Miss Dix,

Your kind favor commenced at Boston Oct. 4th and finished at Saco the 18th came to hand as I was on the point of leaving for New York, and I was exceedingly pained to hear of your illness, but happy to know that when you finished your letter you were convalescent. I hope that by this time your health is entirely restored.

I appreciate the friendly concern which you have manifested for me in these terrible times of pecuniary embarrassment; and am happy to say that I hope that my ultimate losses will be small, but the failure of these Rail Roads to meet the payments of interest punctually on their bonds subjects me to some embarrassment, as my little income is chiefly from that source. But my eyes are much better, and if they can only be fully restored, and I can retain my health, I shall feel quite independent of all fluctuations in the money market, for I feel that I am quite competent to take care of myself.

But really the winter-prospect for the poor is truly appaling; and nothing but a restoration of confidence can afford relief. The panic has been as fatal here as it is in an army; and perducing [sic] a similar effect. A universal terror has seized the public mind, and each man in his efforts to save himself crushes his neighbor and in turn is run over crushed himself. But as you say, I hope the worst is over, and that men will soon begin to look around, and see that all are not killed, and then increasing confidence will calm their fears, and revive the commercial prosperity, and industrial pursuits. Our next intelligence from England,—when they have heard of our bank suspension—will doubtless show us the worst. Let us calmly and hopefully await the result.

My time is passing very quietly, for I avoid reading or writing as much as possible, but still I can not forego the pleasure I feel in hearing from you, and therefore I send you this dull and uninteresting letter with the sincere regards of your friend

MILLARD FILLMORE

Vice President Millard Fillmore. Engraving by
W. S. Edwards from a daguerreotype by
Mathew B. Brady.
Courtesy of the New-York Historical Society.

Dorothea Dix in her forties. From a portrait in the
Trenton State Hospital, copied from a daguerreotype.
Courtesy of Trenton State Hospital.

(Above) Abigail Powers Fillmore when First Lady. Photo by C. M. Bell.
Courtesy of the Buffalo and Erie County Historical Society.

(Below) Caroline Carmichael McIntosh Fillmore, second wife of Millard Fillmore. Portrait by Lars Sellstedt.
Courtesy of the Buffalo and Erie County Historical Society.

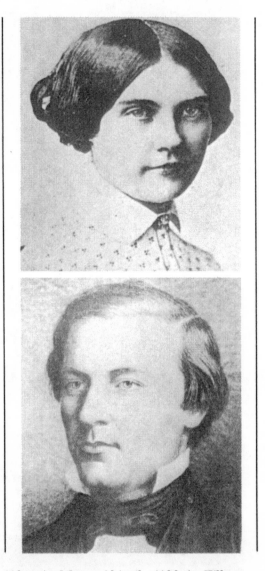

(Above) Mary Abigail (Abby) Fillmore,
daughter of Millard and Abigail Fillmore,
when about twenty.
*Courtesy of the Buffalo and Erie County Historical
Society.*

(Below) Millard Powers Fillmore, son of
Millard and Abigail Fillmore, in his twen-
ties.
*Courtesy of the Buffalo and Erie County Historical
Society.*

Saturday Evening
May 15. 1852

My Dear Miss Dix,

Please to accept the accompanying bouquet as a slight testimony of the respect and esteem, with which your disinterested devotion to the cause of suffering humanity, has inspired you

Sincere friend,
Millard Fillmore.

Letter of Millard Fillmore to Dorothea Dix, written from the White House, May 15, 1852.
Courtesy of Harvard College Library.

(Above) "The Right Man for the Right Place." Cartoon lithographed by Nathaniel Currier during the presidential campaign of 1856, showing Fillmore at center, with John C. Fremont, left, and James Buchanan, right.
Courtesy of the Library of Congress.

(Below) Trenton State Hospital, Dorothea Dix's "first-born child."
Courtesy of Trenton State Hospital.

Letter of Dorothea Dix to Millard Fillmore, July 27, 1854.
Courtesy of the State University of New York, College of Arts and Science, Oswego.

(Above) Dorothea Dix holding her commission as Superintendent of United States Army Nurses. Portrait by T. W. Wood, 1861.
Courtesy of Pennsylvania State Hospital at Harrisburg.

(Below) Millard Fillmore at age seventy-three, about a year before his death. Photo by William J. Baker, Buffalo.
Courtesy of the Buffalo and Erie County Historical Society.

❧ 87. To Millard Fillmore

Five months after her previous letter and six weeks after Fillmore's marriage to Caroline McIntosh, Dorothea broke the lengthening silence to suggest that as an old friend she believed that she was entitled to more than hearsay. Overlooking his slight, she offered her congratulations.

If his remarriage disturbed her to the degree that the Porter rumor had done four years earlier, she left no record of it. But her letter makes it obvious that she was hurt. Their friendship, or at least her feelings for him, would never be the same.

Trenton, March 29th [1858]

My dear Sir and Friend,

Amidst crowding objects and occupations a much longer time than usual has glided away since writing to you, though if I do not mistake you are my debtor if the rule of correspondence is measured letter for letter. I believe under existing circumstances I was rather specially entitled as an old friend, to hear from you, even if the balance had leaned the other way. In this world of gossip and busy rumors I could not know whether I was authorized to offer congratulations till the papers announcing your Marriage settled *oui-dire* [hear-say] into a fact.

Now therefore that I do not hazard mistake, I desire to offer as others already have done, my sincere good wishes for your long years of happiness, and I pray that your domestic life may be cheered and brightened by the society of the Lady who has joined her fortunes with yours for the good and ill of this world's varying experience. If you think my remembrance to her with compliments will be acceptable, I beg you to so express my good will and good wishes as to leave her no doubt of the hearty sincerity with which they are sent.

I hope Powers is well and prospering; also that Miss Fuller is in good health, and that both your sight and hers are strengthened since I last heard.

I am just from Washington; of course I can tell you no news from that hot-bed of political strife and party selfishness: the poor President is tasting largely of the cares and troubles and petty vexations which rank and power usually experience, and no little of the disquiet which results from weak pandering to dangerous advisers, who flatter to gain personal power and attain to individual distinctions, no matter what principles are sacrificed and trampled on the road to office, or the way to wealth.

My Measures for Hospitals in Maryland and Tennessee have passed the several Legislatures. In about a fortnight I shall go to Virginia.

Your friend stedfastly,
D. L. Dix

[Miss D. L. Dix, March 29; rec'd. April 5, 1858, Ans'd. May 17.]

❧§ 55. To Dorothea Dix

After delaying his answer for seven weeks Fillmore accepted Dorothea's congratulations with his customary equanimity. He did not allude to his failure to share his plans with her, but lamely pointed out that he had not yet met Mrs. McIntosh when he had last spoken with her in December of 1856.

Buffalo, May 17, 1858

My Dear Miss Dix,

I should commence with apologies for having so long neglected your kind and welcome letter of congratulations, but it is sufficient to say that it reached me in Albany, amidst the confusion of packing our goods to remove to this place, and that we are not even yet settled in our new house; but we soon hope to be in a situation to see our friends and when we are, I have Mrs. F's. authority for saying, what you know must be true in regard to myself, that none will be more welcome than yourself, and we both sincerely hope that your angelic mission may lead you in this direction, and that should it do so, you would consent to partake of our hospitalities. I need hardly add that Mrs. F. joins me in sincere thanks for your congratulations and good wishes, and that I am sincerely anxious that you should both enjoy the pleasure of each others acquaintance.

Miss Fuller has returned to her mother in Brooklyn, and was quite well when I last heard from her. My son is also very well, and quite prosperous in his business. He is, however, for the present at the Hotel in consequence of our house not yet being settled.

I infer you have never seen Mrs. F. as I had not when I saw you last. I had then no anticipation of the change which has taken place, but I feel that I have no reason to regret it, and hope and trust that I never shall have. Pray come and see how contented and happy we are.

I am gratified to hear that you are still so successful in all your benevolent undertakings. The world seems to appreciate your disinterested charity, and Heaven crowns your labors with success; but my Dear Friend, remember that your strength and power of endurance can not last forever, and that you must husband your resources, and take some care of yourself. I fear for your health; and entertain a constant apprehension that I may hear of your illness.

I am happy to say that my general health is perfect, and my employments for some weeks past, which has prevented me from reading or writing, has exerted a very beneficial influence upon my eyes, and they are decidedly better.

Mrs. F. joins me in cordial regards and

I am, as ever,

Your sincere Friend

MILLARD FILLMORE

8

Growing
Apart

1858–1869

The combination of Fillmore's marriage and Dorothea's far-flung travels and uncertain addresses combined to reduce the volume of their correspondence after 1858. Fillmore's eyes were improved—one of Dorothea's perennial worries—and their worlds were physically, professionally, and socially farther removed.

Even Dorothea's long-awaited visit to see the Fillmores at home in their splendid mansion on Niagara Square did not come to fruition, and their last personal contact was a brief one in New York, probably in the lobby of the Fifth Avenue Hotel in October, 1860.

Yet, their interest in each other did not flag. Her wartime duties left her little time for social affairs and correspondence. And they got out of the habit of writing. A trip to the Government Hospital (St. Elizabeth's) in Washington in 1869 filled Dorothea's mind with memories, and she drafted her last letter to her old friend. Possibly, Fillmore's reply was not de-

livered to her (it is not among her papers). It appears that she
did not write again.

◄§ 88. To MILLARD FILLMORE

Having broken the ice, Dorothea drafted a gracious con-
gratulatory note and expressed a desire to meet the new Mrs.
Fillmore.
After more than a year in Pennsylvania and New York,
Dorothea now planned more distant engagements in Virginia,
the West, and in Canada.
She recalled the closing hours of Doctor Hare's life.

917 Chestnut St.
May 25th, '58

My dear Sir and Friend,
    Your letter received a few days since was read with much
interest, and came just as I was considering the expediency of
writing again myself, in the idea that by some accident my last
two might not have reached their destination. I am sure I need
not multiply words in expressing my satisfaction in reading so
pleasant accounts of your present position, your health, contentment, and prospects of continued, and I will hope, your
increasing happiness. It will afford me gratification to make
the acquaintance of Mrs. Fillmore, of whom I have been favorably impressed through some of her early friends; and also,
should opportunity offer, of being your guest.
    At present I have no idea that my engagements will lead
me to your part of the country; at this time quite the opposite
direction claims my time. I expect to set off next week for Virginia, notwithstanding the lateness of the season; but I pass
thence to the West, and finally to Canada. My letter address

for convenience sake, I fix at Trenton, *permanently;* letters being forwarded thence twice weekly.

Of late I have been joined with other friends in attending the sick-bed and last hours of our friend (your friend), Dr. Hare, who deceased of Pneumonia, May 15th, in the 78th year of his age, and has closed a long life of active labor in his profession as practical and analytic chemist, and in which he centered his energies with rare success and faithfulness. I never knew a more entirely true, honest, and reliable man; eccentric and absent, he still endeared those most constantly to his friendship, who knew him longest and most intimately. During his last illness, the delusion, which had so strongly obsessed his judgment for two years, was hardly referred to, and the stores of literary and scientific knowledge accumulated through his long life were opened in a manner to astonish those even, who were acquainted with his attainments. He spoke of you with animation two days before his decease, and said if I wrote to you he would, as his farewell message, bid "God bless you." He had constantly maintained your cause, steadily advocated your interests, and felt the greatest pleasure in the remembrance of your kind attention to him and in all the personal association he had had with you. "He is an honest man, and we have need of him in these times of recession from integrity," were his concluding words of you.

I have thus executed my commission, and with regards to Mrs. Fillmore, am your friend.

D. L. Dix

[Miss D. L. Dix, May 25, Rec'd. 27, 1858; Ans'd. July 20.]

৬§ 56. To Dorothea Dix

Fillmore pays a tribute to the memory of Doctor Hare, and notes his own contentment and happiness.

Buffalo, July 20th, 1858

My Dear Miss Dix,

Your kind and acceptable favor of the 25th of May came duly to hand, and contained an interesting account of our mutual, and much lamented Friend, Dr. Hare during his last illness. He was indeed a good and great man, honest in his purposes, pure and steadfast in his friendships, and fearless and indefatigable in the pursuit of knowledge. Though we may regret the hallucination which seemed to have seized upon his mind in his latter days, and to obscure his otherwise bright and unclouded intellect, yet we must all admire that characteristic fearless independence with which he promulgated what he believed to be most solemn and momentous truths. I saw him last, at the Scientific Convention in Montreal in August 1857, and his mind was then so absorbed with "Spiritualism," that he seemed to think of nothing else, and I was therefore the more surprised, and I may say gratified, to learn from your letter that he seldom alluded to it during his last illness.

It is a consolation to know that he remembered me in his last hours, and that he spoke so approvingly of my public services. The approbation of one such disinterested man is appreciated more highly by me than all the fulsome flattery that ever issued from a partisan, venal press, or the shouts and huzzas of an unthinking mob.

I beg of you not to be alarmed at the paragraphs going the rounds of the papers, in regard to my eyes. The truth is that they are as well, and I think better than they have been at any time within three years; and indeed I do not suffer from them at all, if I do not use them too much; but I found news-paper reading decidedly injurious on account of the fineness and obscurity of the print, and I requested a paper sent me to be stopped, and by way of softening the ungracious act to the editor, I alluded to the difficulty of my eyes; whereupon he published a paragraph, more in malice than sympathy, I fear, which is now going the rounds, representing me as unable to read the news of the day. Such is too often the reward one receives for having bestowed unmerited favors. The serpent warmed into life by the kind husbandman, turned and stung his benefactor.

I am spending the summer here very contentedly and happy, and should you make the tour of Canada, I shall expect the pleasure of entertaining you as a guest at my house.

Mrs. Fillmore joins me in cordial regards.

Your sincere Friend

MILLARD FILLMORE

✍§ 89. To MILLARD FILLMORE

By September Dorothea had returned from her tour of the South and West and was en route to New York and the Maritime Provinces of Canada.

During Fernando Wood's tenure as Mayor of New York, lawlessness in the city had approached a national disgrace. Armed bands, sometimes but not always identified by such colorful names as "Dead Rabbits," "Bowery Boys," and "Five Pointers," battled each other as well as the New York police, with stones, clubs, and firearms. Outbreaks on July 4, 5, and 6, 1857, involved hundreds of police and militia.

Then, on September 1, 1858, a mob burned the Quarantine Station at Tompkinsville on Staten Island, including a hospital and a row of shanties. The station was said by an apologist of the perpetrators to have been a "pestiferous local nuisance, a menace to health, and a pleasant pauper home for broken-down politicians [New York Herald, March 8, 1914]."

Trenton, N. Jersey, Sept. 24th, '58

Dear Sir,

It is an unusually long time since our usually rather infrequent correspondence has been altogether suspended; and I
recollect too that I am your debtor; and that too for a letter
which relieved me of anxiety created by a newspaper paragraph reporting your rapid failure of sight. You may believe
that I learnt from yourself more encouraging accounts with
great satisfaction. I hope by this time you can note essential
relief from a weakness of vision which has threatened to pass
into a settled chronic form.

I have just now arrived here from the South and West,
where I have been closely occupied for the past four and a half
months, and am enroute to New York City, where affairs connected with the welfare of some southern Institutions now
take me. In a few days following I may be in the British Provinces. My health is in general, good.

I suppose that you and your family have made some
changes of place during the summer; it has become almost
universal to adopt [during] one fourth of the year, an itiner-
ant life. Probably the most positive result and most general
conclusion on settling again in family homes is that Hotels
and Boarding Houses offer but poor substitutes for the comforts of independent households.

I observe that political questions are beginning again to
agitate the popular mind; with what good result I think is not
clearly shown. Sound sense does not appear to be in the ascendant; and no very clear ideas are shown of the true principles which should lead all Republican Governments. Hopeful
minds are becoming discouraged concerning the stability of a
national rule which shall dignify humanity, and procure and
perpetuate benefits honoring and honorable to communities
and the whole people.

The late tendency to lawless deeds in the City of New York and vicinity is really alarming, and I can not but dread the consequences of that apathy which has witnessed the monstrous outrages at Staten Island where the last shelter of the sick and the dying has been invaded and acts worthy [of] the remotest savage life perpetrated, and the heartless and base sustained in their atrocious proceedings.

It is consoling amidst the much that is evil and vicious to know that goodness is wider spread, and more certainly anchored, than evil in our land. Bad deeds are widely printed, while small note is made of daily and incidental well-doing. Therefore the former comes to be magnified as dominant.

Please present my compliments to Mrs. Fillmore, and recollect me as your friend,

D. L. Dix

[Miss Dix, Sept. 24, Rec'd. 29, 1858, Ans'd. Oct. 9.]

❧ 57. To Dorothea Dix

Fillmore expressed his delight with his fine home, his library, and the presence of his wife and friends. He looked forward to introducing Dorothea to his wife and entertaining her in Buffalo.

After being the target of so much abuse Fillmore might be excused for his cynicism regarding political corruption. It was not unjustified, however. Lobbyists were spending large sums for tariff revisions, an exorbitant sum was paid by the federal government for land for fortifications in New York harbor, and expenditures for printing were padded. In fact, the Thirty-fifth Congress, which assembled in December of 1857, is generally regarded as one of the most corrupt prior to the administration of Grant.

Fillmore's reference to the "last Republic" presumably

stemmed from his belief that republican form of government itself was now on trial in the United States.

Buffalo, Oct. 9, 1858

My Dear Miss Dix,

Your letters of late are "like angels visits, few and far between." And I began to conclude that you were too much engaged in your noble work of charity, to find time to write, or that I had passed from your memory as a correspondent. But I was surprised and delighted about a week since to receive yours of the 24 ult. and happy to hear that you were well and prosperous.

We have spent the entire summer at home with the exception of a few days at Niagara Falls, and a short visit at Lock Port [New York].

Indeed I think we are both more contented at home than abroad, and our summer climate, as you are aware, is most delightful in Buffalo. Many of our people, it is true, go away for a month or two, either from habit or fashion to meet society at the Watering places; but really I do not think they find any where a more delightful summer or autumnal climate than this; and when business or a desire to visit some friend, does not call me away, I prefer to enjoy it. My own house is the most comfortable place I can find, and my wife and library, with the occasional friends who drop in, are the most charming society. But among those friends I wish I could see your genial face, and catch your quiet smile. I want you to know my wife and I want her to know you. I trust you would be mutually pleased with each other. If I understand your letter right you expect to go to Canada this fall. Can you not go or come this way and make us a visit? Even if it be but a short one we shall be delighted to see you.

Business will call us to New York the latter part of this month; otherwise we expect to be at home through the autumn; and shall be happy to have you partake of our hospitality at any time without ceremony.

I am taking no part in the political squabbles of the day. I am looking on calmly, hoping for the best and bracing my nerves for the worst; and I confess the worst feature to me is the universal corruption which disgraces official station, and the tendency to lawless anarchy among the people. But I trust to the conservative power of the better portion of community to correct these evils, and save the last Republic from becoming a stench in the nostrils of nations.

Mrs. F. joins me in affectionate regards to yourself, and

I am as ever
Your sincere friend
MILLARD FILLMORE

90. To MILLARD FILLMORE

Momentarily halted by an attack of influenza Dorothea was preparing for one of her most extensive and exhausting tours of asylums extending from Charleston to Texas; Louisiana to St. Louis; and the Ohio Valley. It was obvious that she was approaching it with enthusiasm and dedication.

Somerville, Mass'tts. Nov'b. 15, [1858]

My dear Sir and Friend,

There is a homely familiar saying which may be applied by myself just now *viz.,* "It is an ill wind which blows no good." An attack of Influenza, confining me to my apartment and the House, affords opportunity to open my writing case and reduce by degrees an accumulated unanswered correspondence. Under the influence therefore of a bowl of Gruel, dry cupping and counter irritants, I give my thoughts to my friends, which I regard as quite the best remedy of all.

I have not at all forgotten the cordial and hospitable invitation from Mrs. Fillmore and yourself which closed your last letter, and if leisure days had been in measure with my inclination I should long before now have been your guest. I imagine that my engagements will not any more in the future more than in the past leave me time for social intercourse which comes by incident and accident rather than chosen times and seasons.

I need not assure you that it is pleasant to me to hear from you of your domestic comfort and enjoyment. To know that one's friends are at "peace in their possessions," and removed from the turmoils of civil and political disturbances is no little satisfaction. This period of our National and Metropolitan histories seems especially tumultuous, and affairs are driven on at strange hazards and with more than usual lack of discretion. I find no pleasure in noting the "story of our times," and hope that the efficient able men who are now in the minority may yet be able to stop or steady our headlong career. Meanwhile the industry of the people at large keeps up the financial credit, and the case with which men in the United States gain a subsistence satisfies the less reflecting that the Government is "well enough."

To recur to myself; having spent the past six months in examining Hospital affairs and in attempting and sometimes effecting reforms in Poor-Houses, etc., I am now preparing to proceed to the southern line of States: South Carolina, Georgia, Louisiana, etc., which I suppose will consume several months; so that my objects in Canada and the North Western States are of necessity deferred till another year. And then if nothing as heretofore hinders, I may some day surprise you by a ring at your door, and claim the introduction so long promised to Mrs. Fillmore, and share your family pleasures for a day or two.

Do let me hear sometimes how you are; and direct to Trenton, whence my letters are duly forwarded.

With friendly regards to Mrs. Fillmore I am yours with esteem and friendship.

D. L. DIX

[Miss D. L. Dix, Nov. 15, Rec'd. 17, 1858, Ans'd. Feb. 25.]

⊷§ 91. To MILLARD FILLMORE

From Charleston, an early stop on her tour. Dorothea offered her impressions of the changing American scene.

The strains in Washington stemmed in large part from violence in the Kansas Territory.

"Bleeding Kansas" continued to agitate the nation as it dragged on month after month and year after year. It is not surprising, therefore, that the nerves of congressmen should become razor thin. Name calling and challenges became almost commonplace. Members carried knives and pistols. At a midnight session of the House a personal confrontation between Galusha Grow of Pennsylvania and Lawrence M. Keitt of South Carolina set off a melee in which at least ten exchanged blows. A Washington reporter could later see a comic opera in Mississippi House member Barksdale's loss of his wig and in John Covode's attempt to wield a spittoon as a weapon. But it was deadly serious, and a warning of things to come.

Dorothea's distrust of fanaticism in the guise of abolition had not abated. She saw slavery as a southern problem, and believed that slaveholders might mitigate its inequities if they were given time and were not disturbed by "northern interference."

Her travels in the South acquainted her with proposals of southern leaders for the amelioration of slavery, including the protection of marriage, a prohibition upon the sale of minors, a repeal of laws prohibiting emancipation and the education of slaves. In Missouri, Frank P. Blair had presented a plan for gradual emancipation in the state. A minority of southern people (but not the more vocal ones) accepted the premise that slavery was doomed by the Industrial Revolution and the changing social climate of the nineteenth century.

Obviously Dorothea did not support Edward Everett's nationwide speaking tour in behalf of the Mount Vernon Ladies' Association's drive to purchase Washington's residence (Mount Vernon) and convert it into a national shrine. In all Everett delivered his oration on Washington before 129 audiences and raised $70,000. The project, initiated by Ann Pamela Cunningham of South Carolina, was eventually successful, and the title to the property was obtained from John Augustine Washington early in 1858.

Dorothea offered no explanation for her disparaging observation, but she may have regarded it as a frivolous use of money.

Charleston, S.C., Feb'y. 9th, 1859

My dear Sir and Friend,

The intervals which fall between letters to my friends, fall longer and longer, as the grand[?] claims of my vocation press from various quarters. I do not imagine that repetition of expressions of esteem are necessary when friendships rest on the solid foundation of respect for the principles of those we number on "our list of friends," and therefore I do not feel anxiety either under very long separations from all for whom I entertain friendly regards, nor distrust under interrupted written correspondence. I hope your weakened sight is stronger, and that you can enjoy the satisfaction of being your own reader. I am sure whatever is the fact, you find a cheerful friend beside you, always ready to supply any want or enhance any pleasure. I beg to present my kind regards to Mrs. Fillmore, and friendly remembrances to Powers.

I did not find it possible to accept your invitation to Buffalo the past year, and will not venture to predict my course of travel for the coming season. But it is quite within the range of possibility that I shall be in your vicinity within four months. I have found the southern climate this year unusually variable, and have been really more incommoded by cold than in our severe northern climate.

You no doubt look on with interest upon the course of events which sweep on at Washington; much like the turbid autumn floods of some wild bankless river, rushing overshore, and often wasting and destroying more than it fertilizes and benefits. The conservative principle of our Government is certainly remarkable, since it has not been dissolved by corruption nor the judgment-lacking acts of our President and of Congress. The Extra mural and Intra mural fist-fights seem to have made little impression in the Capital city of the nation; but have had marked effect in the Provinces:—when our law givers fight, say the laboring people, we can not be blamed for imitating their example.

The Abolition fever seems declining, and Southern Citizens may have time to improve the condition of the Negro population, if not disturbed by indiscreet northern interference.

Mr. Everett, I observe, still uses his pen and voice on behalf of that very questionable Mt. Vernon scheme, and the end seems not to be reached by any even near approach.

I must take leave with all good wishes for the uninterrupted enjoyment of your family circle.

Your friend,
D. L. Dix

I am about to proceed hence to Montgomery and Tuscaloosa,
Alabama.
[Miss D. L. Dix, Feb'y 9, Rec'd. 21, 1859, Ans'd. Feb'y 25.]

◄§ 58. To Dorothea Dix

*Fillmore renewed his invitation to Dorothea to visit them
in Buffalo. He also noted that Mrs. Fillmore had sprained her
ankle—it would be only the first of her frequent misfortunes.*

Buffalo, Feb'y. 25, 1859

My Dear Miss Dix,

Your letter of Nov. spoke so doubtfully of your "where-
abouts" for some time to come, that I delayed writing; but I am
now gratified by the receipt of yours of the 9th from Charleston, and I am happy to hear that there is a prospect of our
seeing you here within 3 or 4 months.

We shall be delighted to see you. My wife feels that she
knows you very well and appreciates you as I do and is anxious
to make your personal acquaintance. Pray, if possible, let us
know a little in advance when we may expect you.

Our lives are very monotonous but I can assure you we are
none the less happy. We go little into Society, but my eyes are
now so well that I am able to read and write several hours
every day; and consequently find my time most agreeably employed.

I read the newspapers so little and when I read them at all,
I find so much in the corruptions that disgrace our public bod-
ies, that I am utterly disgusted. Was there ever a time when

official corruption was so rank? When the plunderers of the public treasury stalked abroad with such assurance of impunity and such unblushing boldness and confidence? The character of a successful swindler seems to be a pasport [sic] to public favor, and official confidence. Where is it to end?

About 14 days since Mrs. F. turned her foot and sprained her ancle [sic] so seriously, that for 10 days she was not able to step on it, but now she uses it a little and hopes with care soon to be well again.

I see that you still pursue your mission of mercy; and I hope with success. Your self imposed and unselfish labors are very severe, and I feel a constant anxiety for your health. Our winter here as a whole has been very mild, but so changeable that I think it has not been very healthy. I was in hopes you would find it more pleasant at the South, as I can not doubt you find a very hospitable people.

Mrs. F. unites with me in kindest regards and I remain—

Truly your friend,
MILLARD FILLMORE

◄§ 92. To MILLARD FILLMORE

Dorothea traced her progress from Charleston to Tuscaloosa and Mobile, and noted her plan to go from New Orleans to Texas despite spring floods.

She again returned to her appraisal of moral laxity and corruption. Her letters are becoming more impersonal.

St. Louis Hotel, New Orleans
March 16, 1859

Dear Sir and Friend,

I received your letter at Mobile, arriving from Tuscaloosa, and reply now lest passing time should find no leisure for even briefly expressed words of friendly regard. I am sorry Mrs. Fillmore has injured her ankle; these sprains are troublesome of care, and pain often occurs. But I hope the timely rest from use, which is the main assistant to recovery, will have proved effectual in this instance.

Your remarks on Governmental and general corruption and laxity of all moral obligations are alas too correct to admit any contrary argument. I do not know how it has come that there seems so little *sound* integrity, so little uprightness of heart and life, so infirm principles of virtuous life. Trust and confidence in our neighbours and friends even seems shaken continually by shocking facts and by shocking revelations of history. It would seem that there must be a radical defect in early education when the root so soon withers and perishes leaving the tree to a feeble sickly growth, a life in death.

It does not help our perplexity nor lessen our anxieties that this deadly canker is seen and traced; *cure* is what the whole body politic cries out for when it rouses from its dull lethargy, but the spasmodic rebuke, like spasmodic virtue, is ineffective to heal. Our downward track as a *Nation* is the common topic of consideration and discussion in Europe. We are not solving the great problem of wise, free government: "Every man for himself," a few for their country's rights is now the favorite password; and patriotism is dying not by slow degrees, but through a fearfully rapid decline. I don't wonder my friend that you turn from the daily journals with pain and mortification.

I have been making some of the most perilous journies [*sic*] this winter to which I have ever been exposed. The continued rains and the consequent wide overflow of rivers have left the country one vast swamp, where the creeks and rivers have not quite spread deep water over roads and all highways, iron or

other. I leave here this week for Texas; Austin being my ultimate point, and Galveston, my proximate. Whether I shall
make Lavaca an intermediate place of rest I can not now determine, but I go via Berwick Bay from this port. Returning, I
proceed to Jackson, La., and Jackson, Miss.; after this to Illinois. This supposes no fatal accident. One can not but make
cautious reservations in a country where *human life* is rated of
no account.

Present me cordially if you please to Mrs. Fillmore, and
believe me your friend with esteem and all good wishes.

D. L. DIX

[Miss D. L. Dix, March 16; Rec'd. 26, 1859, Ans'd. May 19.]

᪳§ 93. To MILLARD FILLMORE

*Dorothea had completed her mission to Texas, and after
stops along the Mississippi River en route, had reached St.
Louis. But calls upon her were heavier; not lighter.*

St. Louis, May 16th, 1859

My dear Sir and Friend,

As the winter has passed into spring, and the spring is advancing towards summer, I find the absolute claims on my
time increased rather than diminished, and the season I had
mentally, and more than half by direct engagement, appropriated to social intercourse with friends, is claimed for grave
pursuits and definite duties, which do not now seem likely to
yield to either personal wishes or anticipations.

I see therefore my friend, less and less prospect of being
for some days Mrs. Fillmore's guest at the home you so pleasantly describe, and I must ask that you will hold my visit indefinitely deferred, except indeed some sudden phase is pre-

sented in the face of my affairs. I have been longer detained in
Louisiana and Mississippi by three whole weeks than I anticipated, and have but now arrived here from Natchez.

I am happy in the rather unexpected complete success of
my winter labors. Such being the case, it does not become me
to indulge a wish for remission even of those claims which
"thicken like spring leaves on the trees."

I trust you are still well, and your sight strengthening. I
had subject for such long talks concerning "life in Texas" and
the changing South, that I should have proved a very time-
consuming visitor had I presented myself at the doors of your
mansion in the early days of June, as I expected. Fortunately,
occupation, distance, and lapse of time does not dissolve
friendly appreciation and friendly regards. And so recollect
me, with compliments and abounding good wishes to Mrs.
Fillmore,

Yours with cordial regard,
D. L. DIX

[Miss D. L. Dix, May 16; Rec'd. 19, 1859; Ans'd. May 19.]

§ 59. To DOROTHEA DIX

*Fillmore continued to look forward to Dorothea's oft de-
layed visit. He likened her work to an "Oasis in the desert of
crime."*

Buffalo, May 19, 1859

My Dear Miss Dix,

Several times since the receipt of yours of March 16th from
New Orleans, have I taken up my pen to address you, and as
often laid it down from the apprehension that you were probably in the inaccessible wilds of Texas, where a letter could
hardly reach you. But this morning I was delighted to receive

yours of the 16th from St. Louis, showing that you were again in the land of civilization and that you had been well and prosperous in your mission of mercy. But as no bliss in this world is perfect, so my joy in this case was dampened by your annunciation that your long expected visit here must be indefinitely postponed, unless matters shall present a new phase, which both Mrs. F. and myself sincerely hope they may. You do not indicate your future destination, but will you not pass us and can you not at least give us a call? Be assured that we shall both be delighted to see you; and rest for a day or two in this delightful region can do you no harm, but I trust would do you much good. Pray try it and see!

I am gratified to know that your labors have been prospered, and not only that, but to know that they have been appreciated. For it is a relief in these times when every act of infamy is trumped by the public press, and its poison sent on the wings of the wind to every hamlet and house in the land, to have the dark picture relieved and its deleterious influence mitigated by publishing such acts of disinterested and gratuitous goodness as those mentioned in the enclosed slip, taken from the *Savannah Republican.*

Just at this time, it appears like an *Oasis* in the desert of crime, and I hope that in future these green spots may recur more frequently, and the desert be less offensive and forbidding.

We have nothing new here —My eyes continue better and myself and family are in the enjoyment of usual good health.

Mrs. F. joins me in cordial regards and I am as ever

Your sincere friend
MILLARD FILLMORE

✥§ 94. To MILLARD FILLMORE

*Dorothea returned from the West in the spring and toured
the Maritime Provinces in the late summer. She had deferred
any thought of an immediate visit to Buffalo. South Carolina
now needed her attention.*

*Her reference to the "passage of affairs in Europe" con-
cerned Napoleon III's invasion of Italy, which forced Austria
to cede Lombardy to Italy; France received Savoy and Nice.*

Boston, Sept. 23d, 1859

My dear Sir and Friend,

I shall not venture on proposing to myself a visit to Mrs.
Fillmore and yourself after so many plans have failed, but
truth to say all my social plans usually end in proposition not
realization. I have been occupied every day continually with
cares for Hospitals to be either improved or created, and there
is no probability these claims on my thought will abate. I am
only now returned from Prince Edward's and Newfoundland,
and Nova Scotia and New Brunswick, and must be in South
Carolina to meet the session of their Legislature by the last of
October.

I hope that you and Mrs. Fillmore have enjoyed the summer wherever it has been spent, and that your sight is now
perfectly restored. I hardly can imagine a more serious privation than the impairment or loss of vision.

You are no doubt amazed at the present and recent passage
of affairs in Europe, certainly one can not hazard predictions
when great national concerns seem swayed by passing incidents rather than controlled by mature wisdom. I do not think
quite so badly of Louis Napoleon as most persons, and not
discerning what could serve France better than his rule I am
willing to see that hold place at least till there is chance for

more wholesome and renovating influences. It seems to me that till enlightened education is more diffused through the masses in Europe, it will be difficult to secure permanent extension of the liberty of subjects.

But I can not dwell on these themes. I only intended to report myself with compliments and good wishes to Mrs. Fillmore and yourself, and am your friend with esteem.

D. L. Dix

My letter address is uniformly Trenton, N.J.
[Miss D. L. Dix, Sept. 23, Rec'd. 28, 1859, Ans'd. Oct. 13.]

๛ 60. To Dorothea Dix

Fillmore's vision improved but Mrs. Fillmore's ill health became chronic.

He paid tribute to Dorothea's "labors of mercy."

Buffalo, Oct. 13, 1859

My Dear Miss Dix,

While you were writing me at Boston on the 23d of Sept. I was detained at Newport [Rhode Island] by the illness of Mrs. Fillmore. She had quite a severe billious attack which confined her to her room for two weeks and as soon as she was able to travel, we went over to Boston for a few days, and finally reached home a little more than a week since. She has not yet fully recovered her strength, but we trust she will soon be herself again. I am happy to add that my health is very good, and eyes well.

I perceive your disinterested labors of mercy are bounded by no artificial state lines, nor are they confined to any climate or race. Your mission seems to be coextensive with suffering humanity. In the North in the South; in the East and in the West; and even the wide Atlantic can not say to you "thus far shalt thou go and no farther; and here shall thy energetic steps be stayed"; but in Europe as well as in America you have left the foot prints of your journeys of mercy. May Heaven reward you for all your toils and all your sufferings. When I see what you are accomplishing, not only in the United States, but in Canada, New Brunswick, Nova Scotia, and even in Europe, I can not wonder that your plans for social enjoyment are deranged and broken up; and that we have looked so often, in vain, to see you. But still I do not give it up, and Mrs. F. joins me in renewed and earnest solicitations that as soon as your engagements will permit, we may enjoy that pleasure.

I am taking no part in politics, but looking at the world from the outside, delighted that I have no responsibility, and thankful when anything happens to be done, either by accident or design, for the honor or prosperity of my country.

Mrs. F. joins me in cordial regards and I remain as ever,

Your sincere friend
MILLARD FILLMORE

⤶§ 95. To MILLARD FILLMORE

Remaining at Boston for only a few weeks after her return from Nova Scotia, Dorothea headed for the South to attend to unfinished business. She was in Columbia, South Carolina, in October and in Jackson, Mississippi, by November. Railroads now speeded her travel between South Carolina and Mississippi, and enabled her to go from Columbia to Jackson in three days, a trip which formerly required fifteen days by way of the Gulf and Mississippi River. But she balked at one innovation, the sleeping car. "Nothing would induce me to occupy them," she advised Ann Heath. "They are quite detestable. I did make one night's experiment between Pittsburgh and Cincinnati that will suffice me for the rest of my life. I cannot suppose

that persons of decent habits, especially ladies, will occupy
them unless some essential changes are made in the arrange-
ments and regulations" [*November 19 (1859)*].

Like most of her countrymen North and South, Dorothea
was shocked by John Brown's foolhardy seizure of the United
States Arsenal at Harpers Ferry. His martyrdom would come
later with his trial and his heroic bearing at the gallows, and,
of course, with the Civil War which followed. "All in all," she
noted, "the Southern people are as moderate in their opinions
under such press of danger as could possibly be expected."

State Library, Capitol
Jackson, Missipi., Nov'r. 21st [1859]

Dear Sir and Friend,

From my quiet table in a cheerful recess of the Library,
assigned for my present use, I write a few lines taking up the
broken thread of correspondence so desultory and often interrupted as almost to have lost claim to being considered a correspondence.

I always consider however that a friendship founded in
mutual respect and esteem rests on a basis so solid as to need
for its survival no often renewed attestations of its vitality, so
my friends in special and at large are *put away* in my mind
and regards, to be met by pen communication and personally
always as cordially as if the links of the chain received the
daily polish of letter and speech.

I am here to give impulse to Legislative action on behalf of
the State Hospital. The Governor, the Committees and those I
have seen of the Senate and House are on my side of the question thus far, and I shall close my efforts here in ten days to
repeat the same work at Columbia, South Carolina, to which
place I proceed on the 30th by Express.

I have no doubt that you are looking with regret and anxi-

ety on the present singular state of our state relations and national affairs. This mad scheme of Brown's opened at Harper's
Ferry is the strangest illustration of mistaken feelings overrul-
ing judgment and practical common sense that I have ever
heard or read of. And if the conspiracy is as extensive as
claimed, which I very much doubt, it only proves that there
are more impulsive people than one could have supposed
amongst our impulsive countrymen. It is a little singular that
men who could desire such a plot had so little caution and
prudence. In fact the lack of this is so amazing as to make one
doubt the narrations shown in the public journals. All in all
the Southern people are as moderate in their opinions under
such press of danger as could possibly be expected.

I am interrupted, and can but add very cordial good
wishes, anticipating the congratulations of the season to Mrs.
Fillmore and joining your name with hers in all that a friend
should wish for the prosperity and happiness of another, I take
leave as yours with stedfast regard.

                                                      D. L. Dix

[Miss D. L. Dix, Nov. 21, Rec'd. 29, 1859, Ans'd. March
5.]

ᴥ§ 61. To Dorothea Dix

*Fillmore's view that the sectional quarrel was the work of
demagogic politicians had not changed. Southern demagogues,
he believed, destroyed the Compromise of 1850 in order to
force slavery into Kansas; northern demagogues capitalized
upon sentiment against slavery by pretending that there was a
real danger that slavery would be extended into free territories
and states and founded the Republican party, "fired with a
fanatical zeal against the imaginary wrongs of slavery."*

Fillmore never defended slavery. It was the distortion of

slavery and the fanaticism endangering traditional political institutions which drew his condemnation.

". . . how quietly and contentedly we live, 'The world forgetting; And by the world forgot.'"

Buffalo, March 5, 1860

My Dear Miss Dix,

I fear you will think me a very negligent correspondent, and were I charged with the offense, I think I should plead guilty at once and throw myself upon the mercy of the court like other self-convicted criminals. But I trust that I should find in you a merciful and forgiving judge, when I assure you that, this apparent neglect has not arisen from any want of respect and esteem, but from the simple fact that I felt assured that you had too many proofs of my unabated friendship to doubt it, and I had nothing beyond a reassurance of that worth communicating.

In truth I have spent the entire winter very quietly and very happily at home, without a single wish to be any where else; and I should be very happy if you could drop in upon us and see how quietly and contentedly we live, "The world forgetting; And by the world forgot." But still remembering past scenes with interest, and true friends with pleasure.

When you last wrote, you were on the point of leaving Jackson, Missi., for Columbia, S.C. on your mission of mercy, and I sincerely hope that God has blessed your labors and that your efforts and sacrifices have not been in vain; for this seems to be all the reward you ask or expect in this world.

You have been at the South and you can best appreciate the feeling excited by John Brown's foolish and criminal invasion of Virginia. He doubtless believed what these insane fanatics at the North have taught, that the slaves would rise in mass and join his insurrectionary standard, and the result, I think has had one good effect; and that is to show the people of the North, that the slaves themselves do not regard their condition as so bad that they have any strong desire to change it. This may do some good, but the ill will and jealousy that has been engendered between the North and the South, growing out of this slavery agitation, is greatly to be deplored, and I greatly fear that it will eventually destroy this government. But both sections are in the wrong. Demagogues at the South unnecessarily and unwisely opened this question, after it had been *Settled* by the compromise measures of 1850, by repealing the Missouri Compromise and attempting to force slavery into Kansas, and demagogues at the North, seized upon the fanatical feeling against slavery which pervades the northern states, and under the pretense of resisting the extension of slavery—of which there was really never any danger—have raised up a party, fired with a fanatical zeal against the imaginary wrongs of slavery, and stimulated by the hopes of partisan success, that seems to endanger every thing which I hold sacred in our political institutions.

But enough of this, and permit me to add that, my eyes are quite restored, and Mrs. F. joins me in cordial regards, and I remain as ever

Your sincere friend
MILLARD FILLMORE

◄§ 96. To MILLARD FILLMORE

Dorothea's pride in her achievement is well deserved.

She contemplated a period of less strenuous endeavor, but she changed her mind.

She assumed that Unionists would again organize for the Presidential campaign and implied her support; but she made no mention of Fillmore as a nominee.

Justice John McLean of Ohio was a perennial candidate for the Presidency despite his long tenure on the Supreme Court and his chronic ill health.

Senator Bell was nominated by the Constitutional Union party, made up of a remnant of Whigs. Edward Everett was his running mate. Stephen A. Douglas and John Breckinridge headed the northern and southern factions of the Democratic party, and Abraham Lincoln was selected by the Republicans over William H. Seward.

917 Chestnut St., Phila.
April 10th. [1860]

Dear Sir and Friend,

Yours received several weeks since, breaking a long interval of nonepistolary communication, required perhaps an earlier acknowledgment, but all social claims yield before the obligations of business interests, as you will readily allow. My time and thoughts have never been more continually occupied than the past two years, in which period I have secured something over half a million for Hospital purposes in different States. My Bills have only last week passed the Pennsylvania Legislature, granting $98,000 to old and new Hospitals. In South Carolina my Bill passed after some discussion both Senate and House unanimously; indeed I never had more satisfactory experience of legislation for charitable purposes.

Notwithstanding constant success, now, with six Legislatures in five Southern and one Northern State since last October, I am really relieved that the advanced season puts an end for the present to the heavy work, and that I have a season for preparing for the next year's claims, when I may be less limited to precise times and places of occupation.

But enough of myself. Your report of the improved state of your vision is very satisfactory, but I could not forbear a smile at the very graphic discription you give of your domestic life, "The world forgetting; by the world forgot." I must venture to modify the final clause after a reading of my own, but which it is not needful to submit for your approval.

Mr. and Mrs. [John] Bell have been lately in Washington. Mr. B. has returned to Tennessee, but Mrs. B. with her daughters is residing at the La Pierre House in Philadelphia; all are well. Ideas of the Presidency are often presented to them, and Mr. Bell's friends here imagine that he will be the choice of the Convention which absorbs the *Union* Party. Judge McLean's impaired health would seem in the way of his nomination, which is a good deal talked of. Indeed there seems no lack of Candidates: some eager aspirants; others less ambitious and more meritorious wait quietly the turn of tide. I confess I should be deeply mortified to see Douglas in the Presidential Chair, but we have suffered so many humiliations as a Nation, that we dare not be sanguine of a better result than the last *choice* of the people afforded.

If I had not so often expressed the intention of paying Mrs. Fillmore an informal visit, I should refer to the subject with a little more confidence, but I do not venture to propose any plans. I have the idea that I must be in Western New York sometime this year, and I may sometime ring at your door, and walk in to spend the long-talked of social time which has been heretofore proposed only to be set aside.

My compliments to Mrs. Fillmore and recollect me as your friend. Cordially,

D. L. Dɪx

[Miss D. L. Dix, April 10, Rec'd. 13, 1860, Ans'd. July 31.]

✎§ 62. To DOROTHEA DIX

Fillmore invited Dorothea to join them at Saratoga "during this vacation in your labors." It was a poor choice of words.

Buffalo, July 31, 1860

My Dear Miss Dix,

Your last kind favor from Philadelphia has remained quite too long unanswered; for my life is now so monotonous that I had really nothing to communicate of myself, and could only repeat the assurance, which is hardly necessary, of my unalterable esteem, and the deep interest I feel, not only in yourself personally, but in all your noble and disinterested charitable efforts. I congratulate you most sincerely on the success of your efforts during the last legislative season. Such results compensate in some measure for the disappointment you must have felt after years of toilsome labor to have your hopes dashed by the cruel veto of President Pierce.

I think St. Paul in one of his epistles said something like this: "Alexander the coppersmith hath done me much harm. May the Lord reward him accordingly." But I fancy your Christian love and more than Pauline forgiveness, have not even breathed so severe a censure as this upon the author of that veto. But turning from this hopeless task with the National legislature you have directed your untiring efforts to the states, and there they have been crowned with success. But those for whom you labor can not appreciate your devotion or sacrifices. You must look to Heaven and an approving conscience for your reward.

But I took up my pen mainly to say that Mrs. Fillmore and myself leave this week for Saratoga where we may stay from 2 to 4 weeks and I have a faint hope that during this vacation in your labors we may have the pleasure of meeting you there. I

can assure you that it would give me great pleasure to do so;
and I know that Mrs. Fillmore would be delighted to make
your acquaintance and I begin to despair of ever seeing you
here.

I am interrupted and can say no more. Mrs. Fillmore joins
me in cordial regards and I am, as ever

                                        Your sincere friend,
                                        MILLARD FILLMORE

&§ 97. To MILLARD FILLMORE

*Instead of remaining inactive as she had hinted in her
previous letter Dorothea had invaded Kansas, Missouri, Iowa,
Wisconsin, and Minnesota! "Vacation," she reminded Fillmore, did not find a place in her "notation of time."*

*But she now considered a short visit with them in Buffalo
on her return to the East. But it turned out that they were
already committed to be in New York.*

                              Chicago, Sept'r. 18, 1860
                              from Wisconsin and Minnesota
Dear Sir and Friend,

I have just received your letter of July, duly forwarded,
meeting my arrival after an absence of a month from this point
which has been a sort of Headquarters, whence I have visited
Kansas, Missouri and Iowa, and more recently Wisconsin and
Minnesota.

I have delayed writing because I could say with no certainty at all, when I might reach Buffalo, a place I still have
the intention of reaching at no distant time, *if possible*. My
days and hours are constantly occupied.

I thank you for the invitation to join yourself and Mrs.
Fillmore at Saratoga, not the less that I have only read the

notice of your plans. I have never leisure for excursions, seldom for a visit, now and then, a call for a few hours to see
some old friend measures the times of recreation during the
year usually. I was surprised at your reference to my *"vacation"*
seasons, as such periods do not find place in my notation of
time. I proceed to several points in Michigan next week, and
now *intend* on the following: To reach Western New York,
but this is rather uncertain, and if, as I anticipate, being in
Buffalo should be practicable, I will write. Meanwhile, will
you address a line to meet me at Detroit (Post Office) to say if
you and Mrs. Fillmore are free from engagements from home
about this time (the first week of October, or last few days of
the present month). Do not let the chance of my coming interfere with any already proposed arrangement for your disposition of time.

Excuse this brief note and with compliments to Mrs. Fillmore and cordial regards remember me your friend,

D. L. Dix

[Miss D. L. Dix, Sept. 18; Rec'd. 19, 1860, Ans'd. Sept. 19.]

✑§ 63. To Dorothea Dix

*Fillmore replied immediately to Dorothea's letter of Sep-
tember 18 seeking to determine the date of her arrival and to
try to fit it into their plans.*

He acknowledged that she took no vacations!

Buffalo, Sept. 19, 1860

My Dear Miss Dix,

Your favor dated at Chicago yesterday has just come to
hand and I hasten to answer your inquiry whether we shall be
at home next week. I can assure you we shall be glad to be if
we can have the pleasure of seeing you. But we are under

conditional engagement to go to New York, but the time is not definitely fixed nor within our control; but accidents may prevent us from going at all or delay the time—as I hope it may—beyond your intended visit. In either case we shall be most happy to welcome you to our home.

I ought to have known that you have no vacation, but it seemed to me that when your winter labors with legislatures were over that you ought to have a vacation, but really your labors during the summer are more arduous than during the winter. No one knows what he can do until he tries, but really it seems to me that you are testing your strength to the utmost and that it is due to yourself to take some rest; and I hope we may be able to give you some in our quiet mansion.

But hoping to see you soon I will say no more now. I should add however that Mrs. Fillmore joins me in a cordial invitation to visit us; and we shall both be greatly disappointed if any thing should prevent us from seeing you.

I am in great haste, Your sincere friend,

MILLARD FILLMORE

❧ 64. To DOROTHEA DIX

Fillmore continued to try to coordinate their movements so that they might meet in Buffalo.

Buffalo, Sept. 26, 1860

My Dear Miss Dix,

I wrote you some days since that we had a *contingent* engagement to go to New York, which I hoped might not interfere with your visit here (if you were able to call on us), but last night I received such intelligence as will compel us to leave on Friday or Saturday next, which we shall both most sincerely regret, if it should be the means of depriving us of the pleasure of a visit from you; but as the matter is now settled beyond our control, I thought best to let you know it.

Mrs. F. joins me in cordial regards and

I am as ever

Your sincere friend

MILLARD FILLMORE

◅§ 98. To MILLARD FILLMORE

Dorothea left Detroit without receiving Fillmore's letter of September 26. She arrived in Buffalo on September 29, only to discover that he and Mrs. Fillmore were in New York.

Russell House [Detroit], Thursday 7 A.M.

Sept. 27th, 1860

My dear Sir,

I have this hour arrived and have only time to acknowledge your letter and add that I will if possible be in Buffalo Saturday P.M. from this quarter. I have to go to Amherstburg [Ontario] today and am as usual *short* of time for all my work. I design taking the line on the north side of the Lake. I do not know the hour of arrival; if late at night I should prefer going to a Hotel rather than disturb your household. I pass Sunday with you. Please arrange your journey to New York, etc., therefore from that time without reference to me. I am sorry to have delayed you. Yours cordially with compliments to Mrs. Fillmore.

D. L. DIX

[Miss D. L. Dix, Sept. Rec'd. 3d at N.Y. 1860. Ans'd. Oct. 2]

◅§ 65. To DOROTHEA DIX

The Fillmores proceeded to New York unaware of Dorothea's final plans for Buffalo and thereby missed her call.

5 Avenue Hotel, N. Y.
Tuesday Morning
Oct. 2, 1860

My Dear Miss Dix,

I avail myself of a moment's leisure while Mrs. Fillmore is dressing to attend the wedding this morning, to express my deep regret and disappointment that this engagement should have prevented us from seeing you at our house. Your letter of Thursday, from Detroit, ought to have reached me at Buffalo on Friday, and if it had we would have remained over, but I received it here on Sunday evening.

We were quite desirous of remaining at Buffalo till Monday, but I found the fatigue would be too great for Mrs. F. to come here in one day and prepare for the wedding the next morning.

We had to rise at 3, and although we arrived here at 9½ we did not get our baggage till after midnight. This made the journey a very fatiguing one, but still I regret that we have missed that long deferred and greatly desired visit from you.

But shall we not have the pleasure of seeing you here? We shall be here some days yet.

I received a letter from my son yesterday, saying that you desired me to send any letters to Utica which had come to my care but I have none.

Mrs. F. joins me in sincere regrets at our disappointment and affectionate regards to yourself and I remain, as ever,

Your Sincere Friend
MILLARD FILLMORE

◄§ 99. To MILLARD FILLMORE

Dorothea substituted an inspection of the Erie County Poor House for her visit with the Fillmores. Powers called on her at her hotel, however.

Syracuse, Oct. 5th, 1860

Dear Sir and Friend,

I spent Sunday and part of Monday in Buffalo regretting to have missed the long proposed introduction to Mrs. Fillmore, and which now is an idea more remote than ever. I saw your friend Judge Hall and Mr. Hosmer, and they together with Mr. [Henry W.] Rogers were so kind as to join me on a visit to the County Poor House. The result, it is not needful to explain.

Your son called on me at the American on Sunday, and I asked him to secure some letters which would come to your care. Should any have reached you by error, etc., will you please forward them to Trenton, New Jersey. I should have replied at once to your second letter at Detroit, but did not receive it till I had passed from Amherstburg, when you would already have been enroute for New York.

Your fine city never looked so attractive and prosperous in my eyes as during my late visit. And though my friends were regretting the clouds and rain I did not perhaps the less appreciate the extent, activity and wealth of Buffalo, evidenced in many ways. I suppose you will not return for several weeks to the West, but I shall at all times be glad to hear of your health and enjoyment of your life and home.

The tumults attendant on, and in anticipation of, the coming elections are it is to be hoped not likely to be repeated for many weeks. I am tired of such scenes and the *noise* of this brawling war of words and waste of energies. And it seems to me the politicians of our times are doing little towards winning an enviable place on the page of their country's history.

With compliments to Mrs. Fillmore, I am your friend.

Cordially,

D. L. Dix

[Miss D. L. Dix, Oct. 5, Rec'd. 6, 1860.]

◆§ 66. To Dorothea Dix

The long-delayed introduction of Caroline Fillmore took place in New York on October 11 or 12. Except for Fillmore's single reference to it no details have survived.

The crowd that jammed the hotel was attracted by the heir to the British throne, the Prince of Wales, Albert Edward, who was on a three-week visit to the United States. The eighteen-year-old son of Queen Victoria and great-grandson of King George III charmed New York. An estimated two hundred thousand people lined Broadway to see him seated alongside Mayor Fernando Wood in an open barouche. Thousands more packed the street in front of the Fifth Avenue Hotel to witness his acknowledgments from the balcony of his suite.

Later, three thousand carefully selected guests, including the Fillmores, augmented by two thousand others, who gained admission without invitations, elbowed their way into the ballroom of the Academy of Music to attend the grand reception in the Prince's honor. Surviving a momentary panic when a portion of the floor sank several feet, the festivities were resumed with the loss of only six of the scheduled twenty-one dances. The evening was the most brilliant of the social season and the climax of the Prince's tour of America.

A second day of crowds and visitors forced Fillmore to withdraw to his room suffering from an ear infection. After a second uncomfortable night, he and Caroline departed for Buffalo. Their association with Dorothea had been limited to a single meeting.

Buffalo, Thursday,
Oct. 18, 1860

My Dear Miss Dix,

We left N. York on Monday morning and reached home night before last, and I feel much disappointed at not seeing more of you in New York. But I was very busy all day on Saturday, and the crowd was so great on Saturday evening that no one could go to or from the Hotel; and that evening I took an additional cold in my head and had another attack of the ear ache, from the intense pain of which I was only relieved during Sunday night by suppuration. This has made me almost deaf. Yesterday I could hear nothing with that ear and but little with the other.

Today, however, I am better and hope soon to be restored to my hearing again. But I regard it as not the least of my misfortunes that it prevented me from seeing you again, which I expected certainly to do on Sunday evening.

I knew I ran some risk in coming out on Monday but the day was fair. I had promised to see a man in Troy that evening, and above all I could not bear to remain longer in such a crowd, where every one seemed to regard it as his special business to talk to me, and I could not without difficulty understand what he said.

But enough of this. I merely write to let you know *how* I have been disappointed and sincerely hope, that next time you come this way we may be at home to receive you and enjoy a pleasant visit at our own home.

Mrs. F. joins me in cordial regards and

I remain as ever,
Your sincere Friend
Millard Fillmore

p.s. Did you receive my letter addressed to you at Utica?

~§ 100. To Millard Fillmore

Neither Dorothea nor Fillmore could have had any doubts about their commitments in the Presidential election. Senator Bell and his family were old friends of Dorothea, and his

*moderate Unionist position reflected her own opinion. Fillmore
saw in the Bell-Everett ticket the spirit of conciliation which
he had exemplified during his Presidency.*

*With Lincoln's election a reality, South Carolina, acting
on the theory that a separation from the Union was constitutional, voted unanimously in convention to secede, and invited
other states to follow her example.*

*Her unilateral action elicited a number of hastily framed
proposals designed to forestall such a response. Crittenden's
Resolutions in the Senate and the Peace Convention in Washington are the best remembered of these abortive moves. Fillmore was called upon by a committee of New York merchants
to go to South Carolina "as commissioner from New York to
exhort temperate action and delay." But he refused; conciliation, he replied, would be unsuccessful unless it was offered
by the Republican party. (See Buffalo* Commercial Advertiser,
December 16, 1860.)

Dorothea's letter from Utica is not in the Fillmore papers.

Phila., Nov'r. 10th, 1860

My dear Sir and Friend,

I ought sooner to have acknowledged your last letter but a
series of crowding engagements in the line of my "Vocation"
have more than usually abridged my social correspondence. I
had a letter at Utica dated from New York before I saw you
and Mrs. Fillmore at the 5 Ave. Hotel, and replied to it at once
there. I much question whether communications to that not
systematically managed House chiefly reached the parties addressed, at least if at all, in the season intended.

Now that the Presidential question is settled it may be
doubted if the excitements of processions, speeches and their
kindred train of influences will leave the people in a state of
mind to fall back on regular hours and wholesome employ-

ments. Our Southern friends seem to have enough to keep all their liveliest passions and prejudices in full exercise, and to disturb the quiet which is most in harmony with our free government. It is not easy to see where all the prevailing confusion will lead, and it is vain to speculate on probabilities or possibilities.

I imagine that you are exceedingly content in your retirement from the restless scenes of public life. Have you read Thackery's history of the Georges or of their times. If not I think you will find the lectures of interest. A good many reprints of standard works are announced, and also some new Books, but nothing of very marked interest that I recollect.

I am glad you can give so good account of your improved vision, and hope that both your own and Mrs. Fillmore's health are improved since your return to Buffalo.

I have intended writing to Judge Hall but hindrances have interposed to delay all communication.

I look for a little leisure the last week of November, which may be used for illustrating New York County Poor Houses and their influences.

My compliments to Mrs. Fillmore; friendly regards to your son, and best wishes to yourself. Your friend,

D. L. DIX

[Miss D. L. Dix. Nov. 10, Rec'd 14, 1860. Ans'd. Jan'y. 17.]

◄§ 101. To MILLARD FILLMORE

It is evident that Dorothea was now convinced that a conspiracy existed in the South; that President Buchanan was involved in it, and that Breckinridge was a tool of the conspirators who plotted southern rule over the nation. Resolute action by Buchanan, she believed, might have thwarted it. But she saw only paralysis in Washington.

Reports of secret societies and plots convinced Dorothea
that attempts would be made to seize Washington, cut it off
from the North, and prevent Lincoln's inaugural by destroying
the tracks or bridges along his railroad route between Philadelphia and Washington. She reported her misgivings to Samuel
M. Felton, President of the Philadelphia and Baltimore Railroad, who was at once impressed by the gravity of the situation.

Some years later he wrote a reminiscence of the interview,
which he dated a Saturday afternoon early in 1861:

> I listened attentively to what she had to say for more
> than an hour. She put in a tangible and reliable shape by
> the facts she related what before I had heard in numerous
> and detached parcels. The sum of it all was, that there was
> then an extensive and organized conspiracy through the
> South to seize upon Washington, with its archives and
> records, and then declare the Southern Confederacy de
> facto the Government of the United States. At the same
> time they were to cut off all means of communication be-
> tween Washington and the North, East, and West, and
> thus prevent the transportation of troops to wrest the Capi-
> tal from the hands of the insurgents. Mr. Lincoln's inau-
> gural was thus to be prevented, or his life was to fall a
> sacrifice. In fact, she said, troops were then drilling on the
> line of our own railroad, the Washington and Annapolis
> line, and the other lines of railroad.

If Felton's memory was accurate, his interview with Dorothea could not have been later than about January 20. This
would have been before she had heard of secret societies and
espionage on her visit to Kentucky. If the interview occurred
on her next trip to Washington, it would have been immediately after the bloody Baltimore riot attending the passage of

*the Sixth Massachusetts Regiment through that city on April
19, or six weeks after Lincoln's inaugural.*

*Felton placed guards at bridgeheads and helped to facili-
tate the rerouting of Lincoln's train from Harrisburg, Pennsylvania, to Washington.*

*Surely Dorothea's intervention to alert Felton was not out
of character. (See Tiffany, op. cit., pp. 333–334. Felton sent
a copy of his reminiscence to Tiffany in 1888.)*

*Despite the gravity of the crisis, Dorothea prepared to
leave Trenton for Kentucky to meet an emergency there.*

Trenton, N. J., from
Washington, Jan'y. 12th, 1861

My dear Sir and Friend,

It is a long time since I have written or heard from you;
not that topics on my part have failed, nor at all seasons has
time been short, but the amazing quick succeeding revolutionary movements of plotting Secessionists have held the mind in
suspense. The poor, imbecile and base President has helped on
the present crisis by folly and treason alike, I believe, and
there have been quite enough persons to take advantage of his
infirmity as well as his real unfaithfulness to himself, his Oath
of Office, and to his Country. I never saw the Federal City in
such a state of moral paralysis. I never saw people of common
sense and common capabilities so stupid, helpless and inert.
One strong decided mind, one resolute will could have stayed
all this mischief, and cauterized the head of the Hydra. Now
who can tell where, when, or how the monster may spread its
poisonous breath; and blight the prosperity of a Continent.
One thing is clearly demonstrated: the recent election of Mr.
Lincoln has *not* been either cause or consequence. It is now
evident that worse would have followed at no distant period if

any other Presidential Candidate had been successful. The President, joining with the Members of the Cabinet from the South, was but part of the conspiracy to elect Breckinridge, and during his four years to perfect as silently as surely the scheme for Southern rule; not that Mr. Breckinridge was party to this, save as *their means* of advancing revolutionary proceedings. Mr. [John M.] Botts' letter, which you will have read is seasonable. Did you read a pamphlet I sent you some time since entitled *The South?* It was written by Stephen Caldwell, now of Philadelphia, but a native of Virginia, and is marked by its sound views on practical subjects as I think.

I set off for Lexington, Kentucky, next week; called there by letters urging my services on behalf of the insane. A hospital lately destroyed by fire at Hopkinsville has occasioned the exposure and suffering of many poor people, and it is my duty to go to them. If you write, a letter addressed to me at *this place* or at Lexington, Ky., will be safe from loss.

With compliments to Mrs. Fillmore, I am your friend,

D. L. DIX

[Miss D. L. Dix, Jan. 12; Rec'd. 14, 1861; Ans'd. Jan. 17.]

◄§ 67. To DOROTHEA DIX

Fillmore, too, placed the blame for secession on the paralysis of Congress and Buchanan. But he remained critical of the Republicans for their failure to make reasonable concessions to the South. He believed that the combined action of Congress, the President, and the incoming Republican administration were required to avert catastrophe. He recommended Crittenden's last-ditch compromise plan in the Senate as a basis for settlement—it would have extended the Missouri Compromise line westward to California thereby protecting slavery in the federal territories south of the 36° 30′ line and prohibiting it in those north of it. But he feared it had been offered too late to avert disunion.

His hope that the Republicans would make concessions was unfulfilled. Behind the scenes Lincoln was inflexible. If the tug had to come, he confided, it would be better to have it at once rather than later.

By mid-January Alabama, Mississippi, and Florida had joined South Carolina in secession, and on February 18 at Montgomery, Alabama, six states proclaimed the birth of the Confederate States of America and selected Jefferson Davis as President. A week earlier Lincoln stopped in Buffalo for two days during his slow progression to the capital. As Buffalo's "first-citizen" Fillmore welcomed him to the city, accompanied him to church, and entertained him in his home. Their relations were cordial, but there could have been little mutual confidence. Fillmore was aware of Lincoln's active opposition to him in 1856, and Lincoln, in turn, of Fillmore's support of Bell and his hostility toward Republicanism.

Fillmore's reference to *Fillmore at Home* was to call Dorothea's attention to his Albany speech in 1856, when he warned that a victory by a northern sectional (Republican) party could result in disunion.

As one state after another seceded in the Deep South, the northern and border states looked to the incoming administration for a sign of what might be expected, and Seward's speech in the Senate on January 12 was scrutinized for such a disclosure. Seward was more conciliatory toward the South than he had been heretofore; while he hailed the Union as permanent, he expressed a willingness to accept a constitutional amendment to deny federal intervention to control slavery in the states, and he proposed a constitutional convention to settle

present difficulties. But not until the angry excitement had sub-
sided; "then, and not till then—one, two, or three years hence."

Fillmore obviously believed that such a delay would leave
no nation to require saving.

Buffalo, Jan'y. 17, 1861

My Dear Miss Dix,

I owe you a thousand apologies for my apparent negligence,
but I can assure you that it has not arisen from any indifference, but since the receipt of yours of Nov. 10th my mind has
been engrossed, like your own, by the startling revolutionary
events at the South, which have succeeded each other so rapidly as to keep the mind in a constant state of anxiety.

It was a maxim of the Romans, "never to despair of the
Republic," and I have endeavored to feel so in regard to ours,
but as state after state secedes, and Congress seems paralyzed,
my hopes fail me, and I give up all as lost. It seems to me that
if the President had acted with becoming vigor in the first instance, and the Republicans had shown a willingness to put
themselves right on the record and grant reasonable concession
to the South, that the combined influences would have staid
this treasonable torrent that is now sweeping away the pil-
lars of the Constitution (see page 14 of *Fillmore at Home,*
which I send). But there is no man of the dominant party who
has the patriotism or courage to propose any practicable plan
of adjustment. I did hope for something from Mr. Seward,
but that hope has failed. His suggestion for a *post mortem*
examination after the patient has been dead two or three years,
sounds like mockery more than like the words of a statesman.

I do think that Mr. Crittenden's proposition ought to be
made the basis of a settlement, but I fear it will not be until it
is too late; and that our government will dissolve into thin air
"like the baseless fabric of a dream," without one manly and

patriotic effort to save it. But I dare not trust my feelings to say more.

I am happy to say that my eyes are quite well, my hearing perfectly restored, and my family are in the enjoyment of good health.

Mrs. Fillmore joins me in affectionate regards and I am as ever your

Sincere Friend

MILLARD FILLMORE

P.S. I have read with great interest the able pamphlet of Mr. Caldwell but not Mr. Botts' letter.

&§ 102. TO MILLARD FILLMORE

Dorothea's reports of coercion, secret societies, and treason reflect the prevailing confusion and uncertainty in the border states. She now linked Vice President Breckinridge with a plot to take Kentucky out of the Union.

It is true that Breckinridge was definitely pro-Confederate after South Carolina's firing on Fort Sumter on April 12, 1861, despite his recent election to the United States Senate. He accepted a commission in the Confederate Army without resigning his Senate seat, and the Senate expelled him from its ranks. He later served as Secretary of War in Davis' Cabinet.

Lexington, from Frankfort

Jan'y. 26th, 1861

My dear Sir and Friend,

I have your letter and two pamphlets of interest, especially the first, for which my thanks. I have come to spend a quiet Sunday here in preference to a noisy hotel residence in Frankfort, but return there again on Monday, and also after next week go to Hopinsville, Ky., and Nashville, Tennessee.

I learn from the most *reliable* sources here that the largest part of southern citizens are coerced into a vote *against* the *Union;* that some are by fear led to forswear their allegiance and their principles, others by misrepresentations, and many vote while too much intoxicated to know at all what they are about. I learn some things I don't think it prudent to write touching secret societies, and the connection men [in] power have with them.

Intelligent men of both parties charge the Vice President with participation in the present high-handed treason and base movements of the Southern States, and declare that he is known to express the hope that Kentucky *will go out* before the 4th of March. It is astonishing to what a point treachery has gone in the South—base, low and vicious conduct has the ascendant.

I must bid farewell, with compliments to Mrs. Fillmore. Please address should you write again at Trenton as I am not stationary here long enough to be sure of receipt.

Respectfully your friend,
D. L. DIX

[Miss D. L. Dix, Jan. 26; Rec'd. 30, 1861; Ans'd. Feb. 26.]

◆§ 103. To MILLARD FILLMORE

Despite her despair as secession became a reality, Dorothea projected an ambitious tour of inspections reaching into the spring.

Only once before had she been so unhappy: upon Pierce's veto of her land-grant bill!

The crisis called to mind Cataline's conspiracy.

State Library
Springfield, Ill.
Feb'y. 21 [1861]

Dear Sir and Friend,

I hardly know why I write since I have nothing to say that is important connected with our national interests or our country's welfare. Alas, alas for the fallen Republic! Loss of territory by dismemberment is nothing compared with the loss of "good name." Treachery, corruption, treason, base self-seeking are prominently our characteristics as a people; for as the rulers are designated, so may it be supposed are the people who support them.

I have never before, save once, been so unhappy. When that poor, weak man in power [President Pierce] destroyed by the dash of his pen across the $20,000,000 bill, and crushed the hopes of thousands, and the health-salvation of perhaps tens of thousands, I was greatly distressed. Now, well may the daughters of America sit in sack-cloth and her sons wear the garments of mourning, as pillar after pillar of the great temple of the Republic crumbles in ruins.

But I must quit this theme. God save us the dreadful calamity of civil war. God save those who will not save themselves!

My bills for the relief of the Insane have just passed Senate and House here, and I go to Jacksonville [Illinois] to see the patients tomorrow. On Monday I go to St. Louis (influenced by a letter received yesterday), and probably to Jefferson City to save, if I can, a hazarded bill some person has introduced there.

I am expected to be again in Kentucky in March at the return of the members. Should you write I think a letter would be quite sure to find me somewhere, if to the care of Rev'd. W. G. Eliot, St. Louis, Missouri.

My compliments to Mrs. Fillmore.

Your friend cordially and with esteem,

D. L. Dix

Have you not lately been reminded of Cataline's conspiracy, and more than once of the fall of the Roman Empire? Do you recollect Gibbon's summary of the causes?

[Miss D. L. Dix, Feb. 21; Rec'd. 23, 1861; Ans'd. Feb. 26.]

ᴥᴥ 68. To Dorothea Dix

Dorothea's labors were as endless as those of Sisyphus!

The disparity of opinion within the Republican party precipitated a scramble for office in the incoming Administration, and Lincoln was besieged by patronage seekers. He had not resolved the conflicting claims for posts in his Cabinet when he reached Washington, but Seward and Bates seemed assured of appointments by the last week of February.

Despite the gloomy outlook, Fillmore clung to the hope that Lincoln might avert civil strife and entice the seceding states to return once they had "tried the folly of secession." He trusted that Seward, and especially Bates, would prove helpful.

Buffalo, Feb'y. 26, 1861

My Dear Miss Dix,

I should have thanked you for your very kind and interesting letter from Frankfort, but your future then seemed so uncertain that I delayed writing, and now I have yours of the 23d from Springfield, Ill., by which I perceive that your labors are as endless as those of Sysiphus [Sisyphus] and sometimes almost as discouraging, but I am happy to hear that your health holds out and your courage and perseverance never fail. May God reward you for all your labors and all your sacrifices.

In your letter from Frankfort you spoke reservedly and rather mysteriously of the Secret Societies at the South. Some allusion has been made to them by the papers, but nothing definite or satisfactory. I am sorry you did not give me more information, for I greatly fear that they are nests of traitors and nurseries of secession and rebellion. But, indeed, every thing looks dark and gloomy. The party which has elected Mr. Lincoln is already hopelessly divided, and perhaps after all this is the best symptom of the times. But every thing now depends upon the wisdom, discretion and firmness of the incoming administration. If we can retain the border states, avoid a civil war, and offer an apology for the seceding states to come back, after they have tried the folly of secession, I do not utterly despair of seeing the Union again restored. I know nothing of President Lincoln's administrative ability, but I am better satisfied with Gov. Seward's course of late than I was at first, and I have faith that he and Judge Bates may be found able and reliable cabinet advisers at this time. But I forbear to speculate on the future. The sky is over cast, and my political compass does not traverse. I am therefore waiting the result with as much calmness and patience as I can muster, and as much hope as I dare indulge.

Will you not return to the East by the Northern route and may we not hope to see you at our house?

I regret to say that Mrs. Fillmore, at this moment, is suffering very much from the prevailing influenza, but I hope her illness is but temporary. Did she know I was writing I know she would desire to be remembered.

I am as ever,
Your Sincere Friend
MILLARD FILLMORE

❧ 104. To Millard Fillmore

*Dorothea returned from Kentucky in April of 1861, and
was in Trenton when word arrived that the Sixth Massachusetts Regiment had been assaulted by a Baltimore mob. She
immediately left for Washington. A day later she paused to
inform Ann Heath of her response to the emergency.*

> Yesterday, I followed in the train three hours after the
> tumult in Baltimore. It was not easy getting across the city,
> but I did not choose to turn back, and so I reached my
> destination. I think my duty lies near military hospitals for
> the present. This need not be announced. I have reported
> myself and some nurses for free service at the War Depart-
> ment and to the Surgeon General [*Quoted in Tiffany,
> p. 336*].

*Action followed quickly. She was named Superintendent
of Women Nurses and ordered by Secretary of War Cameron
and Acting Surgeon General, D. C. Wood, "to select and
assign women nurses to general or permanent military hospitals, they not to be employed in such hospitals without her
sanction and approval, except in cases of urgent need."*

*Neither the Army nor Dorothea had any notion that the
"three months' war" involving 75,000 troops would lengthen
to four years and multiply to encompass 1.5 million men.*

*The situation called for a vigorous recruitment, a coordina-
tion of services, a flexibility to handle the unexpected. Dorothea scarcely filled the bill. Approaching sixty and in delicate
health, she had followed the dictates of her conscience without coordinating her work with anyone. But, despite these
handicaps, she assumed the responsibilities of the office without hesitation or reservation, and did not release them until
the war was won.*

Nine months after receiving Fillmore's previous letter in Illinois, Dorothea took time to renew their correspondence. Her frame of mind remained pessimistic, and she found solace only in an intense involvement in her duties. But she invited Fillmore's response.

Washington, Jan'y. 20 [1862]

Dear Sir and Friend,

In these strange dark times one has little heart for friendly letter writing, and indeed I have no time for social intercourse or of letter communication now with long-accustomed correspondents. What human prescience can show our national destiny: Our pride, conceit and arrogant boasting, and even now not rebuked to the measure of wholesome thinking and utterance.

If God were just to correct us according to our offences as a nation I think we should see yet drearier prospects than the past has prefigured. I am not hopeful, for I abide in Washington where no reflecting mind can gather solid reasons for confidence in public rulers, or congressional proceedings.

If you discern any solid cause for encouragement, write and tell me. I need consolation. But that life is really absorbed in *intense* occupation I should find the contemplation of our national condition intolerable.

Let me hear from you then, and present to Mrs. Fillmore my friendly regards, while you accept the renewed expression of my esteem and friendship.

D. L. Dix

[Miss D. L. Dix, Jan. 20, Rec'd. 22, 1862, Ans'd. Jan. 23.]

◈§ 69. To Dorothea Dix

Fillmore replied immediately to compliment Dorothea upon her contributions to the war effort. Comparing her work with that of Florence Nightingale, he cautioned her against overwork lest she suffer a physical breakdown similar to that of Miss Nightingale in the Crimea. He too professed to be downcast by Republican miscalculations and the despotic arrests and imprisonments by the Army when civil courts were functioning.

Buffalo, Jan'y. 23d, 1862

My Dear Miss Dix,

I was no less surprised than gratified to receive your kind favor of the 21st for I saw that you were so engrossed with the misfortunes of others that I did not think you had a moment which you could call your own. Hence I had long since ceased to expect a letter and did not even feel that I had a right to tax you with reading one from me.

I can not help feeling thankful that you have been so wisely placed at the head of the Hospital department of the Army, but I fear that like that other angel of mercy, Miss Nightingale, you may offer yourself a sacrifice for the relief of the afflicted. All I can say is, may your life and health be preserved and may the God of mercy reward you for your disinterested devotion to the cause of suffering humanity.

You say you are not hopeful for you *abide* in Washington, and ask if I can give you any encouragement that shall bring consolation. I wish indeed that I could, but I regret to say that I have never been as confident as many seem to be of the restoration of this Union. I thought some concessions should have been made last winter, that would have given the truly loyal men of the South assured ground to stand upon;

but when I saw the fanatical leaders of the dominant party crying, peace! peace!! when there was no peace and prophesying that this rebellion would be put down in 60 or 90 days, I lost all hope for the Union; and greatly feared that the government of the Northern States would be overthrown, and the Country would first feel all the horrors of anarchy from which it could only escape through a military despotism. But the unauthorized and despotic imprisonments in the loyal states, where the courts of justice are in full operation, and the patience with which the people bear it, makes me fear that we have reached a point where we only want a master to be enslaved. But these things so stir my blood, that I will not write on them. I will try to hope for the best, and reconcile myself to my country's fate, if I can.

I am spending my time much as usual. Domestically very happy, as myself and family are all enjoying health.

I cherish with great satisfaction our long friendship and should be very happy indeed to see you; but you know I can not go to Washington if I can avoid it, and thus far I have been enabled to do so.

Should you pass this way you must not fail to give us a call for we should both be very happy to see you.

Mrs. F. joins me in kindest regards, and

I remain as ever
Your Sincere friend
MILLARD FILLMORE

105. To MILLARD FILLMORE

Dorothea seems not to have answered Fillmore's reply to her letter of January 20, 1862.

Seven years later, her visit to the Government Hospital for the Insane in Washington recalled Fillmore's contributions to

its founding. And she broke her long silence with a friendly
note in which she reported events relating to their mutual
friends.

As in 1862, Fillmore answered her letter, but his reply is
not in the Dix manuscripts. His missing response seems to
have been their final communication. She was now sixty-seven;
he was sixty-nine.

Washington, D. C., Feb. 17th, 1869
Government Hospital for Insane of
the Army and Navy

To Honorable Millard Fillmore,
Dear Sir,

So many years have interrupted a friendly correspondence
that I almost hesitate in recommending a written communication; but this place just now recalls so many pleasant incidents
with which you were connected more or less personally and
officially in the creation of the Institution in which I am just
now for a few weeks a sojourner that I am impelled by unabated friendly regards to take my pen and inquire after your
welfare and for that of Mrs. Fillmore and your son. My time
as formerly is very closely occupied, and social life as much
removed from my path as formerly.

I avoid all political readings and communications, which
are at best always disquieting, and I do not disturb myself with
speculating on what may be the future of our country, since I
have passed that age when one may look for a long term of
added years and what I can not remedy of wrong or avert by
anticipated exertions I think it unwise to contemplate.

I lately heard from Mrs. John Bell, whom you will remember, and who is residing at the Cumberland Iron Works in
Tennessee with one daughter Jeannie and Mr. Bell, who with
good appetite and certain remaining powers seems likely to

live long years a dependent paralytic. Mrs. Judge [James Moore] Wayne is spending the winter with a son in Brunswick, Ga. The family of good Professor Henry are all well, the Professor working as earnestly as ever. Dr. Nichols had the misfortune to lose his wife in 1863, and is as ever devoted to the improvement of the Institution. He has two promising children.

Shall I hear how you are and of your present interests?

My respectful regards to Mrs. Fillmore.

Your friend,

D. L. Dix

[Miss D. L. Dix, Feb. 17, Rec'd. 20, 1869, Ans'd. Feb. 20.]

9
Later
Years

The termination of his Presidency in 1853 was not a retirement for Fillmore, but a start of waiting to see if lightning might strike again. His defeat in 1856 was a retirement from politics. To occasional calls that he break his silence from the platform, in the press, or through an open letter he gave a consistent refusal. Only when writing in confidence to his old friends did Fillmore rail against extremists, North and South, who were creating a sectional impasse.

But the Civil War became a nightmare. It shattered his usual composure and momentarily undermined his faith in the democratic process.

Like most northerners Fillmore was shocked by the assault on Fort Sumter. The nation was threatened, and the crisis called for united action to quell rebellion. At a Buffalo mass meeting he exhorted his audience to rally to the colors. He personally pledged $500 for the dependents of volunteers, the first such offer in the city. He was also instrumental in organizing the Union Continentals, a company of superannuated citizens, to serve as a home guard. Though lacking in military experience he commanded the unit and was identified as captain or major. The company proved more ornamental than useful, but their multicolored uniforms brightened civic functions and their spirited activity encouraged enlistments. Marching at the ceremony marking the departure of the first troops, Fillmore was described as "stately and erect wearing a sword and plume, looking like an emperor." The city had not yet lost its sense of humor.[1]

In November, when the Trent Affair, involving the seizure of Confederate diplomats from a British mail ship, brought a threat of war between England and the United States, Fillmore called for federal aid to restore defenses along the harbor, Niagara River, and canal. Buffalo had not forgotten the devastation that the War of 1812 had wrought upon their village.

But Fillmore's morale was shattered by the almost unbroken succession of military disasters in 1862–1863 and the repeated intervention of the Army in civil affairs. He viewed the arrest and confinement of citizens in military prisons, trials by military courts where regular courts were available, the suppression of newspapers, and other arbitrary acts as evidence that a military coup was in the making.

The war was brought home to Fillmore in a distressing way in 1863 when a nephew was dismissed from the Army for intemperance. Entreated to intervene by the young man's mother, he wrote to President Lincoln requesting a court of inquiry. Ever on the defensive against asking special favors, it must have proved extremely distasteful to him. Lincoln forwarded his letter to the Judge Advocate General for examination, but took no further action.[2]

Fillmore's indignation over the handling of the war came into the open at a Christian Commission Fair on Washington's

birthday in 1864. In an address which opened with a tribute to
Washington and closed with the usual platitudes on the need
for concerted action to win the war, in what may have been a
departure from his text, he lashed out at the war's cost in lives,
liberty, and dollars:

> Three years of war have desolated the fairest portion of
> our land, loaded the country with an enormous debt that
> the sweat of millions yet unborn must be taxed to pay;
> arrayed brother against brother, and father against son in
> mortal combat; deluged our country with fraternal blood;
> whitened our battlefields with the bones of the slain, and
> darkened the sky with the pall of mourning.

While he urged an all-out commitment, he would not
overlook "partisan prejudice, petty jealousies, malignant envy,
and intriguing, selfish ambition." And although he called for
victory, he urged that once it had been attained and the leaders of the rebellion had been removed, "then let us show our
magnanimity and generosity in winning back the deluded
multitude who have been seduced or coerced into this rebellion. This I conceive to be Christian forgiveness, the best policy and only one which can ever restore the Union." [3]
While many in his audience were stunned by his open
attacks upon the conduct of the war, his dissent might have
been tolerated as the aberration of a disappointed and aging
office-seeker, had not the press branded him a "copperhead"—
Civil War jargon for enemy sympathizer or collaborator. The
press linked him with "the bitterest opponents of the war and
its conduct, in the infamous circle made up of such men as
Vallandigham, the Woods, the Seymours and the Brooks." [4]
Hundreds of newspapers were soon deploring Fillmore's want

of patriotism, and some of his oldest Buffalo friends avoided him.

Overlooked in the same address was his citation of women, for their unstinted labor and sacrifice during the crisis, and his special tribute to Dorothea:

And has not America her nightingales he [asked]. Yes, many, though less conspicuous; but she has one who has devoted her life to alleviate the sufferings of humanity, and many a state lunatic asylum attests her disinterested devotion. Since this war began she has given her days and nights without compensation to the services of the hospitals. She is a true and noble type of womanhood, whose disinterested and humane efforts are only equalled by her retiring modesty and feminine delicacy, and when justice shall be done to those noble women who have devoted their best energies to relieve the sufferings "which flesh is heir to," the name of Miss Dix will be no less conspicuous and deserving than that of Florence Nightingale.

But you are all Dixes and Nightingales in your several spheres, and He who judges the heart and the deed will reward you according to your merits.[5]

Two years had elapsed since he and Dorothea had last corresponded, but he had obviously followed her career as Superintendent of Female Nurses.

Evidence that Fillmore's choleric observations could not be excused as a fleeting impulse may be found in his position in the election of 1864. In August he advised a friend that the country was on the verge of ruin, and only a change in administration could avert national bankruptcy and military despotism. He endorsed General George B. McClellan for President.

And in rejecting Lincoln he cast his first vote for a Democrat in forty years of politics.[6]

A final humiliation occurred during the pandemonium following Lincoln's assassination. As the appalling news spread across the city by word-of-mouth from the telegraph office, and by newsboys hawking special editions of the local papers, householders suspended black drapes from their doors and windows. A passer-by on Niagara Square discovered that Fillmore's house remained unmarked and remedied the situation to his own satisfaction by smearing it with black ink. Fillmore tardily displayed the more appropriate symbol of mourning, but his delay was accepted by his critics as additional evidence of his copperheadism.

Nevertheless, Fillmore, at the head of a citizens' committee a few days later, met the Lincoln funeral train at Batavia and escorted it to Buffalo.

A year later, as the city's spokesman, he greeted General Sherman upon his arrival there. In September of the same year he officially welcomed President Johnson during his controversial "swing around the circle" to strengthen his congressional support. Buffalo was unable or unwilling to find a suitable substitute for the venerable ex-President when a host was required for very important persons!

From the platform his broader girth and heavier jowls and slower movements attested to his advancing years, but his back remained straight, his flowing white hair unthinned, and his stage presence and polish were as evident as in his heyday.

Meanwhile, Fillmore gave many hours to his civic and philanthropic interests. He assisted in founding the Buffalo Fine Arts Academy, the Grosvenor Library, and the University of Buffalo. He served as President of the Buffalo General Hospital, and he was a founder and first president of the Buffalo Historical Society. The latter was a favorite of his. He and his associates launched the first systematic campaign to gather and preserve manuscripts and documents bearing upon the region's past. Buffalo's history of its origins, the War of 1812, and its Indian heritage is the richer because of his dedication to the work of the society.

Some of his civic activities extended over many years. Countless others consumed only a few days or hours. At seventy-two he added to a gift of $25 a promise to preside over a Thanksgiving service at the Grace Methodist Church for the "Newsboys, Bootblacks and Poor Children's Fund."

Because of his well-known opposition to Republican policies during the Civil War, Fillmore was appealed to over and over again to support movements designed to overthrow the party's hegemony in the postwar years. By 1868, the Radical Republicans were dominating Washington. They had imposed a victors' peace on the prostrate South, and were preparing to enforce it by an army of occupation. Alarmed by this development, veteran Whigs preferred for President the Democratic nominee Horatio Seymour, a former war governor of New York, to the hero of Appomattox. Grant was now identified with the Radical leaders and was expected as President to acquiesce in their handling of Reconstruction. Fillmore wrote in confidence to Seymour expressing his support, but he refused to heed requests that he enter the campaign in Seymour's behalf.[7]

In 1872, dissatisfaction with military rule in the South and scandals in high places precipitated the Liberal Republican movement. Fillmore was invited to participate in the formal organization of the party, but he declined to reenter the political arena.[8] The party's subsequent nomination of Horace Greeley as Grant's opponent left Fillmore and his old partisans on tenterhooks. Greeley had only recently abjured Radical Republicanism, and he was almost as unacceptable as Grant.

Fillmore appears to have finally supported Greeley as the lesser evil, but the combined backing of Democrats and Liberal Republicans failed to obtain his election. The somewhat tarnished hero was re-elected and Radical Republican rule was assured for another four years.

Fillmore's remarriage had freed him from financial insecurity and enabled him to live in a manner suited to his tastes. He and Caroline were soon caught up in the social whirl of Buffalo, enjoying the company of their friends in their elegant Italianate mansion. They customarily spent a few weeks in August at Saratoga and less regularly dropped into Albany and New York for short visits.

But Caroline's frail constitution failed to sustain her restless nervous energy. In time her weakness became chronic. She spent many weeks of each year convalescing from fatigue and nervous prostration. Hopeful that an ocean voyage would be beneficial, they went to Europe in 1866, but she showed no improvement. They soon returned. Time after time Fillmore canceled plans to travel because of her health. Their Buffalo friends noted her taut nerves and sudden fits of temper, and Fillmore's unceasing concern and attentions. If he ever lost his patience, it was not detected.

By contrast, Fillmore appeared as sturdy at seventy as he had at fifty. He had recovered from the affliction that impaired his vision for several years. He scarcely knew a day's illness and lost little of his old-time buoyancy.

In the summer of 1873 his sister Julia, now a resident of California, returned for a visit, and invited her surviving brothers and sister to a reunion at Ann Arbor, Michigan. Fillmore reluctantly left Caroline, who felt too unwell to travel, and joined the others—Olive, a widow, who lived in Dexter, Michigan; Asher, a farmer near Greenfield, Indiana; Calvin, a carpenter, in Ann Arbor; and Julia—under Calvin's roof. A photograph of the five reveals a striking family resemblance, despite a spread of sixteen years in their ages and the vicissitudes of their many years.

In January of 1874 Fillmore tentatively accepted an invitation from W. W. Corcoran to a reunion with survivors of his Cabinet. It would have been his first trip to Washington since his retirement from the Presidency twenty-one years before. But Caroline's poor health forced a postponement, and the opportunity was lost.

On February 13, 1874, Fillmore had a seizure while shaving. It left him partially paralyzed. Two weeks later he sustained a second attack, and he died on March 8, presumably from a cerebral hemorrhage. He was buried in Forest Lawn Cemetery.

Following his death Caroline's eccentricities became more pronounced. She wrote an elaborate will, then juggled names of beneficiaries as she kept changing her mind. After her demise in 1881 the will was contested, a former coachman, whose bequest had been removed from the will, charging that she wrote the will while insane. The court, however, rejected the claim.

Meanwhile, Fillmore's bachelor son, Powers, obviously embarrassed by his stepmother's foibles, decided to destroy the personal correspondence of his family. Powers' failure to execute his plan and the chain of events which preserved the papers have already been described.[9]

How long Dorothea could have continued the grueling pace she maintained from 1858 to 1861, had not the War intervened, is a mystery. During those years she had raised more than a half million dollars for hospitals. In a five-month period between November, 1859, and April, 1860, she had obtained appropriations in one northern and five southern states. When she brought her crusade to a temporary halt in 1861, it was not because of the obvious dislocations accompanying the War. She saw a more pressing duty—the expenditure of time and talent to save the Union.

Her hurried descent upon Washington in the wake of mob violence in Baltimore in April has been described. Her appointment as Superintendent of Female Nurses by Secretary Cameron would stretch into a four-year service and become one of the most difficult and frustrating undertakings in her career.

When she accepted the commission there were no female nurses in the Army. There never had been. Nursing was a male prerogative, and it was not relinquished by the stroke of a pen. Despite an extreme shortage of nurses, many persons in and out of the armed forces considered the work inappropriate for females. Surgeons recoiled at the idea of fitting women into a hospital routine and, if tolerated, they were frequently assigned to only menial chores. They might wash the hands and faces of the patients, comb their hair, change their bedding. They might prepare drinks and stimulants when ordered by the surgeons, and otherwise busy themselves by scrubbing floors and washing windows. But at the outset they were ordered to leave the ward when male nurses entered to dress wounds and were denied access to the kitchens to obtain "extras" such as tea and sugar. One nurse who purchased a stove and set it up in her tent to provide hot water and occasional snacks for her patients was reprimanded. The stove was confiscated by the surgeon in charge.[10]

It was assumed that women lacked the stamina and fortitude required, and that they would inevitably corrupt the morals of patients and Army personnel in the hospitals.

Thrown on the defensive, Dorothea set out to prove that women deserved a chance to prove themselves. She initiated the recruitment of a corps of "saints" who would exemplify dedication and service. She accepted no young ladies and preferred women who could afford to donate their services and were prepared for duty at any hour of the day or night; "those who are sober, earnest, self-sacrificing, self-sustained, who can bear the presence of suffering and exercise entire self-control, of speech and manner; who can be calm, gentle, quiet, active, and steadfast in duty, also who are willing to take and execute the directions of the surgeons." [11] It was as though Dorothea were describing her own virtues. Her experience should have forewarned her!

When the use of female nurses had been approved by Congress Dorothea formalized the qualifications for admission: "No women under thirty need apply to serve in government hospitals. . . . All nurses are required to be plain-looking women, their dresses must be brown or black with no adornments; no hoop skirts." [12]

Such a formidable list of requirements was extremely unpopular with younger women, and Dorothea was soon in a crossfire between surgeons, who wanted no females, and women who considered her standards restrictive and unfair.

One application which would have amused Dorothea had she not taken her responsibilities so seriously read:

> I am in possession of one of your circulars and will comply with all your requirements. I am plain looking enough to suit you, and old enough. I have no relations in the war, no lover there. I never had a husband and am not looking for one—will you take me? [13]

In the early months before casualties mounted Dorothea insisted upon interviewing each applicant, looked into her housing and other needs, and personally handled the distribution of supplies as they reached Washington. She had always attended to the details of her work. She saw no need to change. Consequently, as hospitals multiplied her office lacked organization and her responsibilities remained poorly defined. She did not take a single day's furlough. Few people noted the friendly, gentle, yet persuasive manner which had often won victories for her in the past; they saw her as opinionated, overbearing, and unreasonable.

After several encounters with her, Chairman of the United States Sanitary Commission George Templeton Strong noted in his diary that she "has plagued us a little. She is energetic, benevolent, unselfish, and a mild case of monomania. Working on her own hook she does good, but no one can cooperate with her, for she belongs to the class of comets and can be subdued into relations with no system whatever." [14]

It was inevitable, of course, that Dorothea should receive the brunt of criticism stemming from dissatisfactions with the hospitals and the practices of the surgeons over which she had no control.

Nevertheless, one nurse who met her during the last weeks of the war while en route to the federal supply depot at City Point on the James River remembered her as "the stateliest woman I ever saw and . . . very dignified in manner and conversation. . . . She was tall, straight as an arrow, and unusually slender. . . . Her dress was plain and neat and her linen collar and cuffs immaculate. She wore no jewel, not even a breastpin." [15] Finding no housing at the bustling depot the nurse obtained permission to sleep in a storeroom, where she fashioned a bed out of shavings and straw. As she settled for the night there was a knock on the door. It was Dorothea in search of lodging. The nurse gave her the improvised bed and, wrapping herself in a blanket, lay on the floor.

A good share of Dorothea's authority was eased from her

grasp in 1863 by General Order 351. While this Order confirmed her appointive power, it allowed the Surgeon General to name nurses to muster rolls in exceptional cases. Taking full advantage of the exception, surgeons frequently bypassed Dorothea and made their own appointments, which were confirmed by the Surgeon General. The Order actually broke her grip upon the appointive power and substantially limited her supervisory control over the nurses. And, while it may not have "broken her heart," as one biographer has written, it was a devastating blow to her pride. But if a resignation was expected by her critics, Dorothea disappointed them, and to the war's close she retained the staunch support of Secretary of War Edwin W. Stanton.

Appomattox did not bring an immediate release from her onerous burdens. Hundreds of sick and wounded continued to require hospitalization, and resignations intensified the labor of those who remained. She continued her work, and added to it a search for missing soldiers when her help was sought by wives, mothers, and sweethearts. By September, 1865, however, Dorothea's work was done.

When Secretary Stanton mentioned a form of recognition for her services—she had accepted no pay—she suggested an American flag. On January 25, 1867, she received a stand of national colors with a copy of the order from Secretary Stanton, "for the care, succor, and relief of the sick and wounded soldiers of the United States on the battlefield, in camps, and hospitals during the recent war." Deeply touched, Dorothea replied that no greater distinction could have been conferred upon her. "No possession will be so prized while life remains to love and serve my country." [16]

The award sweetened her memories of the conflict and her role in it, including the frustrations which once led her to exclaim, "This is not the work I would have my life judged by!"

She presented the flags to Harvard University where they were hung in Memorial Hall, which had been dedicated to the sons of Harvard who had died for their country in the War for the Maintenance of the Union.

With her war duties behind her Dorothea continued to linger in Washington to assist nurses suffering from disabilities to obtain pensions from Congress. And then, unwilling or unable to leave the scene without a last demonstration of her debt to the nation's youth who had given their lives, she threw herself into a drive to erect an appropriate memorial. Learning that a plan to erect a monument at the national cemetery at Hampton Roads was languishing for a lack of funds, she took over the campaign. She was soon accepting contributions from all parts of the North. In twelve months she collected funds to erect a seventy-five-foot obelisk, fashioned from Maine granite of her own selection, surrounded by a stone fence lined with one thousand muskets and bayonets (a gift to her from General Grant). In addition to its stated purpose it fostered monument raising in communities across the country, and incidentally provided a navigational aid for ships in Hampton Roads!

Dorothea was now prepared to take a hard look at the institutions she had inspired in the prewar years. In the North the war had frequently cut or delayed appropriations for asylums, and the growing population and the higher incidence of mental illness, especially among veterans, accentuated the need for action. In the South physical destruction, the diversion of appropriations to military needs, and the waste and inefficiency incidental to military and carpetbag rule combined to undo much that she had achieved earlier.

She hesitated momentarily before entering the South to determine whether the hatred engendered by the conflict would bar her return. But she soon discovered that doors were again open to her and that there were more requests for help than she could answer.

Thus she returned to her travels, slowing only as infirmities incidental to old age required. Even at seventy she remained an arresting figure. As slender as in her youth, her hair graying only slightly, her voice soft and musical unless raised by what she regarded as inexcusable laxity or inefficiency, her motions still graceful and dignified, she was the symbol of humanity for the insane.

An old stereoscopic picture shows her comfortably seated in her living room, presumably in Trenton. The identity is unmistakable—the dark hair, parted so as to reveal her high forehead, the neatness of her dress, the complete absence of jewelry or other ostentation, the almost regal bearing—it could only be Dorothea Dix.

In 1869, as noted elsewhere, she recalled her old association with President Fillmore involving the Government Hospital in Washington. If she thought of him again from time to time, the memories did not elicit a letter. Fillmore's death undoubtedly touched off a flood of memories, but unfortunately Caroline Fillmore did not save her correspondence. Thus the contents of Dorothea's letter of condolence, for surely there was one, have been lost.

In 1881, at seventy-nine, she answered a call to the South and, in a sweep reminiscent of her earlier operations, inspected mental hospitals in Virginia and North Carolina during March and April. She continued her circuit into Georgia and Florida in May and June, and finally returned by water from Savannah. She had accomplished her goal; but it would be her last grand tour.

A few months later Dorothea stopped at the New Jersey State Asylum at Trenton for a few days' rest. Seeing that she was in no condition to leave, the managers invited her to extend her visit. She accepted, and it stretched on to encompass the five remaining years of her life. During these last years she occupied an apartment that looked out on the beautiful and spacious grounds she had helped to plan.

Learning of her failing health, which her physicians diagnosed as the ossification of the arterial membrane, old friends who yet survived renewed their correspondence and made pilgrimages to her hospital apartment. Her visitors noted that she spoke of the present, not the past, and one recalled that she had declared with a trace of earlier vitality, "I think even lying on my bed, I can still do something." [17]

The end came at eighty-five on July 17, 1887, while she was seated at her tea table. She was buried in the Mount Auburn Cemetery near Boston. The service was simple, as she would have liked it. In a letter reporting her death to Doctor D. Hack Tuke, the noted English authority on mental disease, Doctor Charles H. Nichols offered an evaluation shared by her old associates: "Thus has died and been laid to rest in the most quiet, unostentatious way the most useful and distinguished woman America has yet produced." [18]

Afterword

History has not been overly kind to either Dorothea Dix or Millard Fillmore. The former's most recent biographer refers to her as a "Forgotten Samaritan." [1] Possibly the appellation is an overstatement, but it is obvious that she has been neglected. In fact, she is sometimes confused with Dorothy Dix, a mid-twentieth-century newspaper columnist who wrote advice to the lovelorn. Fillmore noted on several occasions that ministering to the insane created no corps of disciples, and that Dorothea's reward would have to be the satisfaction of achievement. By contrast, Clara Barton, Florence Nightingale, and Susan B. Anthony are honored anew each generation by dedicated followers who carry on the missions these renowned humanitarians inaugurated.

Fillmore, too, has suffered neglect. He lived during a generation of giants—Clay, Calhoun, Webster, and Lincoln; Lowell, Whittier, and Holmes; Hawthorne, Whitman, and Poe. Competition was keen.

At a time when historians were agreed that the Civil War

was repressible, that slavery was an anachronism doomed by
the nineteenth century, and that reasonable men could have
resolved the sectional misunderstandings short of rebellion
and war, Fillmore's faith in the goodness of man and his commitment to compromise made sense. The Compromise of 1850
was accepted as a notable achievement. It was assumed that it
might have prevented the many thousands of casualties of the
Civil War and averted the postwar administration of the
South by bayonet. But more recently Abolitionists have appeared as heroes; even carpetbaggers have become respectable.
It is not the Abolitionists who are seen as maladjusted, but
those who made the saving of the Union their highest priority,
whatever their commitment on slavery happened to be. In this
climate of opinion there can be scant recognition for a Fillmore
or, for that matter, a Clay, a Webster, or even a Lincoln. Fillmore will have to wait for still another appraisal.

Meanwhile, the Dix-Fillmore correspondence provides raw
material for a reinterpretation of the principals. Fillmore's letters depict more than "a colorless politician . . . who took a
small man's view of politics," as a historian recently evaluated
him.[2] Indeed, he emerges from the letters a reasonable, com-
passionate leader—he was willing to pardon "slave stealers" at
the risk of pillory from the South and to enforce the Fugitive
Slave Law because it was a part of a national compromise,
despite the wrath of Abolitionists.

He was responsive to Dorothea's counsel despite her
bumptious initial communication, and found her to be a delightful companion and a loyal friend. But he was also practical enough to see that her world was not his way of life when
her friendship might have invited a romantic attachment.

Dorothea Dix's letters were often written hurriedly during
moments between more pressing obligations. But there were

exceptions, and in these she is sometimes dramatic, jocular, or satiric, depending upon her mood and the nature of the subject matter.

As seen through her letters, Dorothea is neither the stereotype of a busybody finding pleasure in dressing down hospital attendants for failing to measure up to her rigid standards nor a machine exacting appropriations for mental hospitals from reluctant legislators. She is a warm and sometimes tender and lonely woman with a longing to share in the lives of others.

Millard Fillmore helped to satisfy this need, and her devotion was his reward.

Chronology

MILLARD FILLMORE

1800   Born in Summerhill (now Locke), Cayuga County, New York (January 7).

1815   Apprenticed to a local wool-dresser.

1820   A law clerk at Montville, Cayuga County.

1821   Delivered first recorded address at Montville (July 4). Moved to East Aurora, New York (September 1).

1822   Read law in Buffalo.

1823   Began law practice in East Aurora.

1826   Married Abigail Powers at Moravia, New York (February 5).

1828   Son, Millard Powers, born (April 25). Elected to New York State Assembly as an Antimason (November).

1830   Moved to Buffalo.

1831   Drafted and obtained passage of statute abolishing imprisonment for debt in New York State.

1832   Daughter, Mary Abigail (Abby), born (March 27). Elected to Congress as a Whig (November); began first of four terms.

1836   Law firm of Fillmore, Hall, and Haven formed.

1841   Chairman of the Ways and Means Committee in the House of Representatives.

1842   Principal author of the tariff of 1842.

1844   Defeated for Governor of New York by Silas Wright, the Democratic nominee (November 5).

1846   Elected Chancellor of the University of Buffalo.

1847   Elected Comptroller of New York State (November 2).

1848   Nominated for Vice President by the Whig National Convention at Baltimore as running mate of General Zachary Taylor (June 9).

Elected Vice President (November 7).

1849   Inaugurated as Vice President (March 5).

1850   Probable first meeting with Dorothea Dix (April).

Took oath of office as President upon the death of Taylor (July 10).

Received his first letter from Dorothea Dix (August 30).

Signed controversial Fugitive Slave Act, fourth of the five bills making up the Compromise of 1850 (September 18).

After rejection of resolutions in support of the Compromise of 1850 in the New York Whig Convention, Fillmore's supporters bolted to form Silver Greys (September 26).

1851   Participated in festivities attending the opening of the Erie Railroad in New York State (May).

Laid cornerstone of the Capitol enlargement (July 4).

Attended railroad celebrations in Boston and Portland linking New England with Canada (September).

Issued Hulsemann Letter approving of popular governments in Europe, and received Kossuth, the Hungarian revolutionist.

1852   Appointed Commodore Matthew Perry as special envoy to Japan, initiating the opening of Japan (March).

Defeated for renomination for President by General Winfield Scott after fifty-three ballots (June 20).

1853   Retired from the Presidency (March 4).

Abigail Fillmore died at Washington (March 30).

1854   Toured the South with John P. Kennedy by way of the Ohio and Mississippi rivers, and continuing through Mobile, Montgomery, Charleston, Savannah, and Baltimore (March–May).

Accompanied by Abby, attended the grand opening of the Chicago and Rock Island Railroad (June).

Abby died from cholera (July 26).

1855   Sailed for Liverpool (May 17).

Met Dorothea Dix in London (July 3).

Met Dorothea Dix in Paris (November 11).

1856   Nominated for President by the American Party (February 22).

Accepted nomination for President while in Paris (May 21).

Triumphal procession from New York to Buffalo (June).

Defeated by James Buchanan for President, carrying only Maryland (November 4).

1858   Married Mrs. Caroline C. McIntosh (February 10).

1861   Entertained President-elect Lincoln in Buffalo (February 17).

1862   First President of Buffalo Historical Society (May 20).

Chairman, Buffalo Committee of Public Defense and Commander of the Union Continentals.

1864   Warned of federal interference with personal liberties in Buffalo address (February 22).

1865   Headed citizens' committee to meet Lincoln funeral train (April).

1866   Visited Europe with second wife.

1873   Attended family reunion at Ann Arbor, Michigan (June).

1874   Died at his home in Buffalo (March 8).

DOROTHEA DIX

1802   Born at Hampden, Maine (April 4).

1814   Made home with grandmother, Dorothy Lynde Dix, in Boston.

1819   Attended secondary school in Dorchester.

1821   Opened elementary day school in grandmother's home.

1825   Published *Conversations on Common Things*.

1830   Served as governess for children of William Ellery Channing at St. Croix, Virgin Islands.

1831   Opened secondary school in her home.

1836   Broken in health, convalesced in the home of William Rathbone in England.

1837   Returned to Boston.

1841   Taught Sunday School lesson to prisoners in East Cambridge House of Correction; appalled by misery of insane there.

1842   Toured Massachusetts inspecting condition of the insane in almshouses and jails.

1843   Released memorial to the state legislature on the condition of the insane (January).

1844   Exposed maltreatment of the insane in Rhode Island.

1845   Memorialized legislature of New Jersey; Trenton State Hospital, her "first-born child."

1845–   Launched campaigns in Tennessee, Kentucky, Ohio,
1846   Maryland, and Pennsylvania.

1846–   Carried campaign into the South: New Orleans,
1847   Alabama, Georgia, South Carolina, Mississippi, Arkansas, and Tennessee.

1848   Took campaign to Washington, seeking a federal land grant for hospitals for the insane.

1849   Additional campaigns in Alabama, Mississippi, Louisiana, Illinois, Ohio, and North Carolina.

1850   Met Vice President Fillmore.

Initiated correspondence with President Fillmore (August 30).

Land grant bill passed by the House, defeated in the Senate.

1851   Land grant bill passed by the Senate but failed passage in the House.

Advised President Fillmore on the secessionist movement in South Carolina (March–April).

1852   Obtained congressional appropriation for the Army and Navy (St. Elizabeth's) Hospital in Washington.

1853   Carried crusade to Nova Scotia, Newfoundland, and Sable Island (June–July).

1854   Shocked by rumors of Fillmore's remarriage (February).

Her land grant bill killed by President Pierce's veto (May).

Grieved by death of Abby Fillmore (July).

Sailed for Europe for rest and work (September 2).

1855   Campaigned in Scotland for better treatment of the insane (February).

Met Fillmore in London (July 3).

Met Fillmore in Paris (November 11).

1856   Toured Italy and interceded with Pope Pius IX for the insane (February).

Toured Turkey, Austria-Hungary, Germany, Russia, and Scandinavia (April–June).

Returned to the United States (October).

Supported Fillmore's candidacy for President (October).

Visited Fillmore in Buffalo (December).

1857   Resumed crusade for the insane in Pennsylvania and New York.

1858   Learned of Fillmore's remarriage (February).
Made extensive tour of South and West.

1859   Returned from South and West.

1860   Met Fillmore and wife in New York City (October).

1861   Observed drift toward armed conflict in Kentucky (January).
Volunteered services to the War Department; appointed Superintendent of army nurses (April).

1865   Concluded her war work (September).

1866   Raised money to construct soldier memorial at Hampton, Virginia.

1867   Returned to mission for the insane, seeking to rectify neglect and deterioration during the war.

1869   Penned her last surviving letter to Fillmore (February 17).

1881   Made her last tour of the South, inspecting hospitals in Virginia, North Carolina, Georgia, and Florida (March–June).
Accepted apartment in the Trenton State Hospital.

1887   Died in her apartment in Trenton (July 17).

Notes

1. BEGINNINGS

1. XLIII, 362–365.
2. Rev. Dr. George W. Hosmer to Millard Fillmore, April 12, 1850, Fillmore papers, Buffalo and Erie County Historical Society.
3. Dorothea Dix to Millard Fillmore, March 26, 1851, Fillmore papers, State University of New York, Oswego. Hereinafter referred to as Fillmore papers, Oswego.
4. Dorothea Dix to Millard Fillmore, August 6, 1854, Fillmore papers, Oswego.
5. Dorothea Dix to Millard Fillmore, August 8, 1854, Fillmore papers, Oswego.
6. Dorothea Dix to Millard Fillmore, November 9, 1855, Fillmore papers, Oswego.
7. Robert J. Rayback, *Millard Fillmore: Biography of a President*, Publications of the Buffalo Historical Society, XL, 1959; William E. Griffis, *Millard Fillmore*, Ithaca, 1915; Francis Tiffany, *Life of Dorothea Lynde Dix*, Boston, 1891; Helen E. Marshall, *Dorothea Dix, Forgotten Samaritan*, Chapel Hill, N.C., 1937.

2. MILLARD FILLMORE—EARLY YEARS

1. Frank H. Severance (ed.), *Millard Fillmore Papers*, Buffalo, 1907, Vol. I, p. 9.
2. *Ibid.*, p. 12.
3. *Ibid.*, p. 14.
4. Fillmore papers, Oswego.
5. Crisfield Johnson, *History of Erie County, New York*, Buffalo, 1876, p. 388. Fillmore, however, seems to have never smoked or chewed tobacco (see Severance, *op. cit.*, Vol. I, p. xxxvi).
6. Mary Powers to Abigail Powers, March 6, 1825, Fillmore papers, Oswego.
7. Millard was frequently spelled "Millerd." Fillmore decided upon the former spelling during his twenties; Fillmore papers, Oswego.
8. Buffalo *Commercial Advertiser,* July 28, 1854.
9. Martha Fitch Poole, "Social Life in Buffalo in the '30's and '40's," *Publications of the Buffalo Historical Society*, Vol. VIII, 1905, pp. 443–444.
10. Robert Rayback, *Millard Fillmore*, Buffalo, 1959, p. 43.
11. Mrs. S. G. Haven, "Recollections [of President Fillmore]," *Millard Fillmore Papers*, Vol. II, p. 489.
12. *Ibid.*
13. Albert D. Kirwan, *John J. Crittenden*, Lexington, Ky., 1962, p. 264.
14. Holman Hamilton, *Zachary Taylor, Soldier in the White House*, Indianapolis, 1951, p. 388.
15. *Millard Fillmore Papers*, Vol. I, p. 431.
16. Ben: Perley Poore, *Perley's Reminiscences*, Philadelphia, 1886.
17. David Donald, *Charles Sumner and the Coming of the Civil War*, New York 1960, p. 188.
18. Allan Nevins, *Gateway to History*, Boston, 1938, p. 120.
19. Fillmore papers, Oswego, August 22, 1850.
20. Mrs. S. G. Haven, *op. cit.*, p. 492.
21. Nathaniel Fillmore to Millard Fillmore, June 29, 1820, Fillmore papers, Oswego.
22. Mrs. S. G. Haven, *op. cit.*, p. 492.

23. February 28, 1853, Everett mss., Massachusetts Historical Society.
24. February 21, 1853.

3. DOROTHEA DIX—EARLY YEARS

1. August 30, 1850, Fillmore papers, Oswego.
2. [August 31, 1850], Fillmore papers, Oswego.
3. September 6, 1850, Fillmore papers, Oswego.
4. Dorothea Dix to Ann Heath, undated, Dix mss., Harvard College Library.
5. Dorothea Dix to Ann Heath, undated, Dix mss.
6. Dorothea Dix to Ann Heath, August 25 and 27 [1824], Dix mss.
7. Dorothea Dix to Ann Heath, undated; quoted in Helen Marshall, *Dorothea Dix, Forgotten Samaritan*, Chapel Hill, N.C., 1937, p. 30.
8. Dorothea Dix to Ann Heath, December 8, 1854, Dix mss., quoted on p. 224.
9. Dorothea Dix to Millard Fillmore, December 26, 1854, Fillmore papers, Oswego; see p. 228.
10. Dorothea Dix to Ann Heath, undated, Dix mss.
11. Dorothea Dix to Ann Heath, undated, Dix mss.
12. Dorothea Dix to Ann Heath, undated [January 1, 1822], Dix mss.
13. Dorothea Dix to Ann Heath, Tuesday [otherwise undated], Dix mss.
14. Dorothea Dix to Ann Heath, January 28, 1826, Dix mss.
15. Dorothea Dix to Ann Heath, undated, Dix mss.
16. Speech before Hamilton Club, Chicago, April 10, 1899.
17. Dorothea Dix to Mrs. Dorothy Lynde Dix, undated; quoted in Tiffany, *op. cit.*, p. 16.
18. W. E. Channing to Dorothea Dix, undated; quoted in Tiffany, *op. cit.*, pp. 22–23.
19. Dorothea Dix to Ann Heath, undated, Dix mss., quoted in Marshall, *op. cit.*, p. 28.
20. Quoted in Tiffany, *op. cit.*, pp. 40–41.

21. Dorothea Dix to Ann Heath, February 24, 1838, written after her return from England, Dix mss., quoted in Tiffany, *op. cit.,* p. 52.
22. *Ibid.*
23. Dix mss.
24. *Memorial to the Legislature of Massachusetts,* Boston, 1842. Reprinted in *Old South Leaflets,* Vol. VI, No. 148, Boston, 1904.
25. Quoted in Tiffany, *op. cit.,* pp. 96–98.
26. Dorothea Dix to Joseph Dix, January 30, 1849, quoted in Tiffany, *op. cit.,* p. 178.
27. Dorothea Dix to Mrs. Robert Hare, January 1, 1850, Dix mss.
28. Dorothea Dix to Ann Heath, undated [1850–1851], Dix mss.

9. LATER YEARS

1. Buffalo *Commercial Advertiser,* May 4, 1861. Quoted in Rayback, *op. cit.,* p. 425.
2. Fillmore to Lincoln, May 16, 1863, Roy P. Basler (ed.), *Works of Abraham Lincoln,* New Brunswick, 1953, Vol. VI, pp. 222-223.
3. *Fillmore papers,* Vol. II, pp. 86–87.
4. Buffalo *Commercial Advertiser,* February 23, 1864. Clement L. Vallandigham of Ohio, the most notorious among the copperheads; Mayor Fernando Wood of New York and his brother, Congressman Benjamin Wood; Governor Horatio Seymour of New York and former Governor Thomas H. Seymour of Connecticut; James and Erastus Brooks of New York City.
5. Fillmore papers, Vol. II, pp. 89–90.
6. Fillmore to John Bell Robinson, August 12, 1864, Fillmore papers, Vol. II, pp. 431–432.
7. Seymour to Fillmore, August 6, 1868, Fillmore papers, Oswego.
8. Henry Demarest Lloyd to Fillmore, June 6, 1872, Fillmore papers, Oswego.
9. See Charles M. Snyder, "Forgotten Fillmore Papers Exam-

ined: Sources for Reinterpretation of a Little-Known President," *The American Archivist*, Vol. XXXII (January, 1969), pp. 11–13.

10. Sylvia G. L. Dannett, *Noble Women of the North*, New York, 1959, pp. 72–73, 88–89.

11. D. L. Dix to Louisa L. Schuyler, Director of Women's Central Relief Association of New York, Quoted by Dannett, *ibid.*, pp. 62–63.

12. Dannett, *op. cit.*, p. 60.

13. Mary A. Gardner Holland, *Our Army Nurses*, Boston, 1895, p. 19.

14. Allan Nevins and M. H. Thomas (eds.), *The Diary of George Templeton Strong*, New York, 1952, Vol. III, pp. 173–174.

15. Dannett, *op. cit.*, pp. 341–342.

16. Tiffany, *op. cit.*, pp. 342–343.

17. *Ibid.*, p. 371.

18. *Ibid.*, p. 375.

AFTERWORD

1. Marshall, *op. cit.*

2. Oscar Handlin, *The History of the United States*, New York, 1968, pp. 555, 557.

Selected Bibliography

I. MANUSCRIPTS

Daniel D. Barnard Papers, Diaries and Letter Books. New York State Library, Albany.

Beekman Family Papers. New-York Historical Society.

Anna Ella Carroll Papers. Maryland Historical Society, Baltimore.

———. State University of New York, Oswego.

John A. Collier Papers. Regional History Library, Cornell University, Ithaca, N.Y.

W. W. Corcoran Papers. Library of Congress, Washington, D.C.

Dorothea L. Dix Correspondence, Miscellaneous Papers and Notebooks, including correspondence from the William Rathbone Family, Robert Hare Family, Anne Heath, Joseph Henry and Francis Lieber. Harvard College Library, Cambridge, Mass.

Dorothea L. Dix, Her Letters During the Civil War. New-York Historical Society.

Dorothea L. Dix, Miscellaneous Collection. Boston Public Library.

Edward Everett Papers. Massachusetts Historical Society, Boston.

Millard Fillmore Papers [including collection of maps used during tour of Europe, 1855-56]. Library of Congress, Washington, D.C.

Millard Fillmore Papers. Buffalo and Erie County Historical Society.

———. State University of New York, Oswego.

———. Harvard College Library, Cambridge, Mass.

Hamilton Fish Papers. Library of Congress, Washington, D.C.

Francis Granger Papers. Library of Congress, Washington, D.C.

Orsamus H. Marshall Papers. State University of New York, Oswego.
William H. Seward Collection. University of Rochester Library.
Daniel Ullmann Papers. New-York Historical Society.
Daniel Webster Papers. Library of Congress, Washington, D.C.
Thurlow Weed Collection. University of Rochester Library.

II. NEWSPAPERS

Albany *Evening Journal*, 1850.
Buffalo *Commercial Advertiser*, 1850-54, 1860-64.
Congressional Globe, 1850-54.
Godey's Lady's Book and Magazine, Vol. XLIII (1852), pp. 362-365.
National Intelligencer (Washington), 1850-54.
New York Times, 1851-53.
Washington *Daily Star*, 1854.

III. BOOKS, PAMPHLETS, ARTICLES, & OFFICIAL DOCUMENTS

Adams, George W. *Doctors in Blue*. New York, 1952.
Albion, Robert G. *The Rise of New York Port*. New York, 1939.
Barnes, Thurlow Weed. *Memoir of Thurlow Weed. The Life of Thurlow Weed, Including his Autobiography and a Memoir*, vol. 2. Boston, 1884.
Barre, W. L. *Life and Public Services of Millard Fillmore*. Buffalo, 1856.
Basler, Roy P., ed. *Works of Abraham Lincoln*. 9 vols. New Brunswick, N.J., 1953.
Beals, Carleton. *The Brass-Knuckle Crusade: The Great Know Nothing Conspiracy, 1820–1860*. New York, 1960.
Brockett, L. P. "Sketches from Humane Institutions; Asylums for the Insane." *The National Magazine, Devoted to Literature, Art, and Religion*. Vol. XI (1857), pp. 315-324.

————, and Vaughan, Mary C. *Woman's Work in the Civil War*. Boston, 1867.

Brooks, Noah. *Washington in Lincoln's Time*. Edited by Herbert Mitgang. New York, 1958.

Carroll, Anna Ella. *The Great American Battle: or, The Contest between Christianity and Political Romanism*. New York, 1856.

————. *Which? Fillmore or Buchanan!* Boston, 1856.

[Chamberlin, Ivory]. *Biography of Millard Fillmore*. Buffalo, 1856.

Curran, Thomas J. "Seward and the Know Nothings." *New-York Historical Society Quarterly*. Vol. LI (1967), pp. 141-159.

Dannett, Sylvia G. L. *Nobel Women of the North*. New York, 1959.

Dix, Dorothea L. *Memorial Soliciting a State Hospital for the Insane, Submitted to the Legislature of New Jersey*. Trenton, 1845.

————. *Memorial to the Legislature of Massachusetts*. Boston, 1842. Reprinted in *Old South Leaflets*, Vol. VI, no. 148 (1904).

————. *Memorial to the United States Congress Praying a Grant of Land for the Relief and Support of the Indigent Curable and Incurable Insane in the United States*. Washington, D.C., 1848.

————. *Remarks on Prisons and Prison Discipline in the United States*. Philadelphia, 1845.

Donald, David H. *Charles Sumner and the Coming of the Civil War*. New York, 1960.

Edgell, David P. *William Ellery Channing: An Intellectual Portrait*. New York, 1955.

Facts and Documents Bearing upon the Legal and Moral Questions Connected with the Recent Destruction of the Quarantine Buildings on Staten Island. New York, 1858.

Foner, Philip S. *Business and Slavery: The New York Merchants and the Irrepressible Conflict*. Chapel Hill, N.C., 1941.

Freidel, Frank. *Francis Lieber: Nineteenth Century Liberal*. Baton Rouge, La., 1947.

Fuess, C. M. *Daniel Webster*. 2 vols. Boston, 1930.

Green, Constance McLaughlin. *Washington: Village and Capital, 1800–1878*. Princeton, 1962.

Griffis, William E. *Millard Fillmore*. Ithaca, 1915.

Hamilton, Holman. *Zachary Taylor: Soldier in the White House*. Indianapolis, 1951.

Hamilton, James A. *Reminiscences*. New York, 1869.

Handlin, Oscar. *The History of the United States*. 2 vols. New York, 1966.

————. *Race and Nationality in American Life*. New York, 1957.

Harrington, Fred H. "Fremont and the North Americans." *American Historical Review*. Vol. XLIV (1939), pp. 842-848.

Heck, Frank H. "John C. Breckinridge in the Crisis of 1860–1861." *Journal of Southern History*. Vol. XXI (1955), pp. 316-346.

Holland, Mary A. Gardner. *Our Army Nurses*. Boston, 1895.

Johnson, Crisfield. *History of Erie County, New York*. Buffalo, 1876.

Kirwan, Albert D. *John J. Crittenden*. Lexington, Ky., 1962.

Leech, Margaret. *Reveille in Washington*. New York, 1941.

LeVert, Octavia [Walton]. *Souvenirs of Travel*. 2 vols. New York, 1857.

Lieber, Francis. "On the Vocal Sounds of Laura Bridgeman [*sic*], the Blind Deaf-Mute at Boston; Compared with the Elements of Phonetic Language." *Smithsonian Contributions to Knowledge*. Vol. II, article 2. Washington, D.C., 1850.

Livermore, Mary A. *My Story of the War*. Hartford, 1889.

Marshall, Helen E. *Dorothea Dix: Forgotten Samaritan*. Chapel Hill, N.C., 1937.

Massey, Mary Elizabeth. *Bonnet Brigades*. New York, 1966.

Maxwell, William Q. *Lincoln's Fifth Wheel: The Political History of the United States Sanitary Commission*. New York, 1956.

Mr. Fillmore at Home: His Reception at New York and Brooklyn and Progress through the State to His Residence in Buffalo. Buffalo, 1856.

Nevins, Allan. *Coming of Lincoln.* 2 vols. New York, 1950.
———. *Gateway to History.* Boston, 1938.
———. *Hamilton Fish: The Inner History of the Grant Administration.* New York, 1936.
———. *Ordeal of the Union.* 2 vols. New York, 1950.
———, and Thomas, M. H., eds. *The Diary of George Templeton Strong, 1835–1875.* 4 vols. New York, 1952.
Nichols, Roy F. *The Disruption of American Democracy.* New York, 1948.
———. *Franklin Pierce.* Philadelphia, 1958.
O'Connor, Thomas. *Lords of the Loom: The Cotton Whigs and the Coming of the Civil War.* New York, 1968.
Overdyke, William D. *The Know-Nothing Party in the South.* Baton Rouge, La., 1950.
Owen, David Dale. *Report of a Geological Survey of Wisconsin, Iowa, and Minnesota; and Incidentally of a Portion of Nebraska Territory.* Philadelphia, 1852.
Parks, Joseph H. *John Bell of Tennessee.* Baton Rouge, La., 1950.
Poole, Martha Fitch. "Social Life of Buffalo in the '30's and '40's." *Publications of the Buffalo Historical Society.* Vol. VIII (1905), pp. 439-493.
Poore, Ben: Perley. *Perley's Reminiscences.* Philadelphia, 1886.
Randall, James G., and Donald, David. *The Civil War and Reconstruction.* Boston, 1961.
Rayback, Robert J. *Millard Fillmore: Biography of a President. Publications of the Buffalo Historical Society* 40 (1959).
Sargent, Nathan. *Public Men and Events. . . .* Philadelphia, 1853.
Scisco, Louis Dow. *Political Nativism in New York State. Columbia University Studies in History, Economics and Public Law.* Vol. XIII, no. 2. New York, 1901.
Severance, Frank H., ed. *Millard Fillmore Papers.* 2 vols. *Publications of the Buffalo Historical Society* X-XI (1907).
Seward, Frederick W., ed. *William H. Seward: An Autobiography. . . .* 3 vols. New York, 1891.
Snyder, Charles M. "Forgotten Fillmore Papers Examined:

Sources for Reinterpretation of a Little-Known President."
American Archivist. Vol. XXXII (1969), pp. 11-14.

Thompson, William Y. *Robert Toombs of Georgia*. Baton
Rouge, La., 1966.

Tiffany, Francis. *Life of Dorothea Lynde Dix*. Boston, 1891.

Tuke, Daniel Hack. *Chapters in the History of the Insane in
the British Isles*. London, 1882.

――――. *The Insane in the United States and Canada*. London,
1885.

Van Deusen, Glyndon G. *William H. Seward*. New York,
1967.

――――. *Thurlow Weed: Wizard of the Lobby*. Boston, 1947.

Weed, Harriet A., ed. *Autobiography of Thurlow Weed*. *The
Life of Thurlow Weed, Including his Autobiography and
a Memoir*, vol. 1. Boston, 1883.

Winthrop, Robert C., Jr., ed. *A Memoir of Robert C. Winthrop*. Boston, 1897.

Wright, J. A. *Historical Sketches of Moravia, 1791–1873*.
Auburn, N.Y., 1874.

Index

CPSIA information can be obtained at www.ICGtesting.com
Printed in the USA
LVOW13s1920060614

388972LV00001B/5/P